GOOD NEWS
~ *for* ~
MARRIED LOVERS

GOOD NEWS
for
MARRIED
LOVERS

CHUCK GALLAGHER &
MARY ANGELEE SEITZ

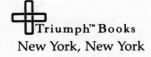
Triumph™ Books
New York, New York

Excerpt(s) from THE NEW JERUSALEM BIBLE, copyright © 1985 by
Doubleday, a division of Bantam, Doubleday, Dell Publishing Group,
Inc. and Darton, Longman & Todd, Ltd. Used by permission of the
publisher.

Library of Congress Cataloging-in-Publication Data

Gallagher Chuck, 1927–
    Good news for married lovers : a scriptural path to marriage
renewal / Chuck Gallagher, Mary Angelee Seitz.
        p.   cm.
    ISBN 0-8007-3008-9
    1. Marriage—Religious aspects—Christianity. 2. Love—Religious
aspects—Christianity. I. Seitz, Mary Angelee. II. Title.
BV835.G34   1991
248.8'.44—dc20   90-47437
                                                                      CIP

Copyright © 1991 by Chuck Gallagher and Mary Angelee Seitz
Published by Triumph Books
An Imprint of Gleneida Publishing Group
New York, New York
Printed in the United States of America
First Edition

Acknowledgment

I wish to acknowledge the special role Fr. Chuck has played in my faith through his insightful understanding of the Sacrament of Matrimony and his personal warmth and love. I hope I might share this with the reader by true and careful conveyance of his reverence for married couples.

Mary Angelee Seitz

CONTENTS

Contents

FOREWORD

Two thousand years ago, Jesus Christ came into the world with a promise. "Give," He said, "and there will be gifts for you: a full measure, pressed down, shaken together and overflowing, will be poured into your lap" (Lk. 6:38).

For those who are joined in marriage, these gifts are waiting, seeking to grow beyond all measure. They are only a soul-search away.

In married couples today, there is goodness, a full measure of goodness, pressed down, shaken together and overflowing.

There's confusion, too. We've been taught to grab what we can, to satisfy ourselves with things instead of people: with hobbies, careers, clothes, cars.

We're choosing egos over love.

That's why there are legalistic prenuptial agreements. That's why there are long-distance two-career families, with husbands and wives living hundreds of miles apart. That's why logic has taken the place of trust and we seek to fill the emptiness with purchases from the store.

Lord, we're making ourselves so unhappy. And we don't even know why.

We need to let go; to trust. To hope and to dream.

We need to face the wrongs we've done and forget those done against us. We need to forgive and be forgiven.

There is no easy recipe for happiness. But there is a promise: of gifts, a full measure, pressed down, shaken together and overflowing. To seek those gifts, we have to reach outside ourselves. We have to have the courage to love, even when it isn't easy.

We begin by cherishing those marvelous gifts God has already given us: our husbands and wives.

This book is written for all the tremendously good couples who are the hope of today's children and the treasure of our world. This book is written for you.

INTRODUCTION

HOW TO READ
THIS BOOK

This book will indeed work miracles. That is, it will challenge you to work them yourselves: to heal each other's hurts, to love each other more deeply than you could ever have imagined, to paint for each other a vivid portrait of God's unbounded love.

Unfortunately, a hurried glance through this book—or any other—won't renew your marriage.

But if you read this book carefully, thoughtfully, applying it to your life, the rewards will simply astonish you. Summer romance, even honeymoon delirium, is nothing compared to the loving, warm, passionate relationship you can share when you invite God—and each other— into your lives.

You won't have everlasting delight by seeking a quick fix for a stagnant love relationship.

You *will* have everlasting delight if you are hopeful, truthful, and courageous enough to look inside yourself for the gift of happiness.

Ideally, this book isn't for only one of you. It's written for couples. If possible, both of you should read each chapter, pray over it, and discuss it between you.

As you read, don't think of yourself as having failed so far. See, instead, how beautiful you are and how much more the Lord is offering you. Growing in love is like learning a language. The more accomplished we become, the more we are able to speak. We are learning to speak the language of the Lord.

That language begins with Scripture. Through the Scriptures, the Lord tells us how we can receive His gifts of happiness and peace. In this book, the Scriptures are applied specifically to you married couples. Their purpose? To help you think about each other more tenderly, to be more open to each other, to talk with freedom and trust. In order for a marriage to grow, you have to go to each other.

In each chapter, you'll find problems and explanations, examples and soul-searchings; questions to help you be open: to yourself, to God, and to your spouse.

Many of the questions will be for you to ponder in private. Others are to be shared with your love. During your discussions, each of you should express only your own feelings. Describe how each chapter relates to you. Never blame your spouse; always treat his or her sharing with gratitude and respect. Remember, your beloved will be entrusting you with his or her most intimate feelings. No gift is more fragile, or more precious.

At the end of each chapter, you will have the option to write to your love. Please take it. When writing, your words come forth just as you intend them: clear, uninterrupted, unchanged by body language. You will discover hidden feelings of pain and joy, fear and comfort, both in yourself and in your beloved.

Chapter by chapter, you'll find yourselves growing closer than ever before. In a few months, read this book again. Its meaning will have grown, even as you have.

If you must read alone, by all means do so. Then put this book under your love's pillow, on top of his or her coffee cup. Speak gently. And pray, really pray, for your love to pick it up.

GOOD NEWS

for

MARRIED
LOVERS

GROWING IN GRACE

CHAPTER 1

WHAT IS LOVE?

(1 Co. 13:1–4)

Imagine you're shopping in the supermarket and a stranger asks, "For you, what is love?"

What would you answer?

Many of us would define love in terms of warmth, closeness, or sexual attraction. But most of us would define love in terms of feelings: maybe the glow, the gratitude, we feel when someone is nice to us. Most of us see love as "what's going on inside me."

We philosophical types might define love in terms of action: love is doing the right thing. Married couples often use this definition. It brings to mind phrases like "Love is doing your duty. Love is living up to your responsibilities. Love is fulfilling the promises you've committed yourself to."

There's a third definition of love, one that isn't burdensome. Nor is it passive and self-centered: contained within

17

ourselves, dependent on our own or our lovers' moods. Instead, it is joyful: reaching out, celebrating the good around us, casting off the mundane weight of everyday troubles.

This definition of love was written by St. Paul in his first letter to the Corinthians. He says love is more important than anything else. He says love is the kind of person you are:

> Though I command languages both human and angelic—if I speak without love, I am no more than a gong booming or a cymbal clashing. And though I have the power of prophecy, to penetrate all mysteries and knowledge, and though I have all the faith necessary to move mountains—if I am without love, I am nothing. Though I should give away to the poor all that I possess, and even give up my body to be burned—if I am without love, it will do me no good whatever.
>
> Love is always patient and kind; love is never jealous; love is not boastful or conceited, it is never rude and never seeks its own advantage, it does not take offense or store up grievances. Love does not rejoice at wrongdoing, but finds its joy in the truth. It is always ready to make allowances, to trust, to hope and to endure whatever comes.
>
> Love never comes to an end. But if there are prophecies, they will be done away with; if tongues, they will fall silent; and if knowledge, it will be done away with. For we know only imperfectly, and we prophesy imperfectly; but once perfection comes, all imperfect things will be done away with. When I was a child, I used to talk like a child, and see things as a child does, and think like a child, but now that I have

18

become an adult, I have finished with all childish ways. Now we see only reflections in a mirror, mere riddles, but then we shall be seeing face to face. Now, I can know only imperfectly; but then I shall know just as fully as I am myself known.

As it is, these remain: faith, hope and love, the three of them; and the greatest of them is love.

Corinthians 13:1–13

To most of us, this Scripture passage is beautiful poetry. We don't believe it's a practical definition of love. Even if we did, our imaginary stranger in the supermarket might not accept it. He'd probably say, "Come on. I wanted something *real*."

That's tragic. This kind of love is, indeed, real. But so many of us pass it by, searching all the while somewhere else.

Paul, the Lover

To understand why St. Paul wrote this passage, we need to understand the apostle himself.

Paul is quite a fellow, isn't he? Let's reflect on Paul, sitting down to compose this letter, thinking about his beloved people in Corinth.

Sometimes we miss Paul's personal dimension. We think of him as a great apostle, a brilliant man who came out with magnificent theology. That's true, but Paul was, first of all, a lover. He was driven to bring Jesus to all to whom his legs could carry him, but it always broke his heart to leave them when his work was completed.

To see how loving he is, read the greetings that close his epistles. They're full of phrases like "Remember me to this

19

person," "Tell that person I was thinking about her," or "I'm sending you this friend of mine; treat him as you would treat me." He closes his first letter to the Romans, for instance, with a lengthy list of hellos. "I hope," he writes, "after longing for many years past to visit you, to see you when I am on the way to Spain" (1 Rm. 15:23). And in 1 Corinthians he writes, "If Timothy comes . . . start him off in peace on his journey to come on to me: the brothers and I are waiting for him" (1 Co. 16:10, 11).

Although St. Paul was always facing forward, he constantly left his heart behind, among the people to whom he had already announced the glad tidings of Jesus Christ. He loved his people so much that he wanted to be present to them even though he had gone on to another town.

His purpose wasn't to expound brilliant theologies, although many of his letters were exactly that. He was simply speaking to his people, and his words were pulled not out of his head but out of his heart.

St. Paul speaks of love, and in doing so, speaks of his ambition for his beloved people. He wants them to be happy, to live in harmony with Jesus Christ. He offers them a way to truly enjoy life.

"Lover": Instruction Book Enclosed?

Paul knew there were no easy follow-the-directions recipes for perfect love. Paul doesn't say, "If you follow these instructions, you'll be a successful woman, a great man." Instead, he says, "Love is . . ." He isn't talking about good deeds; he's talking about a quality of life.

He doesn't say, "Behave patiently"; he says, "Be patient." He doesn't say, "Perform kindly deeds"; he calls us to live in kindness. He simply explains, "If you're a lover, you *are* patient. If you really love, kindness is part of your identity."

Even though he wrote that message two thousand years ago, we still haven't fully understood the message. We're still so very act-oriented. We settle for doing the correct things rather than making them a quality of our personhood. These qualities, of course, can be manifested outwardly. But those outward acts should be significant because they express who we are.

Why should we be kind, for instance, instead of merely performing kind acts?

Because when love is a way of being, it takes the "I" out of "I love you." When I'm a loving person, I naturally make my beloved's life tremendously worthwhile.

Love looks at the other person. Love is not for my self-perfection. Yes, I'm called to be patient, kind, and forbearing. But I'm called to be that way for a reason: to benefit my lover.

Love, according to Paul, is in the very fiber of our being. If we're loving people, anyone who touches our lives will be better off. We simply couldn't resist someone who is living a life of love. In our hearts, we know St. Paul is right, and even hearing that passage is a moving experience.

Love Is Always Patient

Let's look at the qualities Paul lists in his model for love. Which one does he choose first? Patience.

If we were writing that first letter to the Corinthians, would patience have been the first loving virtue that popped into our minds? Probably not. That's why the Lord chose St. Paul, not us, to write that letter.

Often, we're difficult to live with because we're in such a rush. We want that other person to love us immediately.

In a way, we really haven't grown much beyond those little toddlers of ours. They'll ask, "Mommy! Daddy! Can I have some candy?" We'll answer, "Maybe later," and they say, "No. I want it now!" "Now" is always accompanied by a stamp of the foot. We're a lot like our children, except that we keep our feet on the ground.

We're just as now-oriented as they are: "I want you to talk to me *now*. I want supper *now*. I want to go out *now*. I want you off the phone *now*." How often does this simple lack of patience cause friction in our relationships with one another? St. Paul was wise when he wrote that love is patient.

If we could just get "now" out of our vocabularies, our marriages would be so much happier.

Love Never Gives Up

Our urgency isn't confined to small daily concerns. Sometimes we're terribly impatient about serious issues. We withdraw from our loves simply because they aren't changing fast enough. We give up on each other in sex, for instance, or in understanding.

"He'll never change," we say to ourselves.

Or perhaps, "That's the way she is."

Or "Have you ever tried to change a woman?"

Translated, these phrases all mean, "I've tried hard enough."

We've given a great deal of attention, energy, effort, persuasion, encouragement, or affection; whatever we thought was needed. We've reached out to the other person and we haven't received a proper response. Nothing seems to be happening, so we decide to leave the other person alone. We don't do that because it's good for that person, but because we're disheartened and weary of trying.

I think men are special sinners here. We laugh and say if a man is dead set against something, his wife can still bring him around, but if she's against something, there's no changing her. There's some truth in that old saw, and it isn't because the woman is tougher than her man. It's because the man doesn't try as hard to bring her into his life.

Women aren't naturally good at this. They're good because they've decided to work on it all their lives. A woman doesn't give up. She's much more persistently loving. Take, for example, a day when her husband is angry or moody. She tries to put a hand on his arm, but he shakes it off. She smiles, but he frowns. She backs off, then comes back again with a nice word. Perhaps she tries the hand on his arm again or brings him a drink. There is a beautiful quality of patience in our women.

St. Paul was writing about this type of patience. We have to be willing to stay with each other, not to take no for an answer but to try again in gentleness and tenderness.

Love Is . . . Playing Like a Winner

Remember that old macho football and Marine Corps slogan? "Winners never quit and quitters never win." In your family, who lives that slogan, and who does the quitting? Most likely, the wife is not the quitter. She's always in there trying. But her man often quits after a halfhearted struggle.

Perhaps he comes home and sees his wife has had a tough day. She's so down, she doesn't want to talk. She wants everyone to pretend she isn't even there. He gives her a hug and squeeze. He says, "Honey, what's the matter?"

She says, "Nothing."

He tries again. "Ah, come on, really, what's the matter? I can tell there's something wrong."

"No, I'm fine," she says, with that special overtone to the word "fine."

He rolls his eyes and says to himself, "This is tough tonight." Maybe he pours himself a drink and tries again. He is a good man. He puts his hands on her shoulders and she shrugs them off.

At this point, he decides, "Well, I did as much as I could." He takes his drink, goes to another room, and reads the paper. "She'll come out of it," he thinks. "When she wants to talk, she'll talk." But he's really not present to her anymore. He's back in his own world and she'll have to recover alone.

We limit our patience with our husbands, wives, and children to what we think is reasonable. How can something be wrong if it feels so—reasonable?

It is, nonetheless. The devil doesn't tempt good people into doing bad things. The devil always tempts us into doing something less good. Often, we're awfully proud of ourselves because we're avoiding the biggest sins. We haven't robbed any banks or had any orgies.

The devil isn't even asking us to commit sins like that.

He knows better. He catches us with little temptations instead. Good people rarely fall into bad traps; they fall into good ones, but they're still traps.

Love Isn't Reasonable

Reasonableness is one of the most common antilove concepts in our lives. Why? Because it limits patience. We'll be patient only to a certain point. Once that point is reached, we think we don't have to try anymore.

How many times have we used "It's against good reason" as an excuse for not being lovers? The lines we draw between reasonable and unreasonable may differ greatly from person to person, but they're always there.

St. Paul didn't say, "Be patient when it makes sense."

"Love is patient and reasonable"? He didn't say that either. In fact, reason isn't mentioned once in Paul's entire list. He didn't even say love is intelligent. He did say love is patient; it is always ready to make allowances, it endures whatever comes.

We stop being patient because this level of self-sacrifice doesn't meet our needs. Perhaps we get fed up or we don't think we're getting enough consideration. Perhaps anger is starting to churn within us.

"I have really been loving," a wife might say. "What more can I do? He takes me for granted; the least he could do is appreciate my efforts."

We men might think, "How much longer is she planning to sulk? I've done all I can."

Love Works Overtime

We're all good, generous people, but even good people tend to ration patience like gasoline during World War II.

25

Each of us will allot a certain amount of time to coax our husbands out of their bad moods or to help our wives solve their problems of the moment. If they don't respond in the proper time slot, we give up. We've done our best, and now we're off the hook.

Remember, it's not whether your effort is reasonable but whether it's successful. If, like St. Paul, we're lovers, we simply have to keep on until it works.

Patience is other-centered. When I'm a lover, you become my agenda. If, instead, there's something else on my agenda, I can't help but think, "How much more time can I spend with you before I have to leave?" I don't have to leave physically. Maybe my favorite television show is coming on in thirty minutes. Perhaps it's getting late and if we don't wind this up, I won't get my sleep. Maybe I have to make lunches for the kids, fix that faucet, sew on that patch. Maybe if I continue to be patient, I won't read today's paper.

I simply can't have something to do when my spouse needs me. When I find I need patience to deal with my lover, am I other-centered or me-centered? I have to choose my lover. I have to say to myself, "I'll get to that when we're free," not "I'm pretty busy but I'll fit you in."

If you, my lover, need me to be present to you, I simply have to make you my priority. No matter how long it takes, I'm yours. If later I get around to my other plans, fine, but I'm not counting on that right now because you need me.

That can be very hard to do sometimes. Especially if you're well organized, you might be tempted to think, "But I just can't live that way. There are things that have to be done around here. He understands it as well as I do," or "She knows I can't spend twenty-four hours a day with her."

Our lovers know about all our other obligations; they're very conscious of them, indeed. If they still feel they need us right now, their needs are obviously important. Why do we place such tremendous priority on the normal, everyday chores? What if the dishes did go unwashed? What if the kids' lunches didn't get made and we had to take them to school later on? What if we did go to work a little sleepy because we stayed up late talking to our spouses? We'd be happier, that's all.

Still, we keep fitting our lovers into our schedules. Think about it. Are our husbands less important than a set of dishes? Are our wives less valuable than the scores of last night's game?

Of course not. Yet our priorities speak louder than our words.

That's why St. Paul was wise when he chose patience as the first quality of love. If we could just discipline ourselves to give our lovers absolute priority in our lives, our marriages would be so much better.

Love Is a "Give" Proposition

We often think of patience as passivity, but St. Paul's definition has nothing to do with an even temper.

"If I don't say anything abrasive," we might think, "I'm patient." Not necessarily. We may be steaming inside, or perhaps we're people who never get angry. It may not be virtue; it may be indifference.

On the other hand, maybe our husbands do shout sometimes or our wives snap at the children, but they never quit trying to reach out when we need them. That's what St. Paul wants from us. Patience is sticking with each other, regardless of response.

That takes trust and sometimes even strength. We can't say, "I love you, but you have to respond to me pretty soon because I have to feel your love, too." That's like saying, "Hurry up and love me before it's too late, because my love won't last."

Paul says that real love loves regardless. Love doesn't say, "I'll give you my love as long as I feel good about it." It doesn't say, "As soon as I start getting frustrated because you're not listening, I'll stop talking to you. I won't say anything nasty, but I'll wait until you're ready."

We make love a give-and-take proposition. It's not. It's a give proposition: I give love because I love you.

Love Is Kind

Kindness is a very special gift. Probably the closest we can come to canonizing someone in normal, human terms is to say, "She's really kind," or "He's a kind guy."

We don't use that word very often. "Kind" is too special to throw around. We'll say "good" before we say "kind," even though the most outstanding aspect of a person's goodness may be his or her kindness.

We may recognize other qualities in a person and respect them very much, but kindness is something quite different. It's such a wonderful quality in another human being; it's grand to experience it and to be touched by it. We all love to be in the presence of a truly kind person.

St. Paul says love *is* kind. Here again, Paul is not talking about performing a number of kind actions. He is talking about living a kind life-style, creating that atmosphere in the house. When a husband and wife are living in kindness, there is joy, peace, and delight in that home.

This quality should be the one you most desire for yourselves, because it's the best gift you can give each other. To turn the tables, can you imagine any better quality in your spouse than total, unrelenting kindness? Isn't that really a beautiful virtue in marriage?

Kindness is a gentle concern for the needs of others, a desire to make them happy and relieve their pain. Affection is a very strong ingredient in kindness.

Kindness can be present in small, everyday actions, but the same actions may not reflect kindness at all. Perhaps you're being kind when you put out the garbage. Maybe not; maybe you're just being obedient or trying to avoid trouble. You're probably being thoughtful rather than kind.

You might be kind to cook dinner for the family. But then again, maybe not. You could be just a grumpy short-order cook.

The same activity can be good or neutral, depending on the warmth that passes between the two of you. Fixing the faucet or dusting a table can be either a chore or an act of kindness. In the second instance, there is an obvious affection in the way you do it. But in the first, you're just doing the work.

This affection, this tenderness, this gentleness, come from a reverence for the other person. That's why kindness is not present merely in our actions, no matter how good they may be. For kindness to be truly present, there must be warmth in our hearts. We can't be thinking only of what we're doing; we have to be conscious of whom we're doing it for, and our feelings of love must be evident.

How Kind Am I?

Do you see yourself as a kind person, not just one who does kind things? We all do kind things, and frequently, too, but that doesn't mean we're living a kind way of life.

Perhaps you men are thinking, "I really wish I could look at myself in a mirror and say, 'Yes, you are a kind man.' I can't. I know how wonderful that would be for my wife; that would really make her happy. But I just wasn't put together that way. I'm too much of a driver. I'm more of a man's man."

Maybe you wives are finding it difficult to think of yourselves as, above all, kind. "I'm more of an efficient, well-ordered woman," you might say. "I can really do the work."

Don't be discouraged and don't give up. Each of us has the potential to be as kind as Mother Teresa of Calcutta.

Kindness is a virtue, not a talent. Talent, I either have or don't have. I'm either six foot nine with a great deal of agility and a good shooting eye or I'm five foot six and I'm just not going to make it as a big-time basketball player. I either have an IQ of 190 and can earn a doctorate of geophysics at a school like Harvard, or I just can't do that.

Virtue, though, is there for the taking. If I go into the bank and take money, I'm a thief, but if I go to an undiscovered island and find diamonds on the beach, they're mine to keep. Like those diamonds, virtue is a free gift.

I can't say I'm not kind because kindness wasn't given to me. I can't think that some people are naturally kind, and I'm not one of them. Some people have better personalities than others, yes. Some people have less abrasive temperaments or are less driving. But nobody, by nature, is kinder than I am.

When someone is kinder than I am, it's because that person has chosen to be kind and I have not. I have to decide: will I be kind? Notice, it's "will I?" This "will" is not the future tense of the verb "to be." It's "will" in the sense of the Latin word *volo:* I will it, I choose; I decide to be a kind person.

I can't value kindness just because it makes me a better man or woman. I shouldn't make a checklist of my virtues, then study it to decide where I score high and where I need work.

I should take on kindness for the sake of my lover, not for my own sake. That's a very important lesson and a very hard one. We humans really are so self-centered, even in our virtues. I'll say, "Yes, this is the kind of person I should be." Then I go out to further my own integrity. Rather, I should be saying, "This is what she needs. This is the kind of wife my husband should have."

To truly be lovers, we must seek virtue for the right reason: not because it makes us better people, but because it adds joy to our spouses' lives.

Kindness: How Do You Score?

The Lord created marriage as a way to show us His love. Unless kindness is present in our homes, our husbands and wives cannot experience that love.

We can't excuse a lack of kindness by saying everyone has defects, that we'll make up for our lack in other ways.

That's a self-centered response. It's like saying, "Well, I score pretty well when you consider everything." Virtue is not like a chatty magazine quiz: "How do *you* score as a lover?" If we must score, let's score on what the Lord wants us to give our husbands and wives.

We can't say, "Well, I'm kind enough to suit my taste. I don't think I'm bad at it." We have to concentrate, instead, on how others perceive us. Do they believe we're approachable? Do our wives think they have to warm us up—or thaw us out—before mentioning certain subjects? Are they nervous because they don't know how we're going to react? We might discover that we frighten them.

Do our husbands think they have to do all the right things before they can approach us? Are they afraid of us? Yes, husbands can be afraid of their wives.

We should all ask ourselves, "Am I a fearsome person?" We're dodging the issue if we ask merely, "Do I sometimes get mad?" Anger is only a symptom of a larger ill. Must our lovers go through all sorts of contortions, building up the courage to risk talking to us about something important?

Some old jokes have more than a grain of truth. How about the one where the wife has a traffic accident and she's afraid to tell her husband? She's physically bruised and shaken emotionally, but she knows he'll be more concerned about the car.

We can inspire fear in our spouses without shouting. Maybe we're soft-spoken on the outside. Maybe we don't get angry at all, but there is a tenseness about us; our lovers never know when the volcano is going to erupt. It never has because it never has to. Like a nuclear warhead, it's a deterrent.

When we're in the presence of a kind person, we always

feel relaxed and at ease. We can be ourselves. We don't have to weigh our words or wonder how to bring up certain topics.

Those around us best experience our kindness when they believe we're pleased with them. When we're kind, they know we're always on their side. That doesn't mean we agree with everything they say, do, and think. It means that no matter what happens, we're always with them. That type of mentality, expressed both verbally and nonverbally, brings our lovers tremendous security and a sense of well-being.

Tender Loving Care

Our natural activist American reaction is to want to do something about this. We say, "Okay, how do I act kind?"

Yes, that's a worthwhile question. We'll come to it, but first we need to look into our hearts. Our actions of kindness will flow much more naturally from a loving frame of reference. Ask yourselves these questions: "When I'm sitting on the divan, reading the paper, or stirring soup at the stove, how tender am I toward my spouse?"

"How warm am I feeling right at this moment?" If we find a hardness in ourselves or even just a shoulder shrug, we have to change. We have to stop, breathe deeply, and deliberately build up some kind thoughts about our husbands or wives. We have to reflect on those qualities that originally attracted us to them.

There are many practical ways to be kind. What about the kindness of a home-cooked meal? What about the kindness of a truly gentle kiss? Not just a casual peck, but one I give her with me in it . . . or a look across the dining room table that's misted over a bit with gratitude and affection . . . or a hug during the evening, for no reason at all except that I was thinking about her, dreaming a bit about him, and I wanted him to know that.

Often, we men translate kindness into perfume, flowers, and restaurant meals. That's fine, but it's much kinder to be alert on the days we're not going out or buying gifts.

We have trouble achieving kindness because we aren't spontaneous. We tend to practice it only when it's needed: when something is wrong or when we've hurt someone. More important are the small kindnesses we can do every day, not for any reason but just to be kind. Of course, we do have to respond to our lovers' needs, but it's even better to have kindness flowing from our very being. Then we're going beyond healing hurts. We're creating an environment in which our lovers truly enjoy life.

Love Is Never Jealous

We imagine horrible pictures of jealousy: of Jezebel, for instance, who had innocent Naboth stoned to death because her husband wanted his vineyard. We have visions of a woman who tells her husband, "We're going home," because another woman talked to him for thirty seconds; of a man who won't let his wife out of the house unless he's with her.

Most of us don't have that type of jealousy. We're jealous in subtler, more significant ways, and we're jealous more often than we think.

Men will tell me, "That's a feminine problem. I'm not jealous." But often, lack of jealousy is simply indifference. Indifference isn't a virtue.

What makes us jealous? Usually, the small things: When someone talks only to our spouse, for instance, and we feel we're being ignored. If our spouse is heavily praised, we think it's great—providing we get equal time. Sometimes we're jealous when the children bring their needs to our spouse. "Why do they always go to her?" we grumble. "Why don't they come to me?"

Sometimes the jealousy is more serious, an envy of lifestyles: "He has it so good," we think. "He spends money on his clothes and people respect him. I stay home all the time, just like the family dog."

Part of the reason for this jealousy is that we're expected to be that way. Ever since we were little, we've been trained to resent others' good fortune. Sometimes the other person doesn't even deserve our envy. Maybe a neighbor—or husband—goes on trips and stays in interesting places. But once he's comfortable with the idea of checking into a hotel, those "interesting" places all begin to look the same. Whether he's in the Hilton or a nameless motel on the highway, he's still a man away from home, surrounded by four impersonal walls. When he goes on the road, those walls are interchangeable, whether in Atlanta or San Diego, Anchorage or Hartford.

Jealously is antilove. Jealousy is thinking about me. It's concentrating on what I'm getting out of our marriage. It's not finding delight in the other person's delight. It's a mean, ugly little vice.

Too often we excuse ourselves by saying, "Well, that's the kind of person I am. He knew that when he married me," or "She knew I wouldn't want her spending all her time with the kids."

But our lovers never had to live with our jealousy before

they got married. It's much more a part of their lives now that its viciousness is coming to the forefront.

Jealousy, of course, is not necessarily an overall attitude. It can be restricted to one or a few areas of a couple's life together. Maybe I'm not generally jealous of you, but I am jealous of your relationship with your mother, your success at work, or the way the children obey you.

That jealousy strongly interferes with the love and trust that should be between us.

Love Reaches Out

If we're going to be the lovers St. Paul commends, we must concentrate on our spouses. We must see love as a means to bring delight to them, not as a gift meant only for ourselves. When we become other-centered, we become happier as well. Small annoyances no longer bother us, and we become more cheerful and full of peace, no longer consumed with worries and regrets.

We can, indeed, live such lives if we ask for God's help. Each of us is supremely capable of patience and kindness and generosity of spirit.

We shouldn't regard that truth as a reason for despair. We all fail; that's normal. Our goodness is determined not by our failures but by our dreams, our goals for our marriages, and our willingness to try again after we've failed.

In Chapter 2 we'll discuss the remainder of St. Paul's message. But now let's take time to grow in openness to the virtues of patience, kindness, and generosity of spirit.

Search and Sharing

The end of each chapter in this book will include questions for self-search and for sharing with your spouse so the two of you can grow deeper in love. It will also include a prayer.

It's good to respond to the self-search questions with pencil in hand, even though this section of the exercise is private. Most of us think far more seriously when we write down our thoughts.

If your spouse is not participating in this book, do these questions anyway. Often, your growth in love will inspire your spouse to a greater love, too.

When working through the sharing questions with your spouse, each of you should write. Write for ten minutes. If you feel you have nothing to say, the enforced timing will often help stimulate your mind. Begin writing immediately, and if you don't know what to say, say so, and try to explain why.

Your written sharing is really a love letter, so begin with "Dear" and end with "Love." Remember to focus on your own feelings and to never, under any circumstances, lay blame on your spouse. If you can insert the word "that" in your feeling, you are expressing a judgment instead.

This expression is all wrong and a love-killer: "I feel that your low-down, selfish way of life makes me miserable and lonely."

This one is much better: "I feel miserable and lonely when you tinker with the car after work. I feel a yearning to spend more time together."

After you have both written, exchange your letters. Read them twice, then discuss them with love.

Consider these questions privately:

What type of husband, what type of wife, would my spouse like to have? (Make a list.) How can I become that person?

How do I feel about growing in patience, kindness, and generosity of heart? If I am resisting these virtues, why? Am I willing to work and pray for them?

Share this question with your spouse:

How do I feel, knowing that my role as your husband, as your wife, is to make your life delightful and worthwhile?

Finally, let us invite God into our marriages:

Dear Lord, let us always be patient with each other.

Help us believe in each other's goodness, in each other's willingness to grow closer. Let us not lose hope and withdraw our love.

Lord, help us to be kind. Help us to live daily with warmth in our hearts for each other and let that warmth show in our actions.

Let us not be jealous of each other, but, instead, let us take pleasure in each other's good fortune.

Open our hearts to change so that we can give each other the gift of Your generous love. Amen.

CHAPTER 2

YOU ARE LOVE, MY DEAR

(1 Co. 13:4–13)

I was in the supermarket the other day, and a stranger approached me; said he was an author researching some book. He asked me, "For you, lady, what is love?"

"Gee, I don't know," I said. "Love is, well, when you—"

"When you what?"

"I don't know."

He didn't go away; he just stood there, waiting for an answer.

I began to think. We were in the magazine section, and the headlines jumped out at me: "Love: are you getting enough?" "When the thrill is gone: love him or leave him?" "Love or money: what to do when your career comes first."

No, those weren't right.

"Love is, um, like when I was painting the living room, and my two-year-old tipped the paint can off the ladder," I said. "I was soaked, the carpet was soaked; it was awful. I cried. I was too depressed to even clean it up. Harry didn't say anything. He just loaded me in the car, took the kids to mom's house. Then he drove me to my favorite restaurant, paint and all. People were looking at us, and I was so embarrassed, I started to giggle. Harry started, too, and we couldn't stop. And you know, I realized the mess wasn't that bad."

"Hmmph," he said. "Maybe that's an example of love. But what *is* love?"

All right, smart guy, I thought. I'll get you this time. "Love is like this: One day, I just couldn't do anything right at work. I got home late, and was I mad. I was shouting so loud, the dog was hiding under the coffee table. Harry didn't shout back. He just waited until I'd stopped for breath and all the pans were already across the room. I wanted him to say something—one comment. I wanted someone to fight with. But he wouldn't do it. He just said, 'It really is hard, isn't it? I understand.' Now, that's love."

The stranger looked bored. "I'm looking for something more significant than a story, no matter how touching it may be."

"Well, I can't explain it any better," I said. "Love is the way Harry listens to me. Sometimes I rattle on, and I don't know why he doesn't fall asleep. Love is the way he gets up with me at six A.M. He doesn't have to do that. Love is the way he's patient with my kids."

He raised an eyebrow. "That's love? You were supposed to say love is the way you feel when he takes you in his arms."

40

I just winked.

I couldn't read the expression on his face. "If he's that great, you shouldn't have married him," he said with sort of a sneer. "It only goes downhill."

Too bad he didn't warn me sooner, I thought. Years sooner.

Like the cynical stranger in the supermarket, we still think love is somewhere out there; like perfection or saintliness, love is some unattainable state of grace nobody can touch.

That's not true. Love is all around us, and there's more waiting in the wings. God is eager to make us more loving than we could imagine, if only we would ask Him.

Love is what we are and what we can be.

Love Is Not Boastful or Conceited

We have a hard time believing this passage of Scripture was meant for us. Maybe the Corinthians were conceited, but we aren't. On the contrary, Paul knew what he was talking about. We can be conceited no matter what our circumstances.

We are truly good people, but we're good people with bad training—and some natural tendencies that are less than noble. We've been taught to evaluate: Who has it better than we do? Who's smart? Who will make a good manager someday? Which friends will let us down? We've also been taught to place everyone according to rank: Who was the most popular girl in school? Who was most likely to succeed? Who wasn't going to amount to anything?

What does he do for a living? Is she worth cultivating as a friend?

We need to take a good, long look at ourselves, not in contempt or with feelings of low self-esteem. We do have to be honest: We have to know where we fail, so we can change those old love-killing habits and become the people Jesus Christ wants us to be.

When you see your flaws mirrored anywhere in this book, don't think you're a bad person. Everyone does wrong things—everyone. Instead, be proud that you have the courage to face your mistakes. Now you can change them. Don't concentrate on how unhappy you may have made your lover. Instead, read with a sense of excitement, thinking of how much happier your lives will be now.

This Superiority Is Killing Me

When does our conceit cause us to obey the loveless rules of this world? When do we turn our backs on the love that could be ours?

We could think, for instance, that we're superior in logic. "If he'd only listen to *me* . . ." we might think, or "If only she'd take *my* advice . . ."

Maybe we're overly proud because of our academic or professional credentials.

We might be overly proud of our openness or even our reserve: "I'm in touch with my feelings. Now if he would only get in touch with his, we'd have a great marriage." Or "I don't say anything if I can't improve on silence."

We can even feel smug about our insecurities. Usually we call them "feminine sensitivity" or "male ego." We might think, "I'm so sensitive, I'm better at love than he is," or "Where would she be without a good, strong man?" We can also feel superior about our jobs. We men might say, "I have to earn a living. I don't have time for . . ." any number of things. We can use this as an excuse not to work on our personalities at home, or to dodge out of spiritual growth or church work. We're satisfied that because we put paychecks in the bank every Friday, we're superior. Women are learning this superiority, too, but altered slightly: "I don't have time for volunteer work. I have a real job."

Holier than Thou

We can put on airs in our faith too, and sometimes it's easy to get away with that. I grew up in an Irish Catholic neighborhood in New York City. My mother didn't put on airs about her faith, but my sister and I both decided that my mother was the family's good Catholic. She went to daily mass and communion, had attended Catholic schools, was knowledgeable and very active in church affairs.

My father had to drop out of public school in the ninth grade and never set foot inside a Catholic school. He went to confession on Thursday before First Friday, went to communion on First Friday and the following Sunday, and that was that until the next month. He had the old Irish idea that you just couldn't go to communion unless you went to confession. He worked nights, so he wasn't able to involve himself in church activities. He was a good man, but when it came to "real faith" in the family, we looked to our mother.

Only after I had left home, when my dad was dead, did

I realize that he was every bit as good a Catholic as my mother was.

Sometimes we can fool ourselves by looking at the externals. We might feel virtuous if we belong to a prayer group, go to daily mass and communion, or are baptized in the Spirit. We're not putting anyone else down, but isn't there a hint of smugness there?

A good personal appearance is a mark of healthy self-respect, but we can also use it as a tool for conceit. We might think, "I'm pretty attractive. It would be a shame for me not to look my best." We can be equally conceited and think just the opposite: "I don't need to look good to feel good about myself. If you think I'm a slob, that shows how shallow you are." We can also justify spending money on clothes in a conceited way: "I'm going to buy that; it would look great on me."

Addicted To Affluence

We can be overly proud of the way we handle money, whether that means spending it or saving it. We may even be proud of the unselfish priority we give our lovers' needs. That's not pure generosity; it can also mean control. What if our lovers desire to put our needs first? Would we be reluctant to allow them to take the reins of fiscal management because we're better at it?

We may say we're not materialistic because we don't hoard money; we spend it as soon as it comes in. Or we seek to prove our lack of materialism by spending little and letting the money pile up in a bank account. Because we don't accumulate visible possessions, we deceive ourselves into thinking we're not acquisitive.

Most of us think we're not attached to money. Paradoxically, most of us also think we don't have enough of it. Those of us with three-bedroom homes want four, and those of us with four-bedroom homes want vaulted ceilings. Those of us with old cars want new ones, and those with two cars need one for each teenager. Money is an addiction; it's even stronger than heroin. People can break away from heroin, but how many of us can break away from money? Most of us probably think the idea's ridiculous. That's an indication of how addicted we really are.

Money can be a real area of conflict even between good husbands and wives, especially if one of them is not particularly good with the budget. Family finances might scare them or they're afraid to make a mistake: it's such a tremendous responsibility and they just don't have any experience at it. Maybe they simply don't have any natural skills for dealing with bills and mortgages, payments and savings. Then their spouses are strongly tempted to feel superior. They may not be especially good at it, either, but they judge they are.

The Noble Givers

We're yielding to superiority when we see ourselves as the givers in a love relationship: "Oh, he's a great guy. I'm glad I married him, but I'm the one who holds this marriage together," or "She's a wonderful, wonderful woman, but she couldn't make it without me."

This can happen in a number of areas. A woman can be superior in this way when it comes to sex. She may view lovemaking as a time when she takes care of her husband.

Men can feel superior as providers, and not just because they bring home the only paycheck or the biggest one. If they do the budgeting and make sure the family stays on an even financial keel, they may feel overly proud of that, too. This feeling of superiority can be even stronger when the man thinks he's the one who's making the sacrifices. After all, the money all goes to his wife and the children; none of it goes to him.

This feeling of superiority can encompass an entire marriage or only one specific area. In either case, it's not a harmless little idiosyncrasy.

If we're going to live lives of love, we must thoroughly explore this attitude of superiority toward each other. Conceit and boastfulness aren't pretty words, and it's hard to be honest with ourselves about them. None of us like to see ourselves as haughty braggarts. Nonetheless, all of us do have feelings of superiority, no matter how good we are.

It's far better to see our faults and change them than to close our eyes and deny they exist. Besides, we wouldn't fool anyone that way. Deep down, we'd know the truth. Others would, too, and be alienated from us.

"Anything You Can Do, I Can Do Better"

Remember the old Broadway song? It sounds catchy when sung with a smile, but in real life, it's anything but friendly.

Each of us needs to turn to our spouses and silently ask, "Where do I consider myself superior to you?" It's a difficult question, but a necessary one. It's undoubtedly true in some areas of our life together.

We're not speaking now of whether I can drive the car better, or sew a better seam, or change a flat tire on the highway with absolute confidence. Those are skills; important as they are, they pale in significance beside our personal qualities: kindness, understanding, listening, thoughtfulness.

Where do I consider myself superior to you? Sometimes we excuse ourselves by saying, "Well, my superiority is my contribution to our marriage. I'm more thoughtful and my spouse is more understanding. We work as a team."

That's not teamwork; it's competition. Superiority, no matter how gracious, is never a plus in a love relationship. Each of us brings special qualities into our love relationships, and that's great, unless they come with a price tag of conceit.

Sometimes we don't realize the superiority that hides even behind our compliments. We may say, "Yes, you are much more sensitive than I am. But I'm much better at making money." Or "Why don't you do the entertaining when people come over? After all, you're much better at it than I am." Or "Why don't you discipline the kids? You don't lose your temper like I do."

Conflict grows even more intense when we believe we're superior in the same area. Most often, couples clash over their children, because both of them think they know more about child-raising. But when parents clash over strict or lenient philosophies, a child doesn't see a philosophical debate. He sees the trauma of discord in the home and the lack of guidance. It's better for his parents to work together, whether they're stricter or more lenient than one prefers.

Women Are Better than Men?

I don't believe we can grow to adulthood in this society without learning that women are superior as people. We were taught that lesson ever since we were tiny children. Boys may have more freedom, but girls have more attention, more praise, more recognition, more opportunities to participate in family life and to be valued for that participation.

Those attitudes were communicated in very strong terms. Little girls are made of sugar and spice and everything nice, but what are little boys made of? Frogs and snails and puppy dogs' tails. Little girls are dressed in pretty dresses with ribbons in their hair; they're so affectionate and they help Mommy around the house. Our hearts go out to a teenage daughter when she goes out with a new boy. We worry: Does he drink or do drugs? Will he take her into the wrong crowd or break her heart? How often do we worry about our sons' dates?

We grow to maturity in an environment where sympathy goes naturally to the woman. When there's a problem, we're quick to blame the man. This attitude is deeply ingrained; almost all of us assume that when it comes to personal qualities, a woman is far ahead. Not only does this excuse her husband from trying, but it allows her to take over in the home.

Everyone seems to recognize that she's much kinder, more thoughtful, sensitive, and understanding, more loving, and more capable of establishing a proper pattern for everyone. The husband's role is to support her in all this. She isn't always pleased with this attitude, because it puts tremendous burdens on her. Nonetheless, her superiority is firmly established in both their minds, so they live it out.

When it comes to education, initiative, and leadership, we tend to think the man is superior. His wife may have far more talent than he has, but we still expect him to take charge in a public situation. Feminism notwithstanding, we're still reluctant to give women equal opportunities, whether in jobs, church work, or even family finance. This is gradually changing, but we have a long way to go.

When we live this way, we're creating rival superiorities, then passing like ships in the night. We'll say, "I'm better at marriage than he is. But then, women are that way," or "You know, I'm actually much kinder than my wife."

The comparisons are killing us. We have no right to them, either. We can try to increase our virtues, but we can't compare them with our spouses' lack of virtue. Not only does it spell death for love, it doesn't help us to be better people.

Love Is Never Rude

Until now, St. Paul's Scripture passage was serious. What happened here? Love is never rude? That's hardly worth bothering about, is it? Paul was probably tired the night he wrote that. Maybe someone stepped on his toes or his landlady shouted at him.

Wait. Let's think for a moment what a gift it would be to have a spouse who was naturally full of small courtesies. When you put all those courtesies together, they're no longer small.

During your dating days, you were delighted by all the little favors you did for each other. You wanted to show your reverence for each other; to let him know he was important to you, that she counted in your life.

If we listen to the sophisticated doomsayers around us, we'll learn that you just can't keep your best foot forward all your life. Strange; they're telling us we could never be more well behaved than we were as adolescents. If we could put our best foot forward when we were dating, why can't we keep it there after we're married?

Let's ask, how courteous are we as lovers?

For instance, do you open the car door for her from the outside, as you did when you were dating? Or do you lean over and open it from the inside? Do you do it at all? Do you try to please him with his favorite foods, or are you weary of fixing them?

Why don't you take some time to think of all the tender little courtesies you performed for each other in your dating days and in the early days of your marriage? They really make quite a list, and you did them spontaneously, without thinking too much about them. Go ahead; write them down, and when you're through, ask yourself a question. How could it be wrong to perform these little courtesies for her; how could it be a mistake to do these things for him?

Maybe by now, you're squirming in your chair or rolling your eyes toward the ceiling. What an embarrassing idea. People would wonder what was going on. Even your spouse would be puzzled.

But why not do them anyway? People would probably decide you were in love.

The Price of Politeness

Unfortunately, we tend to wonder, "Why do I have to do these things? Are they necessary anymore?" Don't look at them that way; look from the opposite perspective: "How could it hurt my beloved wife, my beloved husband, if I did these nice little things?"

When we think like that, we can't come up with any good reasons. We dropped those courtesies because they cost too much: too much effort, too much trouble, too much thought.

That's why St. Paul says love is not rude. When we're courteous toward our spouses, we're never rude. These courtesies may look small, but they create an atmosphere of kindness toward each other. The two are very closely related.

Let's stop for a moment and think of how often we permit ourselves to be rude to each other. We're not speaking now of omitting the small courtesies, but of being purely and simply rude: the sharp tone of voice, the imperious manner, the orders we give each other, the demands we make.

"That's one of the privileges of marriage," we might say. But look at that attitude from the outside: "Ah, see that couple being rude to each other? They must be married."

Another form of rudeness is name calling. Language doesn't have to earn an "R" rating to be hurtful. Maybe I've cleaned up my vocabulary, but still there's a cynical tone of voice or a biting harshness in the way I say my love's name. It's only a name, I argue. But in truth, I've turned a vital part of my spouse's identity into a curse.

Perhaps I use a term of affection in a bitter tone: "Why

don't you do the dishes—*honey*," or "I hear you—*dear*." If I do this, I rob the endearment of its power. It will never hold the same loving meaning for my spouse again.

The Sin of Indifference

Perhaps we need to examine our habits of rough teasing. Teasing can be a gentle gift, but it can also deliver a fist to the face. How often do we permit ourselves the sin of this kind of teasing?

Maybe I remember embarrassing my wife in front of others. Not too long ago, perhaps, we joked a little, then I said, "I want to introduce everyone to my *first* wife."

At home that night, she told me she didn't like that. Even before she spoke, I knew she was unhappy, but I pointedly told her no one else was bothered by the joke.

If no one had been bothered—my wife included—it would have been all right. But since she was hurt, I should stop that kind of teasing. It's rude to be indifferent to her feelings.

We insist that our children say "thank you" and "please," but when we're angry with our husbands or wives, our "pleases" and "thank yous" become absolutely chilled with ice.

Rudenesses are not necessarily big. Maybe I'm merely on the phone when my husband comes home. "I can't hang up," I think. "If I told my girlfriend I had to say good-bye because my husband was home, she'd think I was crazy." But that's all right. I'm supposed to be crazy about him.

St. Paul knew what he was saying when he wrote that love isn't rude. We've come to tolerate rudeness on a daily basis, and we pay by losing happiness and peace in our homes. We're especially careless of the little courtesies, those small gifts of respect we once gave to each other. Now we're too busy or too "married" to work on them.

Love Never Seeks Its Own Advantage

In other words, love is not selfish. It's easy to be self-centered, to seek our own advantage, no matter how good we may be in so many ways. We certainly want our spouses to be happy, and we'll even help them seek their own happiness. But there's a difference: If they're not happy, we feel sad. If we're not happy, we feel a desperate sense of urgency. Instead of unity, we create a sense of distance, with ourselves irresistibly coming first.

This can happen in sex. We might think, "You want to watch television? Well, *I* want to make love," or "I can't make love to you tonight. I'm angry with you right now, and you wouldn't want me if my heart wasn't in it."

We can be self-seeking in conversation, too. "If your subject turns me on," we imply, "I'll listen. But you can't expect me to listen to a woman's subject," or "You know I don't care about hunting and fishing." In other words, I'm seeking my own entertainment rather than your satisfaction.

This attitude says, "If it's my kind of topic, I'll take part in the conversation." It might not be my kind of topic, but she should be my kind of woman; he should be my kind of man. I should be always wanting to know more about my beloved.

Early Birds and Night Owls

If you enter a home where a day person is married to a night person, you'll probably find lovers trapped in the lonely cycle of seeking their own advantage. Take this case, for example:

"For some reason, he likes getting up early," the wife says. "He whistles around the house when it's pitch-dark outside. I can hardly find my coffee before eight A.M., but I have lots of energy at night. I like to watch the late show after he goes to bed."

"I doze off in front of the television after supper," her husband adds. "I can't seem to help it. She threatens to put a construction sign over me that says: 'Man Sleeping.' "

If she worked during the day and he worked the night shift, they would realize how much they were suffering. But they—and many of us—establish such patterns in our own homes. It's a self-seeking way of life. We're really saying, "I'm not going to change my way of life for him," or "She can't seriously expect me to change the habits I've had for years."

God didn't create day people and night people, though. He made all people in His own image; He made them to be lovers.

It's both ironic and sad: Many husbands feel despair because married passion "naturally" fades, but they arrange their lives so love has little chance to bloom. Likewise, many women feel lonely for their husbands' company, but create schedules that force their husbands to go to bed alone. Then, because these wives go to bed so late, they can't get up to be with their husbands in the morning.

No wonder these people are unhappy. But how do they make themselves feel better? By retreating even further into their estranged schedules.

Of course, these schedules often begin as a reaction to hurt or loneliness. A wife may think, "He doesn't pay me any attention anyway. I might as well read a book," while her husband decides, "I might as well begin that big painting project. She won't want to make love tonight. She'll be reading." These situations call for healing, not retreat.

Who determines the schedule at your house: when meals are served, which activities and social events take place? If you're the one, ask yourself, "Am I being self-serving?" Selfishness often masquerades as efficiency or rightness. Do any of these sound like you?

"I want my supper on the table when I come home. I worked hard all day and I deserve a good meal."

"Nothing is going to happen around this house until the supper dishes are done. Got it?"

"I'm not going to have those things hanging over me. I don't want to think about them for the rest of the night."

"Monday night football is my one form of relaxation, so don't plan anything for that night, and keep the kids out of the way."

"I have a right to enjoy myself and I don't care if you're tired. We're going out tonight."

We can be self-seeking in many normal, everyday ways. We don't necessarily want mink coats or Ferraris. We may just want to go out on Saturday night, and we're convinced everyone understands that.

Love Does Not Take Offense

Anger is probably the greatest source of friction in our homes. Its damage isn't confined to the trauma of fighting or even the chill of indifference. Often, anger is held in reserve as a threat, creating an air of constant tension.

How angry are you? That doesn't always mean, "How often do you shout?" You may be a very angry person, even though you never express your anger.

This is a method of control. After one look at your face, does your lover know he'd better treat you right, she'd better walk softly?

Perhaps you have to explode only once a year, because when you do, it's earth-shattering. The rest of the time, you have only to threaten to get angry and your lover will surrender.

How many wives are afraid their husbands might lose their tempers? Such a husband may control himself manfully, but the effort is so intense, she'll say, "Settle down. I give in. I don't want you having a coronary." Either way, he wins, and when there are winners in a marriage, everyone loses.

The threat of anger is especially effective—so to speak—when used by wives against their husbands. It causes much more hurt than they realize. So many women don't understand a man's desperate need for peace in his home.

When a woman wants peace, she usually means, "Let's talk this through. There's something between us; let's get it out, even if it means a fight." The man's definition of peace, though, is closer to "I don't want to fight about it. If we have to resolve it in anger, let it lie buried."

A husband and wife could avoid many hurts if they would both think through a problem before talking it through. Often, we calm down when we take time to think. We can see our lover's side and we don't blurt out the first angry words that come to mind. The hurt from those angry words lasts a long time and it causes both of us, especially the man, to be wary in the future.

Many of us have learned to talk through our problems, and that's a marvelous improvement over keeping our problems inside, where they can poison a relationship with misunderstanding and resentment. It's not good, though, to voice every angry feeling, no matter how much it hurts.

Let's add thinking things through to our repertoire of marital skills. When we know we're losing control, one of us should just say, "Time out." Then both of us should sit quietly for ten to fifteen minutes, thinking of where we stand on this problem, what we want resolved, and how we can talk calmly and lovingly.

But You Won't Listen Unless I Shout

We've talked about coping with our own anger. Now, how about our spouses' anger? Can we do anything about that?

Yes, indeed, and not with blame or accusations. We can even offer more than sympathy. Each of us can ask ourselves, "How much do I provoke my lover's anger?"

Often, men will blame their wives, saying, "She's always ready to blow up." Why is that? She may be convinced she has to shout to be heard. We look on anger as a small failing, but it's probably our biggest cause of marital unhappiness. Anger is destructive because we use it as an excuse to say things we've been storing inside. We'll let something fester within us until it gets so painful, it spurts out. Then we'll excuse ourselves: "I only said that because I was angry."

Maybe the reverse is really the truth: "I was angry only because I was thinking about that." Besides, one sin does not excuse another. The insults we deliver in anger often take months and even years to heal. In the meantime, those grudges poison the happiness of the person who's holding them.

Love Does Not Store Up Grievances

Love is not supposed to be resentful, but all of us do hold resentments at one time or another.

How many men are like the Greek hero Achilles, who sulked in his tent during the Trojan War because the king had taken away his girl?

"The world just doesn't understand me," we grumble, which may be just as well.

We may think we're nursing our own hurts. Really, we're punishing our wives. We're creating a miserable environment in our homes, even if we do excuse ourselves with a phrase like "Well, I don't do this very often, but sometimes I just can't help it."

We need to find some other way to air those frustrations. Maybe we should talk them out more frequently, long before they have a chance to build up. If we let resentments silently churn inside, they grow into big issues, which could have been resolved so much more easily.

Women do this, too. I remember going home with a man once, a lawyer; when he opened the door and saw his wife's face, he knew a storm was coming. "Honey," he said, "can we have a statute of limitations of five years?"

The Two-Day Rule

Actually, that statute should be much shorter. Why store up our pain and anguish for years when we can get rid of it right away?

How long should we be able to cling to a slight or an injury? No more than two days.

If you haven't resolved a grievance within two days, forget it, and once you've talked it out, don't bring it up again. We can't keep bludgeoning our spouses with the same complaints.

Why don't you make a list of your grievances: grievances against your spouse that are in your heart right now. Be honest with yourself. What grudge do you have against her? What gripes do you have against him?

Think about them, one by one, then decide how you'll get rid of them. You'll be tempted to say, "I'll go ahead and list them, then we'll talk them out. That'll get rid of them."

That won't work in this case. You've probably already talked out a lot of them without success. But even if you haven't, if they're more than two days old, consider them dead. Forget them.

You can do it if you truly want to. You remember them because you think about them and bring them up and mull them over. Now stop the brooding and start to ponder the good things instead. Try to remember the positive aspects of your relationship with each other rather than the negative ones. It's hard sometimes, but it works wonders.

If you're feeling some reluctance, don't be surprised. We really don't want to give up all our gripes. We treasure them; they're precious possessions, like wedding pictures or old war medals. We think about them a lot; we take them out and polish them whenever they start to fade.

They're with us because they make us martyrs. We're like the boy who daydreams about hitting a grand slam home run with bases loaded in the bottom of the ninth in the deciding game of the World Series. We're dreamers, too. We daydream about our hurts and proclaim our innocence.

A Change of Attitude

How often do we air our marital grievances with our friends?

Don't you men put on halos and say, "That's what women do." You do the same thing, a bit more subtly: you talk about women. "Aren't women touchy about little things? They're always complaining," you'll say. But anyone who knows men knows you're talking about your wife.

Somewhere in the conversation, you'll unintentionally stir up trouble by asking, "Is your wife like that?" Perhaps you won't have to. The conversation itself will make your companions aware of flaws in their own wives—flaws they hadn't noticed before.

In the neighborhood or at work, how often do wives talk to one another about their husbands? The conversations take different forms, but they usually all mean, "Does your husband do this to you?"

Often, we're telling our own version of events, slanted by our own feelings. This is actually detraction, and often, it's slander. We're not free to destroy our spouses' reputations.

Worse, talking about our gripes can establish them more firmly in our minds. When friends respond sympathetically, we begin to feel justified. These friends aren't really friends; if they were, they'd work toward harmony, not division.

We each have a choice: we can continue to brood over our slights or mull over our spouses' virtues.

Don't think that you can't stop brooding. That's an attitude of hopelessness. Your negativity is a bad habit, not a personality trait given to you by the Lord. Let today be the day you change. You've probably changed hobbies, your goals in life, your job, even your values and ideals. Why not change your attitude as well?

We're all afraid to let go of the hurts; we think our spouses will take advantage of us. Even if they did, though, we'd be happier than we are now. Brooding certainly doesn't add joy to our lives. Our rights are very cold bedmates.

We have to be absolutely practical: do we want to live loving and happy lives or not? If we choose, we can be sharp-tongued and on target; our lovers won't get away with a thing. Then what have we accomplished?

We can excuse ourselves by saying, "But, gee, if I let go, he'll walk all over me; she'll take me for a ride. Things will just get worse." Nothing could increase the pain more than the way we keep it alive inside ourselves.

Love Does Not Rejoice at Wrongdoing, But Finds Its Joy in the Truth

Sometimes we really do rejoice in wrongdoing: when the kids stand up to Mom or Dad, for instance. Occasionally we rejoice in saying, "I told you so"; "Now maybe he'll listen to me"; "She'll hear me next time and things will get better around here." Sometimes we're glad when we've said something hurtful to our lovers. Rather than feeling their pain, we're smug, at least for a moment. "Well, he hurt me," we say defensively. "She hurt me first. Maybe she ought to know how it feels."

Of course, we don't usually behave this way, but these things do happen, and they happen entirely too often. We'll yield to the temptation to take our lovers down a peg, or we'll be angry with them, angry enough to be pleased when something bad happens. We don't like to admit that about ourselves; it's too petty and mean. That's exactly what it is, and that's what we should remind ourselves when we're doing it. After all, we are people of God; we're truly free to change.

Love Is Always Ready to Make Allowances

This means no retaliation. That's a real gift in marriage, isn't it? Too often, our spouses will do one small thing and we'll want to send in the army. We call it preventive medicine.

Because we're human, there is a streak of vengeance in each of us. We're good people with the strength to conquer it, but first we have to look it in the eye. Most of us don't see ourselves as vengeful, however. We want to believe retaliation is justified. We hold back for a while, but if we don't get satisfaction one way or another, we attack. Sometimes the vengeance is buried: "I'm so furious over this, I can't help but shout."

Let's ask ourselves, "How do we fight?" Are we all-out fighters? Maybe we pride ourselves on that. We're not peace-at-any-price types; we really fight. Then God help us. There are times when a fight is good to clear the air, but too often we fight so we can hurt our lovers as much as they've hurt us.

How do we react to unfairness? Do we seek fair play? Maybe we shouldn't. Fairness in a relationship is not a good thing. Christ calls us all to be givers, not to establish compromises.

In my study of Scripture, I found that Jesus never used the word *fair*, not even once. Fairness is a pagan standard, rather a nicely dressed "eye for an eye" philosophy. When we love, we're not preoccupied with our fair share.

A little child will pout when his parents say he can't have a toy. "It's not fair," he wails. He really means, "I have to have that toy; I'll be miserable if you don't give it to me and I'll tell you it's unfair because that might persuade you." He isn't expounding on abstract social philosophies; he's reacting to his desires.

Unfortunately, our definition of "unfair" is the same. We're saying, "I'm not getting enough"; enough attention, sex, money, time out, or relief from the chores. It really has nothing to do with injustice.

Do we keep score of the hurts in our marriages?

Do we keep score in housework and chores?

How about with money? Do we keep mental ledgers on the amounts our lovers spend? Usually we don't care how much it is, but if we really want something, we often find we can remember those expenditures.

How often do we keep score on time to ourselves? "She spent the whole afternoon at the mall, so why can't I watch the game for a few minutes?" or "He spent the whole afternoon watching that darned game. I have a right to run out for a few minutes to buy *his* socks."

We keep score in sex: "We made love last night; that ought to be enough to satisfy him"; "Why should she complain?"

We keep score in time spent with the family: "We stayed with his family for Thanksgiving; now it's my family's turn," or "Don't the kids have two sets of grandparents?"

We can keep score in religion, too: "I'm more saved than you are." We don't say it that way, but the implication is still there. Deep down, we think judgmental thoughts like "I wish he were more religious," or "She thinks she's so religious; she should just hear herself."

Love Is Always Ready to Trust

Do you trust your spouse to respect and like you, or do you keep parts of yourself secret, afraid they'll provoke scorn or disapproval?

Men, let's ask ourselves a few questions to determine how we feel about trusting our wives: Do I trust her to make the basic family decisions, or do I decide how much to save and whether to sell the house? Do I discipline the children because I think I'm better equipped or because I don't really trust her with them? Do I trust her with money; with all of it or just the amount I think she can handle? Do I allow her to influence my judgment about money? Do I trust her with my mother? When we get into the car, do I automatically sit in the driver's seat or do I trust her to drive me?

Now, that's a real sign of love, isn't it? It's interesting:

few men feel truly comfortable when their wives are driving, but whom do the insurance companies trust?

Wives, ask yourselves: Do I trust him enough to give him his paternity, or do I take his fatherhood away, letting him know the children are my responsibility? Do I trust him to care for myself and our children, or have I limited our family size because I can't handle it all by myself? Do I trust him to care for me better than I care for myself, or do I fend for myself, establishing a home life of my own and expecting him to fit in? Do I trust him to understand me or do I believe only another woman can understand a woman's heart? Am I more personal with my girlfriend than I am with my husband? Do I trust him to love the children as much as I do?

Many times, we don't trust because of past hurts or failures. We can't remain locked in our own pain; that's a slow, miserable death. Our Lord is anxious to renew us, slowly and gently if need be. We must be willing to open ourselves to His healing.

Love Is Always Ready to Hope

How do you know if you're hopeful? It's not hard. The sign of hope is a willingness to change.

I can say I have all the hope in the world, but unless I'm willing to change, I don't have any. If we're hopeless, we decide to continue living in mediocrity and making do with what we have.

Why don't you look at each other and silently ask, "Am I willing to change my relationship with you?" Your answer will show whether you have hope.

Be careful with this one. You'll be tempted to look at each other and say, instead, "Yes, we do need changes around here. Are you ready to make them, dear?"

We humans are constantly aware of the good things others are failing to do and the bad things they ought to stop doing. We fail to realize that if we became more understanding, they'd be under less pressure. St. Paul is calling us, not our lovers, to change.

Love Is Always Ready to Endure Whatever Comes

Time is the biggest deterrent to true love.

We're good people; we really want to love our wives and husbands. So often, though, we think, "He makes it too hard." "She's so difficult to deal with." "I do my best, but how can you expect me to love him when he's behaving this way?" "How can you expect me to love her all my life?"

St. Paul never asked you to love for fifty years. You can't. It's not human to be able, after being hurt deeply, to love day after day after day. You don't have to do that. You just have to love today.

It's not possible to keep talking for thirty, forty, or fifty years to a man who doesn't understand you, but he doesn't understand you today, and that's the only lack of understanding you have to endure. Yes, you can do it today.

We think because we've endured for a long time, we're excused from continuing. Really, that long track record of love is proof we can do it.

"Dearest, How Do You Want to Be Loved?"

Too much of our love is based on our own perceptions. We're saying, "This is the way I want to be loved. There-

66

fore, it must be the way you want to be loved, too." Without knowing it, we impose our style of loving on our spouses.

For example, a man may think sex will make everything all right. His wife may not feel that way, but she needs to know that it will, indeed, make things all right for him. She must heal his hurt the way he needs to be healed.

Meanwhile, her husband must understand that sex isn't enough to heal her hurt. He may become frustrated with her renewing desire to talk, but he must realize how important it is to her.

One way isn't better than the other, and we shouldn't trade off: "How do you expect me to desire you when you won't even pay me any attention?" or "Okay, I'll listen awhile—and then we'll make love."

Love has the power to endure. We don't want to endure. We'd rather our lovers change instead.

St. Paul calls us to the grace of endurance, to accept our spouses and respond to them in love.

You Are Love, My Dear

It would be very beautiful to go back to Chapter 1 and reread that passage from St. Paul. As you do, remember that love doesn't exist in the abstract. This beloved woman or man of yours is your love. Then read that passage a second time, saying the name of your spouse wherever you see the word *love*.

You might read, "Jane is always patient and kind. She is never jealous . . . Mike is not boastful or conceited; he is never rude and never seeks his own advantage . . . My beloved husband, you do not take offense or store up grievances . . . My dear wife, you are always ready to make allowances, to trust and to hope. My darling, you can endure whatever comes . . ."

Just mull that over. Think of specific ways she lives out her kindness, her hope, her endurance; ways you've experienced his patience, his refusal to be rude, his trust. Love never fails, and you don't fail each other.

Then write these down, specifically listing the ways your spouse lives out these qualities. Don't write generalities, but memories: examples of how you've personally experienced her kindness, his patience.

Make a full list. The more detailed you are, the more meaningful it will be. Don't remember only the spectacular occasions. The little ones count, too, and they're more frequent. They definitely add up.

When you're through, take that list and exchange it with your spouse. This can be a moment of great tenderness between you.

Maybe your love won't write his or her list. That's all right. Write yours anyway, then give it to your spouse. See, we keep falling into that trap of fairness: "If he doesn't write his list, mine will be a waste. Why should I bother?" Your list alone will be a great gift for both of you, giving you an increased awareness of yourself and a greater opportunity to truly understand each other.

Now let's celebrate Jesus' words of John 15:17: "My command to you is to love one another."

My letter to you, Dear:

This is a love letter; it should be written in your own words, using the name of your beloved. Don't be afraid to use that name as often as you can. The more often you call your love by name, the more he or she will feel truly cherished. Perhaps you would like to write something like this:

My dearest one,

I can't help but remember the many times you have been patient and kind with me. I remember when . . . You have a great heart and I see there's room in it for me. Thank you for your compliments and for watching with love when it was my turn to shine . . . You know I'm proud of you, and perhaps I'm most proud of the times when you stood back and smiled at my accomplishments when you had so many of your own . . . You are so concerned about me, you treat me with care. You have been unselfish so many times in our years together . . .

My dear, you are so loving. I haven't been aware enough of your eagerness to forgive me for my mistakes. There are so many times when you could have taken offense or stored up grievances, but you chose love instead . . .

You are such a treasure to me, beloved. You are always ready to understand . . . You give me a feeling of self-worth by trusting me, even when I don't deserve it. I have never thanked you for the time when . . . You never give up working on our relationship. Your hope for the growth of our love never seems to end; in that hope, I can see my own value. Your love makes you strong; you have endured all the trials of our life together without bitterness. I remember . . .

I believe your love, dear, will never end. It is more lasting than my finest goals and ambitions, greater than the wisdom of those I admire, even stronger than death itself.

Your love is real to me, and through it, I can see the love that God our Father has for me.

Without you, I would be lost and alone. No matter what I may achieve at work or at home, no matter how many people praise my intelligence, my skills, or my personality, I would be nothing without you, my love. I thank you, dear, for the wonderful gift of yourself that you're giving me. I love you.

Prayer for wives:

Dear God, I want to thank you for the wonderful treasure you have given me: my beloved husband. Help me to appreciate him and to never take his love for granted.

Please give me the grace to love him as generously as he loves me. Help me love him the way You intend: by making his life worthwhile rather than by selfishly focusing on my own life.

Help us both to grow together in love so we can heal each other and protect each other from the troubles of this world. Amen.

Prayer for husbands:

Dear God, I want to thank you for the wonderful treasure you have given me: my beloved wife. Help me to appreciate her and to never take her love for granted.

Please give me the grace to love her as generously as she loves me. Help me love her the way You intend, by making her life worthwhile rather than by selfishly focusing on my own life.

Help us both to grow together in love, so we can heal each other and protect each other from the troubles of this world. Amen.

CHAPTER 3

DO I LOVE YOU
ENOUGH?

(MT. 25:31–35)

It was two days until Passover, two days until Jesus would suffer His passion and resurrection. He was alone with His disciples on the Mount of Olives, readying them—and us—for that time when He would no longer walk the earth as a flesh-and-blood man.

His disciples still had lessons to learn; none of these would be easy. This last one would be the toughest of all. Possibly, with His great knowledge, He foresaw generations upon future generations listening to this very message, squirming in their church pews, wishing they could tune out or at least understand. Then He said . . .

When the Son of man comes in his glory, escorted by all the angels, then he will take his seat on his

71

throne of glory. All nations will be assembled before him and he will separate people one from another as the shepherd separates sheep from goats. He will place the sheep on his right hand and the goats on his left. Then the King will say to those on his right hand, "Come, you whom my Father has blessed, take as your heritage the kingdom prepared for you since the foundation of the world. For I was hungry and you gave me food, I was thirsty and you gave me drink, I was a stranger and you made me welcome, lacking clothes and you clothed me, sick and you visited me, in prison and you came to see me." Then the upright will say to him in reply, "Lord, when did we see you hungry and feed you, or thirsty and give you drink? When did we see you a stranger and make you welcome, lacking clothes and clothe you? When did we find you sick or in prison and go to see you?" And the King will answer, "In truth I tell you, in so far as you did this to one of the least of these brothers of mine, you did it to me." Then he will say to those on his left hand, "Go away from me, with your curse upon you, to the eternal fire prepared for the devil and his angels. For I was hungry and you never gave me food, I was thirsty and you never gave me anything to drink, I was a stranger and you never made me welcome, lacking clothes and you never clothed me, sick and in prison and you never visited me." Then it will be their turn to ask, "Lord, when did we see you hungry or thirsty, a stranger or lacking clothes, sick or in prison, and did not come to your help?" Then he will answer, "In truth I tell you, in so far as you neglected to do this to one of the least of these, you neglected to do it to me." And they will go away to eternal punishment, and the upright to eternal life.

Matthew 25:31–46

The Hidden Poor

This Scripture passage fills us with awe, doesn't it? We also do a bit of squirming. We feel a little guilty; we wish we were more like Mother Teresa. Then we're rather glad we're not. We think of all those we aren't helping: the poor sleeping in the gutters in Calcutta, the junkies in the slums of New York, the abused children on the pornography strips in Fort Lauderdale and Houston.

We feel frustrated. We don't even know these people; what does Jesus expect us to do?

The Lord doesn't expect us all to abandon our houses, resign from our jobs, and give our bank accounts to the poor. He works more compassionately and thoroughly than we can imagine. Before we step outside to care for those on the street, he wants us to begin at home.

When we hear this Scripture passage, we never think about our own families. They're well provided for, we believe; after all, we're already there. We're taking care of them as well as we possibly can.

Let's think for a moment.

We've lately become aware of the hidden poor who live on fixed incomes; the little old ladies in walk-up flats who eat cat food because that's all they can afford. Our husbands and wives are often members of the hidden poor, living invisible and dejected right beneath our noses.

We're not cruel people who are deliberately ignoring them. We've simply slipped into blind thinking. When the Lord speaks of poverty and the desperate needs of others, we look at our lovers' dry, warm homes, their bounteous food and clothing, and say, "Well, she's well provided for; compared to the tough kids on the Minnesota Strip or the bag ladies in Newark, he has it made."

It sounds sensible; fair, even, but you can't fill your lover's needs by saying other people are worse off. It would be like telling a heat-struck desert wanderer he doesn't have it so bad; the other guys who came this way are dead.

It's like the old routine our parents used to use on us— and we use on our children. When they won't eat their vegetables, we tell them about the starving people in India. For some reason, parents think that's a sound argument. Kids don't; they still don't eat.

Sometimes we feel guilty about helping our own families when others have it so rough. We think the Lord wants us to adopt a crisis mentality. He doesn't. He wants us to love one another. He made that clear throughout His ministry. Remember the passage of John 12:1–8, when a woman named Mary anointed Him with oil? Judas Iscariot complained that the cost of that oil should have been given to the poor. Judas said, in effect, "What's this business about taking care of one man?" We all know how Jesus rebuked him.

By taking care of those at home, we aren't sacrificing the needy. We're building spiritual muscle; we're in training to be serious, Olympic-weight lovers. The more compassion we display toward our spouses, the more our hearts will be moved by all people. If we can live with a husband or a wife and not notice his need, her hurts, how can we be sensitive to people who aren't even close?

Why Must Charity Begin at Home?

Jesus' teaching of the Last Judgment is a solemn one. Strong as it is, we can see the justice of it. There's a certain

74

beauty about Jesus' claiming oneness with the downtrodden. We're not too happy with the judgment section, especially when it's applied personally.

We send checks to our favorite charities, thinking these take care of the hungry and the naked, but deep down, we know cold cash isn't what the Lord had in mind. It's good, all right, but obviously He's speaking of something more.

We console ourselves with resolutions; we promise to do better before we hear the reading next time. We're uncomfortable and dissatisfied, but we really don't see much we can do. After all, we do have responsibilities.

So we don't clothe the naked; we don't feed the hungry. It's not because we're bad people; it's not because we don't care. It's because we're good people trying to lift a heavy load with our bare hands.

Faceless People

When we think of the poor and the downtrodden, we see a vast wave of despairing humanity on scale with a Hollywood movie extravaganza: slums where rats are co-equal with tenants; prisons crammed with unfortunates who are condemned to hopelessness and brutality. We see hospitals filled with children with incurable diseases and nursing homes reeking of loneliness.

The most outstanding part of our vision, though, is that these people have no faces.

We feel sorry for them, but they're not real to us. We don't know their names; we don't see their hunger; we don't know when they die.

This total anonymity makes them less than human to us. That's why we're so grateful for people like Mother

Teresa, tending the sick in India. She's contributed so much to a world we believe we can't touch.

We can't touch these faceless poor for the same reason we stay aloof from our lovers. We're trapped; as captive as the most wretched prisoner in solitary confinement in a third world prison. We're imprisoned in a middle-class lifestyle that keeps us enslaved to a false god, money. Money is a jealous god; it demands more and more devotion. We find ourselves working overtime to make money; taking on second jobs, scraping and saving—or charging—to own VCRs and newer cars and dinners out and furniture. All our purchases are fair and reasonable, or would be if they weren't paid for with the loneliness of our families.

Another of our false gods is independence. We think happiness is a solo quest, best achieved by becoming greater, more successful, more creative, more fun-loving, but not more loving of others. If we live this way long enough, we find ourselves angry and frustrated, pounding our fists on the table as we shout, "I am happy! I must be happy, because I finally have all the things I wanted."

Our middle-class mentality keeps us from loving the poor—and our spouses—the way Jesus intended.

What's Wrong with Saying "What's Wrong"?

We don't fully let Jesus into our hearts because we know it means trouble. If we really listen to Him, we will have to change, and change completely. That's why Jesus said no man can serve two masters.

We want to live according to the world's standards, but

we also want Jesus in our lives. It simply doesn't work that way. We must make a choice.

It's rather like a man who's in love with two women. If we men came home and said, "Honey, I can't decide whether I love you or my secretary. Can I have you both?" we'd get quite an answer. Yet we think it's unfair when we have to choose between Jesus and our self-centered ways of life.

But we're not doing anything *wrong,* we think.

Jesus didn't say only the wrong things had to change. He came to earth to offer a complete change, a better way. We can take Him or leave Him, but we can't have Him both ways.

When we're dealing with a moral issue, we tend to say, "But what's wrong with . . ." That's the worst question we can ask. It simply misses the whole point. It's an attempt to excuse ourselves; to wriggle by with the minimal amount of work. It's antilove.

"What's wrong with . . ." says our hearts are set on what we want or what we're already doing. To avoid this trap, we must look at what Jesus is offering rather than what we're losing if we follow His way.

The "what's wrong with . . ." trap caught the rich young man in the Bible, too. Remember him? He asked Jesus what he must do to inherit eternal life. Jesus told him to keep the ten commandments. When he replied that he had kept them since he was a child, Jesus said he could do one thing more to become perfect: give up all his money. The young man went away sad; he couldn't do it. Matthew, Mark, and Luke were all startled enough by the incident to include it in their Gospels (Mt. 19:16–22, Mk. 10:17–22, and Lk. 18:18–23).

Jesus didn't tell the young man his riches were evil. He

didn't say he had to give them up because he was misspending them. He simply offered that young man Himself.

It upsets us to read this passage because we know the rich young man was a good person. He wasn't a terrible sinner who had to be converted. He was already a beautiful person, and that's why Jesus offered him more.

He's offering us more, too.

Jesus didn't come to make us miserable. In John 10:10, He explained why He's here: "I came so that they may have life, and have it to the full."

The rich young man wasn't evil when he clung to his riches, but he missed so much wonder, so much delight in the Lord. It's easy for us, too, to forget that Jesus is never outdone in generosity. Our bread cast upon the waters comes back one hundredfold.

Cleaning House

That's why when we speak of doing good for others, we must start in our own homes. One of the reasons we don't do better in the inner cities is that we don't do very well at 14 Oak Street, 17 Hyacinth Lane, or wherever we live.

We certainly can't excuse ourselves from the call to social justice, but it won't be successful unless we personally love the people in our ministries. At best, our work will be a dutiful responding to needs rather than to people.

We may be indefatigable in the way we spend ourselves and our talents. We may even accomplish a lot of good, but something will be sadly lacking. We won't be spending our goodness on our families and friends: the people

Jesus gave us especially to care for, to respond to, to make the Gospel come alive in their hearts.

If I have a greater concern for the hunger of a stranger than for my lover, something is poignantly missing. It doesn't mean I'm a hypocrite; it means I haven't learned to really love. My service of the poor, then, won't be a gentle, tender, generous Gospel deed. It's likely to be angry, confrontational, and condemnatory. Even more likely, it will be efficient and cold; aimed toward helping a maximum number of bodies and loving hardly a soul.

I Was Hungry and You Gave Me Food

Let's center now on our relationship with each other. Where are we, compared to where the Lord wants us to be?

Our husbands and wives are hungry for the gift of ourselves. Have we given them the food of our company?

We'll begin with the one overwhelming, most important action a husband can take to renew his relationship with his wife. Soon, we'll turn toward women.

Husbands, our wives are starved for companionship. We do indeed come home in the evenings; in a real sense, we're there when they need us, but in another sense, we're not there at all. Our wives are hungry to experience us physically, emotionally, and spiritually.

Most of us have, over the years, grown separate from our wives. We relax over the newspaper or the game on television, or we pursue hobbies like weight-lifting or golf. We feel a sense of indignation when told we're not doing enough. After all, we spend eight hours a day, and probably more, earning a paycheck that keeps the family afloat.

Our paychecks, though, are not our most valuable asset. Our money doesn't provide our wives with the love and companionship they so eagerly desire from us. Even if today's women couldn't earn their own paychecks, our money would still pale in comparison with our qualities as lovers.

Learning to Talk

To be lovers, we must talk with our wives. We can't explain, "But I don't know what to say. She's great, she never runs out of topics."

If she's good at it, let her help. Ask her, "How do you learn to keep a conversation going?" The old saw, "Either you have it or you don't," isn't true. A better one is "Practice makes perfect."

We can't tell the Lord we're not naturally loving. He said, "I was hungry. Did you give me food?" He didn't say, "Are you equipped?" because He knew He would give us that grace when we asked for it.

We can discuss a game for hours; we know all about our businesses. When we encounter problems in conversation, we're simply having trouble with the subject. We can learn to be just as interested in our wives' subjects as we are in our own.

"But it's not natural; we men just don't talk that way," we might protest. It's not natural for a visitor from Spain, Ireland, or Italy to talk about football, but he soon learns, even if he's never seen a football game.

Marriage, after all, is a form of immigration; when we take on a new life-style, we're living in new country.

There's a naturalization process: we have to learn the language, and that language is sharing with our wives.

Let Her into Your Life

A man has to ask himself, "What exactly is a husband? What's it all about?" What it's all about, in plain terms, is belonging fully and totally to one woman. We simply can't do this without a great deal of verbal communication. Real communication, by the way, is one part talking to two parts listening.

When a husband examines his conscience, his number one question should be "How much do I communicate with my wife?" He answers this question not by looking at other men's habits but by looking at his wife. Is she happy? Does she feel thoroughly listened to? That's all that matters.

When you're examining your conscience, don't ask if you're satisfied with your level of listening or whether you're doing your best. Your best can mean "Considering all my responsibilities, I listen fairly well." She may still be lonely.

We men must also learn to reveal ourselves in conversation. We can't speak only when we feel like it; we must always be honest and open. Again, to find out if we're doing this, we turn to our wives.

Ask yourselves, men, "Does my wife feel shut out of my life? Does she believe she isn't a full part of who I am?"

If she feels shut away from you, she is hungry. You must look at her hunger, not at the amount you've already given.

Your greatest call as a husband is to feed her hunger to be understood. You aren't allowed to gauge her appetite, either. So often, we humans want to give on our terms, and only as much as we wish. This turning in toward self is almost as natural as breathing, but it's unhealthy and imprisoning. When we're turned inward, we're not tuned in to our lovers.

Men, when our wives want to go out in the evenings, it isn't primarily to escape the children or the house. Mostly, they want to spend private time with us. How often do we send them out alone instead? How often do we fall into a lonely married holding pattern: we aren't fighting, but we simply stop growing closer? How often do our schedules prevent us from being really present to our wives? We may not be frantic in our neglect; we may be busy recuperating from a bad day at work or resting up for the next one.

Husbands, please take this one to heart; it should make you feel good. It should also call you to action: she didn't marry you for the things you do *for* her; she married you for who you *are* to her.

So often, when you come home from work, your wife is less than thrilled with your presence. She's busy getting supper, taking care of the kids, or getting settled after coming home from work herself. That's wrong; she should be eager for you.

But if she were, how much would you have to give her? Think it over.

Tender Loving Kitchen

Wives, I've just asked your husbands for a constantly renewing commitment of love and caring. Now I'm going to ask something similar of you.

I am going to ask you to take charge of a daily family commitment toward a welcoming, heartwarming meal.

I'm asking you to take the leadership role in this, although you may or may not do all the cooking. It would be far better, in fact, for you and your husband to take turns. We'll discuss that in a moment.

This request is, of course, much more than a commitment to serve dinner seven days a week. A welcoming family meal is a powerful message, declaring that your family values love and unity above all else.

Remember the Last Supper, when Jesus reclined at table with His apostles? It was a leisurely meal, well prepared and shared with love. Jesus had looked forward to it for a long time; He even said so. He broke bread and blessed it and said, "Do this in remembrance of Me."

That's why we tell our children that receiving the Eucharist is like a meal with Jesus. They naturally think of their meals at home. When we break bread together in our "little churches," do we share that community that was present at the first Eucharist?

A number of years ago, someone did a horrible study: It involved the behavior of an infant chimpanzee whose natural mother was replaced with a wire "mother" with a bottle attached. Although the little one's physical needs were met, he was obviously starved for living affection. Covering the wire "mother" with fur helped a bit, but no humane observer could believe it was a good substitute for the real thing.

It's frighteningly easy to become a wire imitation of a real parent. Often, it seems that's all our families want. They prefer a microwaved snack, eaten standing at the counter while the car warms up in the driveway. That's because we've forgotten how important we are to one another.

This habit of consuming spiritually empty calories is symptomatic of a rush-rush life-style that puts priority on

83

the family's itinerary, destinations, and achievements. It sees no value in enjoying one another's company. It says that breaking bread together isn't that important.

If we're in step with society, we don't have time for a sweet, old-fashioned idea like a leisurely meal. It would be great, certainly—but at the cost of piano lessons or soccer or parish council?

Blinded by our options, we find ourselves rushing through our meals so we can chauffeur ourselves or our children to the evening's activities.

As Jesus said, we have to choose. Will we choose things or people?

How do we change? First, we must examine our unconscious beliefs. Our friends, relatives, and neighbors will probably think it's selfish, perhaps even abusive, to let a child walk or bike to an activity when he could have had a ride. But they don't realize the virtue of a life-style where children burn energy while developing muscle and self-reliance. These children are immediately rewarded by a good, warmhearted meal that Mom and Dad enjoyed preparing.

Car pools are another option, especially if an event is miles away. We must take charge of our families, for everyone's sake. Too often, we allow friends, coaches, instructors, and committees to persuade us their activities are more important than our family love and unity.

Some of us must find the courage to slow down. Sometimes creative scheduling won't work and the only real answer is "No, we won't get involved in that," or even "I resign." This may be the hardest decision of all, especially when it baffles and hurts others. We sincerely believe it's more virtuous to put our families on hold while we tend others' needs.

After Jesus rose from the dead, He visited His disciples near the Sea of Tiberias. They were fishing, and when they came ashore, they found Him grilling fish for them. "Come and have breakfast," He said (Jn. 21:1–12).

Cooking is a religious ministry. Too often, we neglect a great calling and choose lesser ones instead.

Cooking is a tangible way to tell all four senses that we are nurturers. In fact, we can't truly nurture unless we cook. That's why every father should cook at least two or three meals a week. Otherwise, he's depriving his children of his company, and depriving himself of fullness of life as a husband and father. It may feel restful to sit on the living room sofa while someone else cooks, but really, it's self-starvation. When they grow up, the children won't have fond memories of how Dad used to sit on the divan, but they will have memories of his special grilled chicken or homemade spaghetti. There's nothing more comforting, more real, than the smell, sight, and taste of good food. The Lord knew that; that's why He cooked.

Who, Me?

Again, wives, I'm asking you to take charge of this program. Most likely, you've been chief cook ever since you were married. If you and your husband are like the couples I know, you keep the social schedule, too. You, and only you, will have the commitment and confidence to get the project going and to keep it afloat. Please do it, for the sake of your children, but especially for your husband's sake.

Even if your husband won't participate, I'm asking you to do it yourself; it's that important. Above all, do it with love and generosity. Perhaps if he sees how much he's missing, he'll be eager to change.

Resentment, natural as it may be, won't help at all. Most of us probably have a sales job to undo: We've let our husbands know how much of a burden cooking is. Now we have to convince them—and ourselves—what a beautiful, rewarding gift it is.

Of course, many husbands would rather pull an engine out of the car in the rain than tackle the family dinner, but who's going to teach them if we don't? We shouldn't demonstrate merely that we can cook as quickly or creatively as Julia Child; that only shows them how futile it would be to compete. We must show them how to cook with affection and enthusiasm. Example is the only way to truly teach a lesson of love.

A full dinner can be an intimidating request for many of us. It can make us feel we're giving up hard-earned ground. We might think we're being "returned to the kitchen"; doing KP after losing the war of the sexes.

I'm not asking you to do KP. I'm asking you to take shelter from the pressures of the world in your own private oasis. You and your husband need a place of peace and fellowship and harmony, and that place should be the dinner table. It should happen every night.

Please don't think of how much time and effort it will cost. That's the world's way, and it's loveless and lonely. Battle lines and lists of "you can't make me's" don't make us happy—and they don't make us victorious. They only make us miserable. If we live in love, our lovers will respond in kind. We'll achieve far more than an uneasy détente.

A Gift to Your Beloved

A family meal is very important for the children and for your husband's pleasure as a father, but that's only the tip of the iceberg. That warmhearted family meal is primarily a gift of yourself to your beloved spouse.

What do we do when we want to really celebrate an anniversary? Most of us put the children to bed and have a romantic candlelit meal. When we want to tell friends we care for them, we invite them to dinner.

Let's invite our husbands to dinner. Men do talk better nonverbally, after all, and the way to his heart is still through his stomach. How the meal looks, how it tastes, how much effort we put into it, are all ways of saying, "My love, you are important to me."

Your husband is the most important part of your life, just as you are his most important part. Your time together is precious; you don't have much of it. Most of his day, and perhaps yours too, is spent at work. How do you prepare for that important time of togetherness?

One of the best ways is to plan a beautiful meal. When you spend that time anticipating his company at the table, you'll be much more sensitive to him. That meal will be the high point of your evening. Of course, you shouldn't get so lost in the cooking that you miss the purpose behind that meal: to respond to his hunger for you.

Please don't compare your family to others' families, and don't fall into the trap of saying, "But no one really cares," or "That kind of meal just doesn't fit our life-style." Instead, trust in your husband's goodness. Most husbands are generous people; they really do love their wives. They'll come around with love.

You might explore just how many chores the kids can

truly do; you can teach them to shop or snap vegetables. You might also discover that some of your adult or family activities really sapped energy rather than adding to everyone's quality of life.

My Beloved or My Life?

It's a hard choice: our activities or each other? Our struggle with that choice shows how comfortable we are with our independent, hassled life-styles.

Most of us attempt to compromise on family meals, although it doesn't make us happy. We plan meals according to what's fastest, not what's most meaningful or brings us closer to each other.

The same is true with conversation. Too often, our answers are timed for speed: "How can I get back to my paper?" "How can I get to that television?" "If I say the wrong thing, we'll talk too long and I'll miss my show."

Both husbands and wives keep their freedom at the expense of their relationships. Too often, they schedule their lives the way they wish. They accommodate their spouses when it seems terribly important or when there's an emergency, but basically they live side by side rather than in unity. They try to avoid clashes, and usually, that's what they do. They're not fighters, but are they lovers?

We husbands must make a contribution to married passion: we must get involved in that conversation. We wives must make a contribution, too: we must commit ourselves to making dinner happen.

Your life's success is determined not by your happiness but by your beloved's. How much is your spouse getting from your marriage?

It isn't enough to ask, "How does our schedule improve the quality of my own life?" or "How does our conversation please me?" We must be lovers. We must ask, instead, "Am I filling my beloved's hunger?"

I Was Thirsty and You Gave Me Drink

Paternity and maternity are thirsts. How often do we control our lovers' childbearing and child rearing? Perhaps we're worried about finances, poor health, or the long burden children will lay on both of us.

We have to be very careful, though, when presuming our spouses agree. Just stop and think. We've heard this before, but perhaps we haven't paid too much attention: Plants and pets and flowers are ways of expressing our desire for life. So often, we substitute them for children.

So often, we women assume that our only real value in the world is to bring home paychecks. We devote our days to indifferent business acquaintances, doing tasks that no one will remember ten years from now. So often, we do this to feel fulfilled and important.

So often, our men work for the same reason. They choose overtime over children and wonder why they feel so empty.

So often, we take away a man's pride in being a father. We say that's a sexist attitude, and we decide it's worthless.

Even more often, we take away a woman's pride in motherhood. We ask her at parties, "What do you *do*?" If she works outside the home, she's then supposed to produce a sophisticated speech that implies that work is more important than people. If she doesn't work outside the home, we decide she doesn't have anything to add to the conversation.

So often, we're so very, very thirsty, and no one even knows how to give us a drink.

My Dear, We're a "10"

Is my wife, my husband, thirsty for love? There's no doubt about it: our spouses' throats are parched. Each of us should ask ourselves, "How do I rate today as a lover?" Just today, not generally.

Rate yourself on a scale of one to ten. Don't explain why you chose a number: "I only rate a two today because my spouse was bad-tempered," or "I only rate a one because I had a terrible day."

Now then, how does today compare with my average Monday love? What's my number on Thursdays? How do I rate myself regularly as a lover? How do my spouse and I rate as a couple?

When we say, "How are we doing in our marriage?" it usually means, "Am I satisfied?" Sometimes it means, "Are you doing well enough for me?" When we truly rate ourselves as partners, we don't even face ourselves. We face our lovers instead.

Right now, forget how he's doing, how she rates. What's your score? Wives, ask yourselves this: if you were a man, would you like to have a wife like yourself? Husbands, ask yourselves: if your daughter brought home a man just like you, would you say, "Wow, is she going to have a great life!" or would you chase him out with a stick?

We really are good people, and we do make resolutions: "I need to talk to her more." "I ought to spend more time with him." "I need to pay more attention to her." "I ought to get home earlier." "I ought to be more positive." "I shouldn't shout so much." "I shouldn't nag." "I ought to listen better."

Those are good resolutions, and they come from our sincere desire to please our lovers. But do we ever really take the plunge? Do we ever go all the way and resolve to be full-fledged, no-holds-barred, all-out lovers, with no ifs, ands, or buts?

We tend to compromise just a little. We admit we're wrong in a certain area, so we'll clean up there and do a little better. But we don't go for broke.

Let's forget negative words like "fairness" and "compromise," and add in words like "passion." We want to be lovers, not judges who look at the defendants' records and decide what's fair.

When we're lovers, we don't ask, "Am I satisfied?" or "Am I doing all right?" Instead, we ask, "Is she totally loved?" "Does he experience every ounce of love I have?"

Only this depth of commitment will slake our beloved's thirst.

You Are Wonderful

I hope you recognize what a tribute this book is to you. There are so many people whom I can't teach this strongly and openly.

I don't want you to feel like a failure or to think you're goofing. I want you to see how beautiful you are and how much more the Lord is holding out to you. It's like learning a language. The more accomplished we become in a language, the more we are able to read and the more full of thought we become in that language. As we learn the language of love, the language of the Lord, we become more aware of our possibilities.

I don't want you to close this book, discouraged, or feel that you have such a long way to go. Instead, celebrate how far you have come and how good you truly are.

If you weren't already blessed in your love and openness, you wouldn't still be with me here on this page. So thank God, because you are wonderful.

Consider these questions privately:

How do I worship materialism and independence? In what ways do I follow the world's standards instead of God's?

What will I do to feed my wife's hunger for my companionship? What will I do to feed my husband's hunger for affection?

How do I rate today as a lover? How do I rate through the week? How do we rate as a couple?

Share these questions with your spouse:

How are my schedule, my priorities, and my conveniences excluding you from my life? How do I feel about my answer?

What will I do, dear, to make our love life a "10"?

What are some of my best memories of time we spent together?

Express your love:

Husbands, when you come home from work tonight, take a good look at this woman the Lord chose for you. Feel how delighted you are to be with her this evening . . .

You are so happy with her, you don't want to be anywhere else. You want to spend time with her; to find out how her day went, to hug her and see her smile.

Wives, prepare tonight's meal as if it's the last one you'll ever make for him. Sprinkle it with love. Use the best tablecloth; use candles. Tonight is your night to celebrate because the Lord has given you this man to love and to love you.

When it's appropriate, you can suggest a commitment to a special family meal.

Don't worry about doing this every day. You only have to do it tonight. When tomorrow comes, that will be tonight. You won't have to face a long and weary future. You'll merely get to celebrate tonight—again and again.

Finally, let us invite God into our marriages:

Dear Lord, thank you for this wonderful gift of my wife. Help me realize she is the most important part of my life. Let me delight in her; let me enjoy our time together above all other things. Help me tell her how much I love her, not only with those words, but with every word I speak. Help me give her the gift of myself: my enthusiasm and affection for her, my eagerness to be with her. Amen.

Dear Lord, thank you for this wonderful gift of my husband. Help me realize he is the most important part of my life. Let me delight in him; let me look forward to seeing him when we are apart. Help me enjoy our time together above all other things. Help me show him how much I love him, how worthy he is of my time and my attention. Help me show him that he is indeed the center of my life. Amen.

CHAPTER 4

WELCOME HOME, BELOVED

(MT. 25:35–46)

Joe felt smug.

He had died and it was time for the Last Judgment. Jesus was coming in glory to divide the faithful "sheep" from the unfaithful "goats." The sheep would be heirs to the Kingdom of God. The goats would have a less enjoyable fate.

All around him, people were whispering. One muttered, "Does tithing count?"

"Sort of."

"It'd better. I gave Him a small fortune."

"Did you, now? Are you going to tell Him about your Swiss bank account?"

Somewhere else, a voice whispered, "I think I'm okay. I took care of my mother."

Another voice answered, "I wish I'd taken care of your mother. Now I don't know where I'm going."

But Joe was cool. He'd been a great Christian. And if God didn't believe it, he had witnesses.

It was almost his turn. He saw Jesus Christ coming in dazzling splendor: His robes shining white, His face just like Joe thought it would look. Joe straightened his tie. He looked to the right, trying to see that heavenly chair labeled with his name.

Funny; Jesus' face looked sad. Terribly sad.

"You must go away from me," He said. "I didn't want it this way, Joe, but you insisted. Your own curse is upon you, for I was hungry and you never gave me food—"

"Wait a minute," Joe said. It wasn't Christian to interrupt the Lord, but this had to be an exception. "I was on the parish council when we built a soup kitchen. I drove the truck that collected clothes for the poor. Don't you remember? It gave me a bad back."

Christ nodded. "I remember. You'd just opened your business and you had your company name painted on the truck. That bit of volunteer work wasn't as painful as you pretend. But I'm not talking about a small sin like that. Joe, you spent fifty years telling me I was a worthless human being."

Joe gasped. He couldn't speak, and that itself was a miracle.

"Every night before dinner," Jesus said, "I tried to talk to you, and you snubbed me so you could read the paper. After dinner, I followed you around, but you turned up the television so you wouldn't have to listen to me."

Joe was indignant. "You weren't even there."

"I was your wife."

"My wife?" Joe digested that. "She wasn't poor or hun-

95

gry or *anything*. I gave her a five-figure allowance. Besides, she didn't even *like* me. She used to run off to church meetings and shopping malls."

"After the first ten years, she couldn't stand it anymore," He said. "She could only take so much indifference. And speaking of charity, you weren't all that generous."

"I gave ten percent to the church," Joe said. He was beginning to feel belligerent. "I have the receipts."

"I'm not talking about money," Jesus said. "How often did you take her out? How often did you surprise her with a new dress? How often did you compliment her or brag her up to your friends? How often did you stand up for her when people made fun of her weight?"

Joe didn't know what to say.

Jesus looked distressed. "Joe, I love you. I always have and I always will. But you made a free choice: you cursed yourself."

Joe dropped to his knees. He'd never groveled before, but staying out of hell was worth it. Fire would be bad enough, but he suspected hell's worst torture was boredom. Who wanted to hang around in a furnace for all eternity? "I won't sin anymore," he whined. "I promise. I'll do anything. Anything—"

"You'll have to change your life," Jesus said.

"I'll do it. I'll do it!"

"All right. I'll give you another chance," He said. "Now then, second chances are different for everyone. Yours is this: Every evening you'll have dinner with your family, then build a nice fire in the fireplace and enjoy their company. You can play games or talk or whatever you want. Furthermore, you'll look forward to seeing your wife. When you come home, you'll hug her and tell her how beautiful she is."

It sounded boring, but not as boring as hell. "You've got a deal," Joe said.

"Of course," Jesus added, "you'll have to stop working all those hours. You'll have to give up those conferences and professional associations. Your business won't make the Fortune 500, and you won't be on the leading edge this time around."

"No Fortune 500?" Joe said. "That's not fair."

Jesus raised an eyebrow. "You're talking to me about fair? You won't make the big time because you'll be home, being happy."

"Oh, that. I can make it work. I can—"

"No, you have to choose."

Joe got mad. "Why don't you just see how well I do?"

Jesus shook his head. "Joe, I have another option. I'll give you your business back. You'll still be in the Fortune 500 and you can spend as much time as you want working on the prestige of your business. In fact, I'll give you the rest of eternity to make the top 50."

"Really?"

"You'll have subscriptions to *The Wall Street Journal* and *USA Today*. You'll have the cable TV sports channel and your own private workshop. I'll give you an executive gymnasium and a Ferrari."

"Hey!" Joe said. "That's not so bad." He was feeling smug again. He'd always known he was a good negotiator.

"You can make your own schedule," Jesus added. "I'll keep everyone out of your hair."

"Now you're talking," Joe said.

"I had other plans for you, though," Jesus said. "There are people only you can touch. Follow my way, and your life will be so wonderful—"

Joe's heart sank. He envisioned a lifetime of shouting

teenagers and cribbage games. "No, no," he said. "I'll take your final offer."

Jesus laid a hand on his shoulder. "Joe, you just chose hell."

Welcome Home, Stranger

Most of us aren't scoundrels like Joe, but we must make the same choice he did. Will we follow our own ways of life or Jesus' way? Will we choose things or people? Will we be mercenaries or lovers?

In Matthew 25:35, Jesus said, "I was a stranger and you made me welcome." Strangers are living in our own households. We know their faces intimately, but we don't understand their hearts.

We men and women come into marriage with a myriad of goals and values. That's normal, but fiercely clinging to those differences is a love-killer. We may think our ways are right, but rightness isn't the issue. Love and happiness are the issues.

So now let's read the list below, putting ourselves into each area and thinking, "Where do we stand? How much have we changed to become one couple? How much are we willing to change?"

Be wary of finger pointing here. It's easy to say, "Yes, if he'd only stay home a little more," or "If only she'd learn to save a little." Think, instead, "Do I really want to give up my own values?"

If you don't beware. You're forcing your spouse to remain a stranger in your home. It doesn't mean you won't be nice. You'll allow dissenting opinions. You'll each retreat to your own corners, clinging to your beliefs instead of to each other. You'll be separate but equal. Remember when they used that line before the civil rights movement? It didn't make anyone happy, did it?

So now read these over carefully, opening your hearts to change—and love:

Right or Wrong?

Money. One of us might have a freewheeling "spend it now" philosophy while the other saves for a rainy day. One thinks we have enough; the other believes we need more. One is careless; the other is a precise household accountant.

Housing. To one, a house could be the center of life; to the other, it's only a place to sleep. To one, it's "mine"; to the other, it's "yours." For one, a house needs square footage; for the other, cozy comfort is best.

Faith. For one, it's an experience; for the other, it's a practice. In one of us, it's increasing; in the other, it's stagnating.

Friends. To one, they're pleasant but not that necessary; to the other, they're vital. To one, they're only social acquaintances; to the other, they're like family.

Families. For one spouse, they're people to enjoy on holidays; for the other, they're part of daily life. For one, they're a support network; for the other, a problem.

Children. To one, they're "yours"; to the other, they're "ours." To one, they're a pleasure; to the other, a burden. To one, they mean responsibility; to the other, love.

Life-styles. For one spouse, livelier is best; the other seeks peace. One wants a busy social life; the other is a homebody. One likes single pursuits; the other wants to go out as a couple.

Charity. For one, it's terribly important; for the other, it's only an option for spending extra time and money.

The neighborhood. To one, it's just a place where we plant ourselves; to the other, it's part of our way of life.

We can live with these differences for years.

No Surrender

We want to be alike, but how can we achieve it? The doubtfulness causes pain, so we just surrender. "He's going to believe what he wants," we think, "so why bother?" "She's going to get her own way, so I'll get mine, too."

That's hopelessness at work. It's also stubbornness, camouflaged so well we don't recognize it. It's probably good to surrender at this point, because we haven't been trying to meld with our lovers. We've really been trying to change them.

Do any of these sound familiar? They can be thoughts, not comments.

"I can't believe your attitude about your family."

"Gee. I wish you'd dress more carefully so I wouldn't be embarrassed."

"You sure have the wrong attitude about sex."

"I don't appreciate your opinion about children, about money or the neighborhood or charity or . . ."

Or, summed up, "You need to be thinking my way."

Of course that doesn't work, so we back off in frustration and disappointment. We had the right idea: becoming one in our goals and values. We simply had the wrong method.

It can be frightening to think of changing to your lover's point of view. After all, you're right. You sincerely believe that. So first, work on the areas you can easily change.

Then when you get to the tough subjects, try to see his point, her view. Talk it through until you understand where your lover's coming from. There could be hidden hurts—or hidden wisdom. Suppose, for instance, that your husband embarrasses you by wearing torn-up jeans to a party. He may be happier than you are; he's not self-conscious at all. He's merely looking forward to seeing his friends, and he knows they'll be glad to see him no matter what he's wearing. He'll have a great time, but you'll spend the evening worrying about the run in your hose. You don't have to dress like he does, but you do have to understand his heart. Why not let him teach you to be carefree?

I Lacked Clothes and You Clothed Me

In other words, my husband, my wife, was naked. Did I clothe her? Did I shelter his body?

"I don't have to clothe my wife. She does pretty well by herself."

There's more to clothing her, men, than waving good-bye as she drives off to the mall. So many of our wives say, "He never notices how I'm dressed. I could color my hair chartreuse and he wouldn't comment for three weeks. Even then he'd say, 'Have you done something different?' "

Men, hair is not a little thing. It's so important to care. We must notice, for instance, that she's dressed up to-night, or even that she's wearing her favorite pin. For all the concern we show, she could be wearing leaves. Each of us must take pride in our beloved's appearance.

We men can be very unaware of our lack of concern. Most of us would respond, "I do notice her. I think she looks great."

You must notice her vocally. You must compliment her until she believes the compliment. That takes a lot of work.

How many wives are so self-sacrificing, so beautiful about not overspending? Perhaps she's so concerned about watching the family budget, she won't buy anything for herself. She'll buy for the children, but she finds her own clothes in the rummage sales.

That's a wonderful sacrifice on her part, but where is her husband? He shouldn't let her wear those old clothes. If she won't buy for herself, he must buy for her. That's especially true of party clothes or Sunday dresses. So often, a wife will buy a skirt, perhaps, that she absolutely needs, but she won't buy anything beautiful.

You men may be lifting eyebrows, saying, "How could I ever buy women's clothes?"

As with everything, you learn with practice. Buying women's clothing is an art form, only better; it can, indeed, be learned. First, do what she does when she buys for you: wait until she's gone, then go through the closet. Find something that fits her and look at the size on the label. If that doesn't work, look for a sales clerk who's about her size. If you need styling advice, ask the clerk. That's part of her job.

You don't have to buy an entire outfit each time. You could bring home a piece of jewelry or a scarf; something you know will go well with that blouse. Maybe you've heard her say she doesn't have shoes to go with that suit. She can exchange something that doesn't fit, but if you never buy her anything, there's nothing to exchange.

Again, husbands, don't just give her money and let her buy what she thinks is best. What she wants most is your praise, and she simply can't buy that. When you give her clothing, you're saying, "I think you're beautiful. I'm buying this pretty dress so you can see yourself the way I see you."

In the beginning, there will be times when she opens your gift and gasps, "You've got to be kidding." She'll probably be right, too. You'll learn not to buy *that* again.

Unfortunately, we learn not to *buy* again. That's wrong. Clothes, after all, are very important. They announce us to one another, saying, "I'm this kind of guy"; "This is the type of woman I am." Our clothing tells everyone how we're feeling. Our women especially communicate this way.

Do our wives look sloppy when they're not going somewhere? They dress so indifferently because they think we don't really care. When we give them an after-work hug, do we really notice what and whom we're hugging, or would a lamppost do? We can't expect our wives to get dressed up for us if we never pay any attention.

Stripped by Insults

We could use money to make our husbands and wives naked; to strip them of clothes, hairdos, accessories, and the like. Perhaps we make pointed comments like "How much did that cost?" Our robbery could be subtle; it could voice itself in gestures or comments to our friends: "It's a good thing I don't spend like he does"; "I'm glad both of us aren't clotheshorses."

We can also fail to clothe our spouses in ways that don't involve wearing apparel. Men, is your wife criticized by

103

her friends and neighbors, perhaps because of the size of the family or because her parents live with you? Is she put down because of her faith, her tenderness toward her children, or her love for you? Most likely these put-downs are subtle barbs, which are much more devastating than frontal attacks.

Husbands, do you stand aloof while her friends strip your wife naked? Do you think they're just petty little women's insults and you shouldn't get involved?

Popular wisdom says, "A smart man never gets between two women." Do you believe that? Do you merely nod your approval when she tells you about her anger and hurt? Many of us will even show self-righteous indignation. Then we change the subject. When we do this, we're fooling no one. Our wives know we aren't serious about their pain.

Wives, do you do the same with your husbands?

"Well," you might answer, "I really do care about him. But a lot of times his problems aren't real; they're just his male ego at work." In other words, they're just petty insults; men ought to be able to handle them. Now you're treating him like he treated you: soothing him and thinking men are so silly when they act like that.

Do you see the irony? This time, you're leaving him naked; you seem so above it all, so secure.

A Black Belt in Marital Arts

Sometimes we don't hear about these insults through the grapevine. Sometimes we're right there on center stage when someone attacks our lovers. What do we do then? If we say nothing, we're letting her stand there, naked and hurt; we're allowing him to be vulnerable and unclothed.

We can't just comfort our lovers later. We must stand up right away and tell that hurtful person, "This is my wife; you don't talk to her like that." "This is my husband; I love him and there is no way I'm going to let you get away with that."

Sometimes we're most valiant in the car on the way home. We say, "Did you hear what she said to you? I'd like to give her a piece of my mind."

But we had that chance. Certainly we didn't want to sour the evening; we don't want people to dislike us. But do we want to protect false friends at our lovers' expense?

Public digs and insults happen all too often. After a while, they become less motivated by malice than by habit. They become habits because we don't say, "Stop."

Not all criticism comes from outside, however. Sometimes we ourselves are the hurtful people who strip our spouses. Sometimes we criticize our lovers in front of friends, relatives, or the children. Sometimes we merely criticize them in private; that's harmful enough by itself.

We must be very strict with ourselves; criticism isn't a luxury to indulge. All too often we make excuses for this failing.

We may say, "Me? I'd never do that kind of thing. I never criticize my husband"; "I never say anything negative about my wife."

Scientists would be interested to hear that "never" isn't an absolute. By "never," we really mean "not at parties" or "not before strangers." We feel perfectly free to criticize in front of the children, with our mothers, buddies, or very close friends.

Many people think it's reasonable (remember that love-killer?) to admit that their husbands don't have the best tempers in the world or that their wives don't know how to balance a checkbook. They might tell the children in a condescending tone, "You know your father has his moods; you know how Mama loves to shop."

We're stripping our lovers when we do that. We're exposing them to embarrassment and shame. We're tempted to defend ourselves: Our children, relatives, and friends are close to the situation. After all, my mother knows him; the children live with us. A friend understands.

Quiet criticism before friends and family does far more damage, though, than the angriest screaming match in a shopping mall full of strangers. After all, we'll walk away from those strangers. Although they may never forget us, we won't see them again. But our children are right there, and they'll remember that Mom isn't so special; that Dad is a grumpy man. Our friends and relatives will remember, too. Every time they see our lovers, they'll recall the defect that upset us so.

If I was having a bad day and said my husband was selfish and inconsiderate, they'll remember it long after he brings me flowers and soothes me with tea. If I said my wife was a spendthrift, they'll believe it no matter how carefully she budgets.

I Was Sick and You Visited Me

How do we treat each other when we're sick? Is our lover's sickness an inconvenience? If it lasts beyond a day or two, is it an intrusion? How sensitive are we to each other's needs in sickness: our wives' ache for attention, spelled out in little services; our husbands' fear of appearing weak? So often, our men don't want to seem coddled, but they still need that care.

Have you ever seriously discussed what it's like to be sick and what your spouse could do to please you then? We try to please each other, but too often, we don't know how.

How does your husband want to be treated when he's sick?

"Very, very carefully," you may say. "It's like tending a wounded bear."

Why? Perhaps that last time he had the flu, he felt humiliated because you were fussing over him. He became annoyed, so you backed off, neither of you understanding each other's feelings.

How does your wife want to be treated when she's sick?

"Not how. How much. She wants me there all the time, even when she doesn't need me."

Perhaps she wants all those little attentions she tried to give you. She doesn't want you at her bedside holding her hand; she just wants more of you than you're giving. She feels lonely, thinking her physical pain doesn't matter to you. Why not talk to her about it?

Perhaps we have trouble sympathizing with our lovers. Then caring for her needs, or his, become chores. Do we schedule a sick lover with our other responsibilities, or do we feel real compassion?

Since we're good people, we try to guess why our lovers act so oddly when they're sick. But often we can't, so we shrug our shoulders and give up. "Men and women are different," we tell ourselves. "It's like east and west: never the twain shall meet. So I guess I'll just do as I'm asked."

When we surrender like this, we're giving up any real effort to take each other into our lives. That would mean change, and sometimes we don't want to change. We prefer our own attitudes, values, priorities, and goals. We'll let our lovers work on their own goals; we won't interfere with them, but neither will we give up our ways of life.

We'll modify the things that don't really matter, but when change threatens our personal goals, that's going too far. We miss our overriding goal as a couple: to take our husbands and wives into our own lives; to become one.

We really haven't changed all that much since we were single. In many ways, we're the same people we were on our wedding day. Marriage calls us to become more than that. A marriage is not composed of two people who get along well with each other. It's composed of two people who become part of each other.

Sickness is an important part of marriage. It happens periodically throughout the year; of course, it will happen increasingly as the years go by. So we must concentrate on being "married" when we're sick as well as when we're healthy.

Sickness is hard, even if it's a normal, everyday kind of sickness that doesn't threaten life. When we're sick or not able to take care of ourselves, we become fearful. We feel out of control; we feel like burdens, and unattractive ones at that.

When our spouses are sick, do we treat this sickness of heart as well? We're specially called to face it.

I Was Ugly and You Thought I Was Beautiful

Part of tending the sick is lending dignity to human defects: bedpans, burns, wounds and bandages, sores, and the like.

In marriage, tending the sick includes tolerance for each other's small flaws. How do we respond to baldness, thinness, fat, bucked teeth, warts, an extremely heavy beard, a large nose, or excessive height?

Do we ignore these little flaws? If so, we're really reinforcing the idea that they're disfiguring.

Maybe we tease our lovers about their flaws. It proves we're open about them. After all, it's just affectionate teasing.

It's also a good way to avoid revealing our feelings. Don't we all know a man who goes out of his way to joke about his baldness? "Everyone can see it," we think. "He doesn't have to tell us."

Why is he making such an effort to do so? Because he knows we see it and he's afraid we'll mention it first. If he cuts in with a joke, no one else will be able to hurt him. After this goes on awhile, everyone decides baldness is funny.

That may be all right for acquaintances, but couples are called to do more than evade an issue. Do we comfort each other, really comfort each other, about our flaws? It's extremely important to handle this well, because these little defects make a significant difference in our spouses' lives.

We men tend to think such insecurity is for women only. Deep down, we know better. We may not panic if we're caught without makeup, but we worry about our hair, our physiques, and the clothes we wear.

Our flaws may not be visible, either. Maybe we're afraid of flying, or snakes, or of driving a car. Maybe one of us is an easy crier. Maybe the other one can't cry at all. We wives may suffer from premenstrual syndrome; either of us could get unnerved in a crisis.

What's happened here? We've each married a person with a flaw. How sympathetic are we?

Sometimes, not very. We think, "He believes he's so calm, but when trouble starts, I'm better off without him," or "She's had these cramps every month for twenty-five years, so why should I get upset?"

We humans have a very high threshold of others' pain.

We need to be sensitive to our spouses' needs. First we must realize what those needs are. It's not hard; all we have to do is think awhile. The evidence is everywhere.

It's easy to say, "Yes, she's always that way," or "I know exactly how he's going to behave." How are we using that knowledge? We shouldn't be trying to change our lovers, but we should be responding to their needs. Jesus said, "I was sick and you visited me." I was hurting and you reached inside to heal the hurt.

You Make Me Sick

If we choose, we can use our illnesses to manipulate our spouses. It's an effective way to get the attention we need, to inspire feelings of guilt, or change plans that seemed unchangeable.

This is one of our most typical and most vicious ways of controlling each other. We might withhold affection or sex, or begin showing signs of an emotional crisis. We're saying, "Look how awful I feel. How can you do this to me?"

These games can become a part of daily life. Sometimes we don't even realize we're playing them. It's not as if we're creating false illnesses. We really do have headaches, aching backs, or soaring blood pressures, but do we use them to control our lovers?

Do we respond to the love he or she offers when we're ill, or do we expect our lovers to meet our own standards?

I Was in Prison and You Came to See Me

This one can't possibly apply to matrimony—can it? After all, we didn't marry criminals.

No, we didn't marry criminals, but our spouses are still in jail.

Men, listen. How many of our wives are imprisoned by the children? How often do our women feel cut out of life?

There is a slice of your wife's life from age twenty-one until fifty that just disappears. Those kids are always there like a cloud over her head. She can't think of anything else.

If she works in the home, she lives and breathes kids from dawn until bedtime. If she works outside the home, she lives in a state of exhaustion, worrying about everything from child care to when she's going to find time to sleep.

Did you ever see a woman with five little children trying to cross the street? She can never get them all together. She finally grabs the fifth, and number one disappears. That's the way life is in the house, day after day after day. Just getting out takes what it once took to invade Normandy.

The heart of the problem isn't her mere physical presence in the house. That's bad enough, but the intellectual prison she's experiencing is worse. Even if she works outside the home, whom does she spend time with at a family picnic? The children, of course. There may be years when it's difficult to have an adult conversation.

How often do we excuse ourselves from talking to her about work, the federal budget deficit, or the decline of American manufacturing? She won't understand, we think; it's too complicated. Then we make our analysis come true by starting in the middle.

Some of our wives may have grown up believing they're not smart, but that's not true. It's our job, then, to convince them otherwise. Most of our wives believe they're too fat, skinny, short, tall, ugly, too blond, brunette, red, or gray. We don't reinforce those negative opinions, so why should we reinforce these?

We have to realize that we ourselves have installed some of the bars in our wives' prison cells.

That's Twenty Years, Lady—And No Parole

It's no wonder so many young women today are skeptical of motherhood. Today's mothers see themselves sentenced for twenty to thirty years with no hope of parole. They have the whole burden of child-rearing because we're part-time fathers.

We tend to shrug that off, saying, "Well, that's the way life is." We're appreciative, even sympathetic. We try to reward our wives with affection. We give them guilt offerings: presents, vacations, or nights out.

We men don't take full responsibility for our parenthood. We're relief pitchers, waiting in the bull pen. We'll come in if she gets hit in the late innings, but until then, it's her ball game.

By now, you're tempted to say, "I pitch in when the going gets rough. But I can't do it all the time. I have my responsibilities." You do. They're called Johnny, Mary, Frances. When was the last time we reevaluated our paternity?

Maybe we think we're not that way. Unfortunately, every man reading this book is indeed that way, to a greater or lesser degree. We're not bad people; it's the way we were trained. It's also the way we live. We can't fool ourselves.

"But I couldn't do more if I wanted to. She likes things the way they are. If I tried what you're suggesting, she'd tell me to go away."

If this is true, you need to find out why. Maybe she doesn't believe you'll do as well as she does. Maybe she's right; maybe not. Maybe she wants you to pretend to care, but she doesn't want real changes.

That's when you both need to talk. She is probably afraid to change because she doesn't believe you'll stick with your new role. She's afraid you'll start with a big fanfare, then let her down. Your change has to be a real commitment.

Maybe you're the one who doesn't want change. You think the present system is fine: "I do my share; I work long and hard to support this family. Now you want me to do my wife's work, too."

If you put it that way, yes, I do.

I Love You, Dear. Now Will You Change the Baby?

You can't say "I love you" to your wife if you're not a father to her children. It's just not believable. I'm not speaking just of time spent with the children, either. I'm speaking of the whole mentality in the home. We men have always been tempted to see the home as a refuge. It's a place of rest and relaxation where we gather the strength to slay tomorrow's dragons. We want to be our best when we go out in the world.

We should want to be our best when we're at home with the people who love us.

You might say, "That's not realistic. My boss won't understand that."

Your boss is no sacrament. You and your wife are, though. You're supposed to belong to her. Let's hope you don't belong to your boss.

So often, we men say, "You know, honey, I love you, but I have to do what my boss says if I want to keep my job. You know I'm only doing it for you."

She doesn't want a Daddy Warbucks who'll take care of her as if she's a little girl. She wants a lover; a partner. Those children must be your mutual way of life.

You're not filling her needs when she does most of the work and you merely give her the money to do it. That's when the home becomes a prison; that's when it all presses in on her.

If you're really as much of a parent as she is, the children are not a burden. She realizes how much you're missing when you have to go to work. She won't feel that way, though, until *you* realize how much you're missing.

Your attitude is what makes her life a prison or a blessing.

The Chain Gang and the Whip

Wives, are your husbands in prison? If they're employed, they probably are. Their jobs take away almost all their spare time. They're on treadmills, wearily going no-where, unless it's to newer or bigger treadmills. Some-times they don't even realize it.

So often, we blame men for not being persons. How can they afford to be? They have to callus themselves to keep their careers going. Those calluses are difficult to remove when they take off their ties.

When they spend eight or more hours a day being cold and efficient and impersonal, that personality is going to stick.

Our men spend day after bitter day at jobs in which they can have no real fulfillment, no real meaning, no sense of purpose. We doubt him when he says, "I'm only doing it for you." But in a sense, that's sadly true. If it weren't for you and the children, he probably would have walked out a long time ago, because there is nothing there for him.

So often, we wives take his job for granted. Maybe we have a "what can you do?" mentality. Some of us hope, "Maybe it will be better for our children." There will be no "better" work world in the future. The only change will be this: your daughter will be thrown to the corporate lions too. Perhaps you're already there yourself.

Your husband was a child once. His dad and mom worked hard so he'd have a better life. He has a completely different job, but he's still as crushed as his own dad was.

Materially, this generation's families are doing better. We have better homes than our parents did while we were growing up. Our children's educations are far superior to our own. We have more vacations, better meals, and more expensive clothes, but our husbands aren't any better off. We need to see the poverty behind the wealth; we need to see those heavy balls and chains attached to our husbands' well-dressed ankles.

They Must've Been Good for Something, Ma

Is the male portion of our population becoming obsolete? Maybe the man is like the appendix. The appendix has no function in the human body. At one stage of our evolution, it had a purpose. Nobody knows what it was, but it must have been good for something.

Is our society outgrowing its need for men who are still human beings? Do our standards of income chain them to jobs that grind out their personhood?

Wives, when was the last time each of us evaluated not his job, but where he is as a person and how the job determines that?

We can't sit back and say, "We really have to be personal. If we love each other enough, life will be beautiful." That becomes cruel if we establish conditions where one party can't even be a person; where all his faith, hope, and energy go into earning that paycheck. Then we blame him because he's let us down.

Often, it is indeed the man's fault. He's happy in his niche. He's pleased to be The Boss, whether that boss is foreman or president of the company. He's happy to be working overtime. He's proud to be a professional, and he doesn't want to change because he doesn't want to be intimate.

That's when we wives are called to visit our men in prison.

Capital Fodder

How often do we, ourselves, chain our men to their jobs? They're imprisoned so we can buy the children what they need in order to have a better life. Ironic, isn't it?

We are beginning to realize that no parent wants to raise children to be cannon fodder. The whole notion of war is becoming more and more abhorrent, but we are raising children to go into the meat grinder of the American system. We are putting role models in their living rooms and at their dining room tables. We might as well say it: "Son, this is what you become: an income machine. Daughter, this is the kind of thing you're going to marry, and you will have a good life. And yes, dear, you can become a machine too."

The culprit is our expectations: the homes we think we need, the possessions our children are supposed to need, the expenses we've created. Now, I'm not speaking against basic living expenses or good things for our children. I'm speaking against a middle-class American mentality that looks only at purchases and never at the peace and happiness of the buyers.

Use this mentality to buy the best house you can "afford" and a couple of new cars, and the prison walls grow even thicker.

"It's too late," many of you will say. "I'm trapped in the system. I can't get out of it."

What are you doing, then, to compensate?

Earlier, I told husbands to save their best for home. Be careful, wives, that that remains his gift, not something you feel he owes you. You don't want to judge him. Besides, no matter how good his intentions are, maybe he doesn't have anything to give when he comes home. Maybe he has to be filled before he can even say anything to you. He needs human warmth: compliments, gratitude for both his job and chores at home, knowledge that you enjoy his company, peace and cheerfulness.

What are you doing to alleviate the injustices in his life?

The National Conference of American Bishops keeps calling us to be national and even global peacemakers. What about the peace and justice our husbands need at home?

You might say, "He does his job and I do mine. I do have sympathy for him, but I work as hard as he does. It's a lot tougher being a woman today."

We're not running a contest to see who has it tougher. What's important is this: my husband's in prison. As a matter of fact, there's a great deal of evidence that men's lives are much less fulfilling. There's coronary disease, ulcers, violence, the death rate, even the sex-change operations. Many more men want to be women than the other way around.

Do we wives see we're called to treat our husbands in a special way? Do we see he has greater needs and is less free? He is less able to express his needs or to even accept the knowledge that he has any.

What Do I Need? Nothing, Dear

Visiting our men in prison can be difficult. Often, our men don't really know what they need. It's not because they're refusing to be open. It's because needs are a weakness in the business world. The average man has been trained not to have any needs. At least if he does, he fills them himself.

Dehumanization isn't always crude and obvious, like slavery or physical abuse. Our men are very civilized, but they honestly don't know what they want because they aren't supposed to want anything.

Wives, not husbands, are supposed to want things. It's a man's job, they think, to respond to his wife's needs.

Now, that sounds generous and loving. It isn't necessarily so. It can be a way of saying, "I won't let you in; I don't need you. I will take care of you, but I won't allow you to take care of me."

Our men have to say to themselves, "No, that is not the Lord's will. I can't treat my wife like that." Our wives have a real thirst to be important in their husbands' lives.

Wives, can you see the pain in our men's lives? Can you see behind their eagerness to fill your needs at the expense of their own? That isn't a sign of freedom. It's a sign of imprisonment. Wives, you are much freer than he is to express your needs. So often, your freedom and his imprisonment grow into a marital pattern. You ask something of him, he responds, then you guess what would be good for him.

Husbands, don't be proud that you ask her for nothing. That's a way of putting her out of your life, of not responding to her fully.

I See Your Hunger, Dear; I See Your Thirst

Let's take out the twenty-fifth chapter of St. Matthew's Gospel, verses 31–46, and read it through again. Be thinking as you read: "When is my husband a stranger?" "How is my wife in prison?"

The subjects mentioned in these two chapters can be a start for you, but we've left many more areas unexplored. Use your imagination. The deepest needs may be all but invisible.

"Where does my wife thirst? She is just parched. Maybe she's been parched for so long that she can't even speak to me. Her voice is cracked." "Does my husband feel naked when I don't support him?"

Wives, I ask you especially, please see the tremendous needs your husbands have for freedom. It's true, you're frequently in prison because of the children. But you're in minimum-security institutions. Your husbands are smothering in the Black Hole of Calcutta. There is no way to pretend that those imprisonments are equal.

Our men do have a responsibility to break free, but understand how difficult it is for them. There's a tremendous difference between believing you'll be released and knowing you'll never escape. There's a tremendous difference between solitary confinement and having trustee privileges.

I'm asking you to recognize the bitter life men lead. How can you ease the pressure?

One for Him and One for Me; One for Him and . . .

When we're working on our marriages, we must be careful when it comes to "fairness." We're always tempted to say, "When do we get to him?"

That's his problem.

Now, when it comes to imprisonments, our men have further to go; they're dehumanized. That's why I'm asking wives to reach out to heal them without worrying about fairness. If you say, "I'll change if you will," we'll get nowhere.

Should you change or not? If the answer is yes, it doesn't matter whether he changes or not. That's a hard saying, isn't it? But it's God's honest truth.

Of course, many of our men don't tell their wives about their hunger and entrapment; as good and generous as their wives are, they don't know.

We men don't tell our wives because we want to be macho. We think, "It's my job to take care of her. I don't want to put any burdens on her."

Men, we absolutely must let her know. That's the only way we are going to be cured. If our wives really understood the prison we're in, they would make many different decisions about money and the children.

A Different Kind of Marriage

In Matthew 13:11, the Lord said to His disciples, "To you it is granted to understand the mysteries of the kingdom of Heaven, but to [others] it is not granted . . ." or, in other words, "I'm telling you some things I don't tell the world." Too often we live the world's way with holy water. We have the sign of the cross hovering over our heads, but the world is imprinted in our hearts.

The Lord is really saying, "I'm offering you a different kind of marriage." He's offering you a greater marriage than others have. His offer isn't a marriage in which you get along better, but a marriage in which the whole value system is different. It's not a marriage with improved communication, but a sacrament of unity which celebrates different decisions about the outside world.

He's offering you a happier marriage. All you have to do is begin. Being with simple actions like defending your wife if somebody criticizes her. It's your call not to tolerate such insults. It's not just a matter of nipping rudeness in the bud; it's a matter of identification. By standing up for her, you let your wife know she can always count on you because you're her husband.

Or begin by welcoming your husband into your life. Learn to understand why he thinks the way he does about family, children, religion, housing . . .

There are so many graces in this Scripture passage. Ponder it in your hearts, so you can freely let the sacrament of Matrimony be present in your lives.

Look How Much You've Grown

Don't look at this soul-search as a weighty obligation. You shouldn't have to gather courage for it. Rather, look on it as an opportunity. Because you have been so good as a husband or wife, you've now discovered even more potential. You have even more ability to respond to the needs of your lover and to the Lord. What you have just read has meant something to you, and that's a gift from God. The fact that you thought, "Gee, I should do something about this" shows how tremendous you are. It's in no way, shape, or form an indication of any failure. It is a definite sign of your success.

It's best if the two of you can talk these ideas over. You can't become a good wife, for instance, by yourself. Why? Because you're not "a wife." You're *his* wife. He needs to be fully involved in your plans. Men, each of you belongs to this special woman. If you decide in private how to be a better husband, you're missing the whole point. Your change must be based on what she's seeking from you, what responses she desires, how she believes you can improve the quality of her life.

If your spouse doesn't want to read this book, don't be judgmental. Try to talk to him about what you've read, ask her how she thinks you should change. Don't hit your lover with a statement like "I see you're dehumanized by your job, dear." He'll say, "What are you talking about?" or something even less polite.

Say, instead, "I read this book today, and it says . . . Do you feel like that? Does it hurt your feelings when I . . . ? How would you feel if I changed in this area . . . ?"

And of course, never, ever say, "I think you should . . ."

See if you can get your spouse to write on the sharing questions below, or at least talk about them. And pray. Our Lord is a loving God who wants us to be happy in our marriages; He will certainly hear your prayer. Trust, too, in the goodness of your lover. Our spouses are good men and women who perhaps have been hurt in the past and are afraid to be open and trusting. Your sincerity and willingness to change create a greenhouse effect in your home: it becomes a place of light and warmth where souls can bloom.

This book is not an intellectual treatise on Scripture. It's not a think book; it's a love book. It's written so you will feel more tender toward each other, be more open to each other, speak more freely. It's intended to help you think of subjects that need to be talked over.

In order for it all to work, you have to go to each other, so turn to each other and enjoy.

Consider these questions privately:

Is my husband, my wife, a stranger in our home? Am I willing to change that?

How is my spouse naked?

How do I treat my lover when he or she is sick? How can I improve?

Do I comfort my lover for those little flaws?

How is my beloved spouse in prison, and what can I do about that?

Share these questions with your spouse:

My love, when do I treat you as a stranger in our home? How does my answer make me feel?

When do I feel most vulnerable? When would I like your support?

How do I plan to make you feel clothed, dear? Am I on target?

How do I want to be treated when I'm sick? . . . How am I going to change to fill your needs when you're sick?

How am I in prison? . . . What will I do to free you from your prison, my love?

Finally, let us invite God into our marriages:

Dear Lord,

Thank You for giving me the grace to realize I've been hurting my beloved spouse. Please let me see this truthfully, and let me see with equal truth my goodness and generosity of heart. Help me understand how much You love me, just as I am.

Lord, please make me willing to change. Help me understand that You want me to be happy and that following Your way will enrich the lives of both myself and my beloved.

Help me fill my beloved's life with love and warmth and acceptance.

Help me treat my dear spouse as I would treat you. Amen.

RECONCILIATION
AND HEALING

CHAPTER 5

HOW DELIGHTED IS
YOUR LIFE?

(LK. 6:27–29)

It would be an exciting day, not only for His disciples but for Jesus as well. He had passed the entire night on a mountain, praying to His Father. Now it was dawn and He would choose twelve followers to be His apostles. Afterward, He would meet that tremendous crowd who waited at the foot of the mountain. He would care for them as He always longed to do, curing bodies and souls. Then He would preach. He already knew what he wanted to tell them:

> . . . I say this to you who are listening: Love your enemies, do good to those who hate you, bless those who curse you, pray for those who treat you badly. To anyone who slaps you on one cheek, present the

127

other cheek as well; to anyone who takes your cloak from you, do not refuse your tunic. Give to everyone who asks you, and do not ask for your property back from someone who takes it. Treat others as you would like people to treat you. If you love those who love you, what credit can you expect? Even sinners love those who love them. And if you do good to those who do good to you, what credit can you expect? For even sinners do that much. And if you lend to those from whom you hope to get money back, what credit can you expect? Even sinners lend to sinners to get back the same amount. Instead, love your enemies and do good to them, and lend without any hope of return. You will have a great reward, and you will be children of the Most High, for he himself is kind to the ungrateful and the wicked.

Be compassionate just as your Father is compassionate. Do not judge, and you will not be judged; do not condemn, and you will not be condemned; forgive, and you will be forgiven. Give, and there will be gifts for you: a full measure, pressed down, shaken together, and overflowing, will be poured into your lap; because the standard you use will be the standard used for you.

Luke 6:27–38

This passage of Scripture is magnificent, isn't it? If everyone could live this one, there'd be no unhappiness left in the world.

Just think about it. It would mean an end to the get-ahead mentality that leads to such aggressiveness and aggrandizement. We'd all stop looking over our shoulders to see who was trying to take advantage of us.

The Golden Rule is such a wonderful plan for living.

Jesus makes a great deal of sense. Everything He says is so down-to-earth—but not so easy to accept. I know a tremendous number of lovers who can listen peacefully to that message. At least, I think they can.

One person who can't, though, is myself. I think if we're honest, most of us will admit the same. Jesus' "turn the other cheek" message is most comfortable when we keep a safe distance.

Is Anyone Listening?

We can almost imagine His message being given in a major television address or United Nations forum. We see global implications; national policies, whole societies of people who really ought to be taking notes.

We're right; it does apply across the board. But it starts at home.

That means we must place His message in our own lives. Furthermore, we can't wait for others to get the ball rolling. Jesus spoke to each of us individually. It's not as if He finished His sermon, then muttered, "Whew. I'm glad that's over. I hope someone gives it a try." Instead, He's whispering in your ear right now; He's delivering a personal message into your heart. It's something to the effect of "I'm serious about this, and I want you to go first."

He's holding this message out as a gift, not delivering it like a jail sentence. He really wants us to live our daily lives this way; it's not just for emergencies or special situations.

Most of us don't live spectacular lives. We live ordinary, humdrum, garden-variety lives. If we take Jesus' words to heart and practice them daily, we will be spectacular. We won't make headlines, at least not often, but we'll be extraordinary to those whose lives we touch.

There's No Place like Home

For husbands and wives, the Gospel message starts here. Jesus wants us to pay strictest attention to His words when we're in communication with each other.

It's unfortunate but true: Sometimes your lover is your enemy, at least for an hour or two. That's when she's angry with you; he won't talk to you.

Isn't it odd? We can accept Jesus' message intellectually. I don't think any of us can deny that the Lord is right. He really knew what He was talking about.

When we think of enemies, though, we think of someone with a gun. We think of the business world, where all too often people are out to knife one another. We think of the competitiveness of politics or the academic world, or maybe just the everyday swirl of social contacts. The Enemy is someone apart from us, even if just a neighbor. It's sad, even frightening or angering, to think our enemies share our beds.

Our enemies are people who hurt us emotionally; who take away things we believe are ours, like money or free time, or who make our lives less rewarding than they ought to be. Who's in the best position to hurt us in these ways? Our spouses, of course.

Often enough, we make the tragic mistake of retaliation. We follow the world's way instead of letting go as the Lord suggests.

The Lord said, more or less, "It's easy to be nice to a husband who's romancing you." When he's buried in the newspaper or glued to coverage of the Super Bowl, though, he becomes your enemy. Are you afraid to be nice to him then? Perhaps if you are, he'll never change.

So on we go. We travel round trip, the world's way. We salute the Lord's way intellectually and give it points for being ideal, but deep in our hearts, we don't believe He's right.

"The Lord says such beautiful things," we think. "I wish we could all listen to Him. But I can't do it alone. Then I wouldn't be a Christian; I'd just be a doormat."

Praise Her? She's Just Doing Her Job

An enemy is not a strange creature from outer space. An enemy is a wife who's on your back, who never seems satisfied. How do you treat her then? Are you hesitant to follow the Lord's message, afraid you'll encourage her?

Luckily, it doesn't work that way. There's a difference between encouraging anger and encouraging love.

So often, our women nag simply to let us know they're there. If they didn't shout, they think, we wouldn't listen to them. They wonder if they really come first. We say they do, but we seem to put our jobs first during the day, while the television and our responsibilities come first at night. Perhaps we take dinner for granted. We're certainly glad to have it, but we don't often praise our wives' efforts. Maybe we should, but after all, people don't *really* thank each other for daily chores. Our wives don't thank us every day for going to work.

No wonder a wife gets upset sometimes; no wonder she just can't hold back any longer.

She's frustrated, lonely, and hopeless. She's also a good learner. You see, we trained her by our lack of responsiveness. We taught her that the only way to get our attention is to create a fuss.

The Lord has told us in no uncertain terms that we must love, even when someone is making us angry and taking our peace away. In other words, when someone is an enemy, even if that enemy is a wife.

Besides, why get into an argument? It merely upsets both parties, and makes everyone feel guilty and uncomfortable.

The basic question is simpler: Will we accept the Lord in our lives? Will we really live His way, or will we follow society's footpath?

Will we continue to take each other for granted?

A few paragraphs ago, I wrote about the husband who comes home from work to vegetate at the kitchen table. I hit him pretty hard about that. Now I'm asking you, wives, to praise him for it.

Yes, he does come home at night, but that's not enough, you may think. Consider this: His presence is his gift to you. Of course, he's only doing what he's supposed to do, but he doesn't have to come home to you every night. A lot of men don't. He deserves praise for his faithfulness.

We must begin by seeing our spouses as the Lord sees them: as wonderful, beautiful children created by the Father to be our beloveds. Then we can't help but find delight in them, from the smallest shrug of their shoulders to their biggest accomplishments at work. Our husbands deserve praise just for being themselves.

We pledged to praise each other when we were married, yet we're very grudging with our compliments. We reserve them for special occasions, even when we're in a good mood. When we withhold our praise, though, we're treating our lovers as enemies. We're holding off, wary and distrustful, not wanting to commit ourselves. We're not reacting in anger or malice; we're simply withholding the beautiful gifts we have to give.

Normal, Everyday Saints

Why don't we live the Gospel more fully? Partly because we think we're not supposed to. At least, not right now: not while we're doing the dishes or going through the bills. We're supposed to live the Gospel on Sundays, perhaps; at prayer meetings or when a friend is in trouble. The rest of our lives are filled with normal, everyday events. Because we see them that way, that's all they are.

We draw a sharp line between the great bulk of the world and those few items that fit into a spiritual category. Those spiritual items are important to us; we may practice them fervently and faithfully, but the world takes up most of our time. Our worldly pursuits, too, run on different standards of morality.

In the spiritual category, Jesus is Lord. We enthusiastically accept what He has to say. We pay serious attention; after all, He's the ultimate authority. In the worldly category, though, we let Him in reluctantly and carefully. It's almost as if we have a silent prayer: "Please teach us to pray, Lord. That's all; thanks." We don't want His idealism ruining our relationships with other people.

The rules we use to govern our worldly lives are gathered from our peers. We strive toward good common sense. Common sense is defined as whatever the average, normal person would do under the circumstances.

But Jesus didn't come to proclaim good common sense. He came to proclaim the glad tidings. He came to tell us salvation was at hand. If we'd let Him, He would change our lives, but we often don't give Him free reign.

Jesus is calling us to Himself as whole beings, not just when we're in church or doing volunteer work. The glad tidings apply to every facet of our existence and every relationship under all circumstances. If we accept Him wholeheartedly, it will be a conversion experience.

The Gospel is not something in a book; it's something that lives in our hearts. So we must ask ourselves: "Do I love my enemy?" "Do I love my husband when nobody else would?" "Do I love my wife even when she's rubbing me raw?"

It's Good News—But It's Still News

We must realize that Jesus didn't come to rehash all the worldly wisdom that had accumulated by 1 B.C. He didn't come to repeat ideas everyone already liked. He didn't come to hit the best-seller list with a compendium of clever sayings and heartwarming aphorisms. He came to teach something entirely new, something totally different, something that had never been preached before.

Today, His message is just as new—and as difficult to accept. Our world still doesn't believe the Good News. Husbands and wives are still treating each other with fairness and common sense. When everything's going smoothly, they're smooth; when things are rough, they're rough, too. They're not responding to each other, they're responding to themselves. They're unconsciously deciding, "I feel upset, so I'm going to behave that way."

Jesus is saying, "Let's do it differently. Let's not talk about how you're feeling or how she's treating you. Let's talk about loving her, not because she deserves it, but because I'm asking you to."

He's asking us to question ourselves: "Do I love her when everyone would say I ought to withdraw? Maybe I won't be nasty, but I won't hear a thing. I'll just let her voice roll off me like water off a duck. Then she'll learn."

When we behave this way, we're playing a power game with each other. We're saying, "I won't punish you if you act the way I want." We're forcing our lovers to meet our approval—or else. "My obligation toward you is absolved," we add, "if you don't live up to your obligation toward me." What's left isn't love, it's business.

It's not good business, either. We're trying to "teach" our spouses to treat us better, but we're really teaching them anger, hopelessness, and resentment.

We're behaving like little children then. We're not trusting our lovers' goodness. We're saying, "I really don't believe she'll respond; I don't think he cares enough to change. Furthermore, I really don't believe in Jesus' way. I have to use force; it's the only thing I trust."

Perhaps you're thinking I'm right, but still, it's a big change. It could leave you looking foolish and vulnerable—and besides, it might not work: "If I'm nice to her when she's in a rotten mood, she'll die of the shock."

What a way to go.

You Sure Are Nice, Dear. What Do You Want?

I'm not promising instant success. It might take some time for our new behavior to affect our lovers. After all, we established that other pattern of coldness and anger. At first, our lovers might not notice we're acting nicely. They might be suspicious, waiting for the other shoe to drop. So we must be patient, knowing it takes time to undo the previous training. But soon they'll respond to the love we pour out as we follow Jesus' message.

Sometimes we'd rather look for another way to happiness. Sometimes we even prefer hard work. We keep the house clean and painted, we cook or do repairs, take good care of the children and carefully watch the budget. Yes, we're very good to each other.

That's still a policy of loneliness. We need to add compassion; constant, relentless love. Both men and women crave that type of love. Let's be generous with it. Our lovers need our goodness the most when they're angry or unhappy, and having trouble being lovers themselves.

How could weak human beings ever succeed at such an idealistic program? Basically, because we're not just human. We're the Lord's own people. We have been chosen to reveal Him through the way we love one another. Jesus has raised us to the dignity of children of God. That wasn't a reward for good conduct. It was a free gift, made possible by His passion and death upon the cross.

We must see beyond our lovers' humanness: beyond the pouting, the shouting, or the anger. We must see that immortal being whom God calls His son or daughter and whom Christ died to save. Above all, we must rise above our own feelings.

Feelings are neither right nor wrong, and we shouldn't deny our resentment or hurt. But we must decide whether to love, and that decision can't be based on our own feelings. It must be based on others' needs. We must ask ourselves, "What expression of love does my spouse need right now?" "Right now" should be in the middle of an argument, during a cold war, or whenever is hardest. It's a tough thing to do; no question about it. If it came naturally, Jesus wouldn't have had to tell us about it.

Love One Another

Often, husbands and wives are more in love with the Lord than they are with each other. They'll pray, "Lord, I will do anything for you."

He answers, "How about loving your wife when you're angry with her? Why not love your husband when he's not so lovable?"

They're startled and disturbed. "I thought you were going to ask something spiritual."

Our God is terribly practical. That's why He came to earth. God chose to speak to us in our language, in our way, so there would be no barriers between us. So, too, when He calls us to love one another, He wants our love to be practical, not idealistic. It's not for part-time use or for certain extraordinary people.

Jesus came to earth to preach about real love, love we can have every day. It's for each and every one of us.

Our God is not a selfish God. He didn't say, "You must love me just as I have loved you." In John 13:34 He said, "You must love one another just as I have loved you." Our Christianity isn't best tested by what we say to the Lord. It's tested, first, by what we say and do to our spouses, then to our children, our fellow believers, and, finally, the world at large.

Often, we do fulfill the Gospel message. Our only problem: It's not the Gospel of Jesus Christ. It's our own gospel, the one we want to follow because it's comfortable.

Christianity takes some knocks from the cynics. Often, these onlookers see people who profess to love God and their fellow men but are filled with tension and anger.

The cynics have a point. No one will believe a wife is really a lover if she doesn't passionately love her husband. It doesn't matter how many good things she does for friends and neighbors. Likewise, the world won't believe that a husband loves people if he doesn't love his wife, even when she's angry.

The real test of marriage is not during the romance period, when everything is sweetness and light. Then it's easy to do things for each other. We bend over backward to please each other; we compete to determine who's the most generous.

The real test of marriage comes when we're disillusioned with each other. How do we respond when our spouses aren't responding to us? How do we reach out when they're pushing us away? How do we speak to them when their language is harsh and rejecting?

Bless Those Who Curse You

It's tragic but true: sometimes we curse each other. We want to provoke anger; to put him down, to hurt her.

Some of us are too proper to use so-called bad language. But bad language is not the use of certain nasty words. It's the intention behind the statement. We could cut someone to ribbons with perfectly respectable language.

When we curse people, we're blighting them; we're taking away their blessedness. We're showering their sky with maledictions. We're depriving them of our approval.

Sometimes a curse is best accomplished through silence, or by politeness or pleasant chitchat.

We can also degrade our lovers through sarcasm, which is far more cutting than a filthy word. We can demean others by superiority or scorn. We can humiliate them by the simple, unspoken assumption that they're not worthy of our attention.

I remember seeing someone spit on Bishop Fulton Sheen as he walked into a hotel. Very calmly, he wiped it off his face. Then he asked the police officer who was holding his assailant to release the man. I was very impressed by this, and rightly so. But it's much harder to respond gently to words that are spat at me in the sanctity of my own home.

Pray for Those Who Treat You Badly

Do we pray for those who maltreat us, or do we handle them ourselves, without any help from God? Do we wish God would help us, but doubt that He will? Do we feel that prayer is such a weak little tool when used toward a cold, selfish spouse?

When we do pray, what do we pray?

"Lord, make him straighten up. Make her see how she's hurting me."

Instead, let's ask the Lord to bless them. How about a prayer to celebrate their goodness, to make us see the log in our own eye rather than the splinter in theirs?

Next time we struggle through a difficult prayer, let's ask the Lord to help us respond rather than react. Let's seek the graces of tenderness and love rather than the knee-jerk defensiveness of coldness and rejection. Let's pray to the Lord for understanding when our lovers are our enemies.

We must ask Him to help us respond on His terms, not ours. We must listen and wait as He gentles our hearts, pares the calluses off our tenderness, and encourages us to be happy and loving.

This type of prayer breaks the vicious circle of negativity. Soon we will see our spouses responding to our love with love of their own.

To Anyone Who Slaps You on One Cheek, Present the Other Cheek as Well

We slap each other too, don't we? Not physically, thanks be to God, but we find other ways to let our lovers know we're upset. It reminds me of the old Irishman who used to sail his hat in the door before he stepped over the threshold. If it didn't come flying back out, it was safe to walk in.

So often, our homes are the same way. Sometimes we're only three steps inside the door when we sense trouble.

For a while, we put up with it. After all, he's not a bad man; she's a pretty good woman. Everyone has bad days and bad moods—once in a while. But sooner or later, we reach the end of our rope. "I've run out of patience," we think. "I've had enough. If you don't quit pretty soon, you'll put *me* in a bad mood, too."

We don't always put it into words. Sometimes we say it with our blood pressures, with angry looks, or the way we slam the pots and pans. Our lovers know these signals: "Oh, oh. He's crossed his legs." "She's tugging her ear; here it comes."

Again, we're measuring out our generosity. It's as if marriage is a recipe, and too much love will ruin the batter. The Good News is this: the more you add, the better it gets.

So often, though, we find ourselves searching for some minimum standard of behavior: "What is the least I can do and still have reasonable peace at home?"

We must get away from that miserable trap of being satisfied with the minimum. We aren't satisfied with the minimum in anything else. We don't say, "More clothes? No; I don't want 'em. I'll wear what I bought last year." We don't say (at least, without a twinge), "A vacation away? Why would I want one of those? I had one two summers ago." And we certainly don't say, "I'm earning minimum wage, and that's enough."

Yet we're comfortable with our limited generosity. We believe we're virtuous because we don't lose patience right away. Actually, we're not concentrating on our lovers at all. We're simply being "good."

Jesus is telling us, "Stop concentrating on yourself. Don't see things in terms of how much is 'reasonable'; see your lover's needs instead." He really intends for our unbounded love to be an everyday occurrence. He's telling us to love the enemies in our own homes.

We want to listen to the Lord, but we have learned this world's lessons all too well. When we think He's being extravagant with our rights, we do the kindly thing: we tune Him out. We decide He's not talking about us. If He is, He really can't be serious. He'll understand, we think, when we don't live up to His godlike ideals.

Our problem, then, isn't failure. It's that we don't even try.

To Anyone Who Takes Your Cloak, Do Not Refuse Your Tunic

Do you really give your tunic to the spouse who takes your cloak? There's a good way to find out. What happens when you're both in the car and it's time to pay for gas or a toll? Do you look at each other, waiting for the other one to pay?

Free giving doesn't always involve money. It can involve our lives at home. Maybe I have my chair, and God help you if I catch you in it, or at least you're going to feel the grace of my generosity in letting you sit there.

Do we really give the tunic when the cloak is taken, or do we just establish a nice way of life in which both of us can keep our cloaks? Maybe my cloak is smaller than my lover's, but I like smaller cloaks—they look good in comparison. Maybe I look better in my cloak, so naturally I have a big one.

The Lord is actually speaking of generosity here. He's not talking about the garment. How often do we tell our spouses, "Hey, that's not fair"? Remember, you can go through the whole Gospel and never once hear Jesus praise fairness.

The Lord has great ambitions for us, and scorekeeping is not part of His plan. Yet we carefully measure the minimum amount of satisfaction we'll tolerate in a relationship, and we spend tremendous amounts of energy making sure we get it. We all recognize how sad and even futile it is when a divorcing couple divides their property, each of them trying to get an edge on the other one. They go into every last detail.

Too often, that can be just as true in a marriage, even a good marriage. It doesn't necessarily involve property.

Usually it involves tension versus comfort, recreation, and the like. We may be perfectly willing to concede a greater amount of time, money, or energy, but we're going to get at least a minimum amount of what we want. Nobody had better take that away from us or we'll let them know about it.

The Lord is speaking of this when He says, "To anyone who takes your cloak, do not refuse your tunic."

Mission: Impossible

From time to time, we hear stories of the saints who loved their persecutors. We tend to wonder if these people were for real. They were; now go and do likewise.

I am asking you to be saints. The community of faith needs you; you embody our sacrament of Matrimony and we need you in top shape.

It may be difficult for you to realize that you are, indeed, a sacrament. But it's true. The Lord always calls us to greater things than we could imagine on our own.

Once we realize our importance in God's plan, we're called to action.

Do we live God's plan with each other? Remember, the man you're angry with is half that sacrament; the woman you wish would go away is the other half. We wouldn't treat the Eucharist that way.

See How Good You Are?

Do we ever turn the other cheek with each other?

Yes, we often do. It's not fair to ourselves, nor is it helpful, to call ourselves failures. There are many times when we are most understanding and compassionate toward each other.

I'm not suggesting that we're reprobates and it's time to shape up. I'm saying, let's expand our goodness. Let's make a real campaign of being our best.

A lot of times, we are, indeed, at our best. We're great with each other. But we don't think we could do that all the time.

We sometimes think if we can't be perfect, we might as well give up. That's hopelessness, though, not the Lord's way. Jesus didn't say either we're flawless or we flunk. He expected our goodness to be a journey of growth.

We should ask ourselves whether we're turning the other cheek more frequently than we did last week, last month, or last year. We should ask: "Am I limiting my growth in goodness by thinking I'm already generous enough, or am I willing to push myself a little beyond today's success?"

That's all. Don't tell yourselves, "I won't be impatient with him again, ever"; "I'll turn the other cheek with her from now on." The step beyond today's success, however small or large it may have been, is a big stride ahead.

Consider these questions privately:

Do I love my spouse when everyone would say it's all right not to?

When am I my spouse's enemy?

What specific steps can I take in order to do better than I did today?

Share these questions with your spouse:

I remember a certain time when you reached out to me, even though my actions or words were pushing you away.

Let me tell you about it . . . How does that memory make me feel?

Which parts of my life did I once think were worldly, and now realize are spiritual? (Make a list and explain why.)

My dear, you are God's immortal son or daughter. I can see this because of your goodness, which shines forth when you . . . I remember when you . . .

Finally, let us invite God into our marriages:

Dear Father, I ask you today for the grace of trust. Help me realize Your plan is one of happiness and strength, not hopelessness. Help me see my lover's needs, not mine; lift me beyond the trap of my own hurts and resentments. Let me see the pain behind my spouse's anger; fill me with mercy and forgiveness.

Please give me the patience to wait while You gentle my heart, replacing the hardness with tenderness, and the rigidness with happiness and love.

Thank you for my wonderful spouse, who is so good to me. Bless my spouse and fill her (him) with peace. Amen.

CHAPTER 6

WE ARE INSTRUMENTS OF HIS LOVE

(Lk. 6:30–38)

"I don't want a marriage counselor," she said. "I want a divorce."

This guy didn't look much like a psychologist, she thought bitterly. He was too young, his hair was too long, and he was entirely too cheerful. He looked more like a man who made furniture. "Don't smile at me," she told him. "We're talking about misery here, you know."

"I understand," he said. "I understand it all."

For a strange moment, she believed he did. Behind the smile, his eyes were full of compassion. But wait a minute. He hadn't heard her story yet. "How can you—"

146

"You don't have to leave him, you know," he said. "I know how to repair your marriage."

"You do?" For a moment, she felt a surge of excitement. Then practicality took over. No; it was too late now. She wouldn't indulge fool's hopes.

"Don't think that way," he said. "Listen to me."

"You know what I'm thinking? But—you can't read minds."

"You're the one who said it. Now then, dear, I want you to turn the other cheek."

"Turn the other cheek? No one does that."

His gaze was steady; she could see he didn't agree. She began to feel a little guilty. "I mean—well, I know we're supposed to, but we can't really do it. It's not realistic."

He didn't hesitate. "You need to love Joe. He's acting the way he does because he's starved for love."

"Him? Starved? Not Joe."

The counselor went on as if he hadn't heard. "You need to be good to him, even when he hurts you. You need to say nice things to him; things that make him feel good about himself, especially when he's cold or sarcastic. I also want you to pray for him."

"Pray that God straightens him out?"

"No, pray that our Father blesses him, makes him happy, gives him peace. It wouldn't hurt if you prayed for yourself, too."

She shrugged.

"When he insults you or snubs you, don't fight with him. When he trespasses on your rights, don't hold back. Give him what he seems to need."

"Now you're insulting me," she said. "That's nonsense."

"No it's not. All I'm saying is to treat him the way you

wish he'd treat you. It's not enough to love him when things are all moonlight and roses. Any woman could do that."

"Moonlight and roses?" she said. "We haven't had moonlight and roses since the garden show in seventy-nine."

He didn't look happy. "I'm not excusing him. But if you're good to him when he's good to you, that isn't love. That's common sense. His wife should love him more than that. Now then, I want you to give him everything he needs without expecting him to return any favors."

"And what do I get out of it?"

"How about holiness?"

"I don't want holiness. I want love."

"Love is the same thing."

She didn't understand that at all. "You're saying it's all my fault."

"No I'm not. Not at all. I'm complimenting you. You have the goodness and the strength to turn this marriage around—with the Father's help, of course. If I didn't have faith in you, I would have said, take a cruise. Pretend things are going well and be satisfied with the mediocrity other people have. But if you do what I'm telling you, you two will have the best marriage on the block. You'll have such a good marriage, everyone will think you're crazy."

"I almost believe you," she said.

"That's almost good. Why don't you pray about it?"

"Pray about it? Who, me?"

"Yes, you." He walked her to the door. "I think you'll do well. In fact, I know you will."

"Am I supposed to make another appointment?" she asked.

"No. I'll see you in church."

She stood outside on the sidewalk. "Church? He doesn't even know if I go to church." She flung open the door to confront him with it. Of course, he wasn't there.

What Kind of Saint Are You?

There's no way around it: Jesus' words sound frightening when printed in black and white. In fact, they sound like madness. That's because we humans see them from our own viewpoints: "What will that do for me? How can I protect myself? How can I get what I want and need?"

As I said earlier, the question should be: "How can my spouse get what he or she needs?" Through you, of course. God gave you to your spouse to fill those needs.

At this point, some of you have thrown up your hands in something like panic. "Hey. I won't even pretend that sounds good. I don't want to be that kind of saint."

That's a good point, one we have to face. Because, you see, we've misunderstood. Very naturally, we don't want to become nonpersons who serve someone else—like slaves.

The Good News is, we're sons and daughters of God, and He has no intention of turning His precious children into slaves.

When you're thinking of your spouse's hurts and needs, you're creating a loving atmosphere in the home. That atmosphere creates loving people. Because you're more loving, your spouse becomes more loving; everyone is happier. You are both rewarded much more richly than if you struggled to a "compromise" the world's way. You've cast aside mediocrity and, instead, created a place of miracles, where cold, unfeeling, or argumentative relationships can mellow into something wonderful and beautiful.

Later in this chapter, I'll explain how to grow a loving spouse. But first, let's continue Jesus' lesson of Luke 6:27–38, on treating others as you'd have them treat you.

Give to Everyone Who Asks You

Jesus next said, "Give to everyone who asks you, and do not ask for your property back from someone who takes it." Other translations of this Scripture passage say, "Give to everyone who begs from you."

We may not like the idea that our husbands and wives have to beg from us, but all too frequently it happens, even in good marriages. How often do our lovers have to beg us to pay attention? Are they afraid to initiate lovemaking because they know we might reject them?

Too often, our lovers must remind us to show affection. Why should a wife have to remind her husband it's her birthday or their anniversary? His lack of thoughtfulness forces her to beg for love.

There are so many things our spouses like us to do, yet never seem important enough for us to remember. We're sporadic with our thoughtfulness, which makes our lovers suspicious, sometimes rightly so. When a husband brings home flowers, his wife is tempted to say, "You've quit your job, haven't you? Or have you done something else?"

If a wife dresses up for her husband or cooks him a special meal, he runs through a list of occasions to discover if he forgot one. When he realizes it's just an ordinary weekday, he thinks, "I wonder what she's up to."

Sometimes our thoughtfulness is a form of apology: "I'm sorry I fought with you," or "Let's be friends again." Why don't we expand our repertory? Let's add, "There's no particular reason for this; I'm just so glad I have you. Let's have a party." The Lord doesn't want His people to wear long faces or think only about "serious" spiritual things. He wants us to be happy. We can consider that a divine command.

We force our spouses to beg when they want something we don't approve of, when their needs are a burden on us, or when we think their requests can't really be important to them. Sometimes we make them beg because we're still concentrating on our own satisfaction. We might even withhold something deliberately because our spouses aren't responding to us, and turnabout is fair play. For whatever reason, we humans do a lot of withholding. When we do give, it may be grudging, partial, or seldom. Again, we're not bad people. We're good people who don't see our bad habits. Now that we do, we're free to change.

Do Not Ask For Your Property Back from Someone Who Takes It

Back when feminism was called "women's lib," women's college courses sometimes included assertiveness training. One such exercise was an elaborate marriage agreement that started with Monday's breakfast dishes, wound through income, illness, and overtime, and finished with the last speck of Sunday night dust. In the less enlightened classes, women who promised to do more than their fair share got lower grades.

I'm not saying wives should do the "women's work" with a (hopefully cheerful) smile, nor am I saying it's wrong if they do. The love-killing danger of this score-

151

keeping mentality transcends such trivia. Male and female, old and young, we've all been trained by subtle yet deadly exercises.

How often have we established life-styles with definite give and take? In a typical family, the husband does his share; the wife does hers. When an emergency happens, a spirit of generosity kicks in. Perhaps she's sick and he does all the cooking, or he's had a terrible day, so she doesn't tell him the bathtub's stopped up. When the trouble passes, though, it's business as usual. These lovers expect their spouses to resume their fair share.

Generosity Is an Everyday Virtue

We're often quite generous with each other. I don't want to imply otherwise. But often, we think generosity is for special occasions and we limit ourselves to those.

Most men graciously pitch in with the dishes, the children, or the housework, but pitching in is exactly what we're doing. We're helping our wives do their own jobs, make no mistake about it. Now, we're not working grudgingly; we may be joyful and enthusiastic, even delighted, but we're not taking responsibility.

That can also be true of joint projects: painting the house, for example. In this case, both of us expect our lovers to recognize our goodness in wielding that paintbrush. We want them, at least implicitly, to admit we're walking that extra mile.

We wives can also limit our generosity. Maybe we work in the home, raising our children, and our shift runs from 6:00 A.M. to 5:00 P.M. When our husbands come home, we're off duty. At least, we feel we ought to be. We may not go anywhere, but we're vividly aware that that's our time to ourselves. If our husbands want time for themselves, too, how do we react?

On the other hand, maybe we husbands think time after work is our time off. When we come home at night, it's time to relax. We know we're supposed to talk to our wives, so we give them a suitable amount of conversation. But when they start encroaching on our hobbies, our television shows, or our rest, what do we do?

What if both of us work outside the home and want to rest in the evenings? Weary tempers can flare faster than summer brushfires. How do we change those irritations into love?

Sometimes our "property" is an attitude or belief, and our spouses are ideally placed to take it from us. Clashes in child-raising philosophies are an all-too-frequent example. Often, we think our ideas are the right ones. If our lovers start to "interfere" by using their own methods, how do we respond? Do we feel they're taking the children away from us? Are they robbing us of our authority?

Maybe a wife, for instance, likes the children to have good table manners, but her husband is more interested in a relaxed and pleasant meal. He makes it clear that's the kind of meals they'll have.

Perhaps we think our spouses are too strict, so we make it up to the children. Maybe we let them know we're on their side, or maybe we simply voice that disapproval to our spouses.

What if a wife likes the symphony while her husband prefers the movies? What if she wants to go out and he wants to stay home? What if she wants to talk things out and he wants to think things out?

In a sense, we're like dogs clinging to a bone. Our attention is totally centered on what's being taken away from us. Maybe we growl self-righteously about it, and maybe we just clamp our jaws.

Such bones of contention can be sources of conflict and unhappiness. The Lord wants to free us from that. He's telling us to stop being possessive, not just about money or belongings, but about attitudes, preferences, and styles of living.

Let's stop and examine ourselves now: what hidden demands do we have of our spouses?

Do we have mental lists of their responsibilities, which can only be postponed under special circumstances? What happens when those special circumstances are over? Is it business as usual, with our spouses shouldering the same loads once again? Do they have to carry even more for a while to pay us for our help?

"Remember how nice I was to you?" we imply. "Well, now you can let me off the hook."

Jesus reminds us, "If you love those who love you, what credit can you expect? Even sinners love those who love them." If you love your spouses when they're lovable, how different are you from any other couple? How are you a sacrament in anything but name?

What Is the Gospel?

The Gospel wasn't just the fruit of a few extraordinarily pious, holy people who had mystical experiences with God, then wrote down His orders. The Gospel comes from the believing people of the Church, who, in their faith experience, lived a certain way and wrote down that way.

Whenever we read the Gospel, we should be saying more than "Help me find my way through life; help console me; help enlighten me." We should be saying, "Where am I in the midst of my fellow believers in the Church? Am I living up to their expectations of me?" not "Am I satisfied?" Scripture is a book of the church. It should immerse us in the lives of our fellow believers.

Too often we look on the Bible as private property. We interpret it ourselves, then live out the messages we've perceived. When we do this, we're cutting it off from its roots. The Gospel is not meant to be read on our terms. It's meant to be read on our people's terms.

"Treat others as you would like others to treat you," say our people. The significant Others in our lives—and that's Others with a capital O—are our spouses. We're specifically called to treat them as we'd like them to treat us, but too often we wonder if they deserve our generosity.

We're making excuses, then. And we're also afraid.

"I don't want to look like a fool."

"I don't want to be taken advantage of."

But, wives, if your husbands want to take advantage of you, they can. There's no way you can stop them. Their goodwill and their desire to love you are all that stop them. Husbands, if your wives want to take you to the cleaners, they can, any day of the week and twice on Sundays. Their love for you is all that stops them.

There's no way you can control your spouses. Their goodness is a freewill offering.

Prickly Pair

We're so untrusting; we have been so carefully trained to be prickly, defensive, and above all, in charge. When we can't control others' responses, we become afraid. We worry: are we getting our share? Yes, we're less defensive with our spouses than with others, thank God. But our training has been so thorough, we unconsciously bring it into our homes.

I hope these truisms are dead and buried:

"Women. Can't live with 'em and can't live without 'em."

"Honey, a man's just out for what he can get."

Unfortunately, these subtler ones aren't:

"My husband takes me for granted. I ought to go on strike for a couple of weeks. He'd sure learn a thing or two."

"My wife doesn't know what a hard day is. She has time to talk on the phone, and she still thinks she's rushed."

"He thinks he's got it rough. I'd like to see him keep up with my day."

"She didn't *have* to go to work; she chose to go. She's doing what she wants to do. And now she's complaining about stress."

I'm not suggesting a debate about who's right and who's wrong. I'm calling for a surrender of defenses, a throwing down of arms, and a lasting, peaceful embrace. It's indeed not a fool's hope. It's God's plan, and as they say in the South, He wasn't just whistlin' Dixie.

The Lord is saying, "Let go; be free. Don't treat others as they treat you. That's the world's teaching."

"But I'm afraid. My spouse is hurting me. If I don't look out for myself, who will?"

The Lord isn't as heartless as we sometimes think He is. "Why, I will, of course," He answers. "I'm looking out for you right now, if only you could see it."

The more we require, the less satisfied we become. We see how much we're not getting, and that certainly doesn't make us happy. The Lord is offering us happiness. He's offering us fullness in life. If we follow His way, there will be much more joy in our marriages. Our husbands and wives are not bad people. They will certainly respond to our goodness if we'll only let it shine forth.

If the truth be known, we're never satisfied when we force goodness from our spouses. If a wife reminds her husband it's their anniversary, and later he brings her flowers, she certainly won't be surprised and will probably feel lonely. If a husband outshouts his wife to such an extent that she apologizes for starting the fight, it's a hollow victory indeed.

We desperately want our spouses to love us freely. When we force "love" from them, no matter how subtle we are, we're fooling no one.

Besides, if we wait for our lovers to earn our trust, we'll have a long wait indeed. Our lovers simply cannot prove they're trustworthy. They, like all of us, have faults; none of us is perfect. Our trust must be our gift to them.

We All Have a Stake in Your Marriage

No matter how adeptly we extort good behavior from our spouses, we still can't make them into the people we want them to be, nor can we force them to do things they really don't want to do. Many a fiancée, for instance, thinks, "Oh, I can make him stop drinking (attend the symphony/enjoy family life/change in other ways)." Of course, she can't. Only he can change himself. Likewise, a husband can't force changes on a wife.

Our sacrament calls us to love our spouses, whether or not they earn it.

Your relationship is not just a marriage; it's the sacrament of Matrimony. Practically anyone can be married, but your relationship is more significant than a document in a file drawer somewhere in city hall. We, the church, have a stake in your marriage. Your good relationship nourishes us, and its rough moments drag us down. You are our inspiration and our community, and we need you to be your loving best.

Perhaps you're satisfied in your marriage. That doesn't necessarily mean you're answering your call to be sacramental.

All too often, I'm afraid, we compare our marriages with the failures around us:

"Thank God our marriage isn't like Joe and Mary's. They just endure each other. They never go out together, and when they're home, they're in opposite corners of the house. Now us, we're not perfect, but we still have some passion in our marriage. At least we still fight."

Contrast this with "Thank God our marriage isn't like Joe and Mary's. I can't believe how they treat each other. They're always shouting, then somehow they make up. Now us, we're not perfect, but we still have some peace in our marriage. At least we don't fight."

Which of these couples is right? Neither one, fortunately; not that it matters. Even if we could be absolutely sure our marriage is better than someone else's, that still means nothing. Our spouses live with us, not with the people we're comparing ourselves to.

Maybe we're not judgmental about others. Maybe we're just a little smug:

"We have a date every Saturday night. We go to dinner, take in a movie. We don't know any other couple who does that."

The idea's a great one; there's absolutely nothing wrong with it. The pride in that sentence can be blinding, though. Let's ask: Who has the most fun—us at the movies or our neighbors at home? If we aren't sure, maybe we should keep working on loving each other.

Put the Pedal to the Metal

Let's not ask ourselves, "Am I a good wife?" or "Am I a good husband?" if it means, "Am I living up to certain minimal standards?" or "Am I doing all right?"

Let's do ask, "Is this the best I can do? Am I really going all out, foot to the floor, every moment of every day?"

Don't ask, "Does he gripe?" "Is she reasonably pleased?" It isn't enough to wonder, "Am I living up to my responsibilities?"

Ask, instead, "How delighted is his life?" "How full is her life?" "How can I add to that enjoyment?"

If you compared many of today's marriages to schoolrooms, you'd find a lot of students content to earn Cs, sometimes a D here and there or even an F. But we didn't marry to get passing marks. We each have the capability to make our marriages an A+.

The Lord said, "Treat others as you would like people to treat you." We don't want others to do the minimum for us. We need so much more than that. We want to know that our husbands and wives are eager for us to be happy. We want to know that they'll treat us kindly, do little things for us, make sure our lives are filled with wonder because they love us so much.

If You Do Good to Those Who Do Good to You, What Credit Can You Expect?

We all know our good qualities. When do we exercise them? If it's mainly when our spouses are appreciative or when they're good to us, we've changed loving into banking. We're lending to each other and expecting repayment.

The Lord says, "If you lend to those from whom you hope to get money back, what credit can you expect? Even sinners lend to sinners to get back the same amount."

Now, I'm not implying that your husband's a sinner, but most of the people at work will lend him lunch money, because they know he'll pay them back. The woman across the street will give you an egg or a cup of sugar. She might even baby-sit for you; of course, you'll baby-sit for her too. There's nothing wrong with that, until you apply it to marriage.

We're capable of so much more, yet so many couples practice a system of trade-offs. They may be very good people; it may be all they know. How are we different?

Some of us will give it some thought, then answer, "We go to church; I don't think they do."

That's a good start, but we need to examine more than our Sunday church attendance. Do we live Christian lives during the week? Are you living your sacrament right this minute?

If you live as a sacrament, you and your spouse will naturally benefit more than anyone else does. You're living for more than your spouse's sake, though. The church is only as credible as you are.

The words of the Bible are great and certainly necessary, but people aren't drawn to God because they're impressed with His book. They are drawn through a love relationship, beginning with His love as it is lived in *you:* your warmth and acceptance, your willingness to seek the happiness of others instead of yourself. That's best demonstrated by the way you love your spouse.

Love Your Enemies and Do Good to Them

In full, this passage says, "Love your enemies and do good to them, and lend without any hope of return. You will have a great reward, and you will be children of the Most High, for he himself is kind to the ungrateful and the wicked."

Our defensive instincts urge us to reject this teaching. We want to say, "Wait a minute. That's a nice thought, but we have to live in this world. My spouse is a good person; better than I am, most likely. But if you let people get away with rude behavior, they'll just get worse."

That's a little crude, but it gets to the point. In subtler terms, it's what we've been taught by our mothers and grandmothers, the people in the office and the boys in the shop. It's all around us.

How do we overcome the tendency to listen to, heaven forbid follow, such love-killing advice? By telling ourselves, "I am not that kind of person. I am a loving person, and I will be a lover no matter what anyone else says or thinks." We have to draw lines. Each of us has to know where those lines are, and we can't allow ourselves to step across them.

We must teach ourselves that sulking, shouting back, the cold shoulder, forgetfulness of anniversaries—whatever—is unacceptable in the Lord's plan. We'll still make mistakes. We're human and God loves us, humanity and all. But we must resolve not to lower our standards, even when we can't live up to them.

Prayer is a great self-improver. It opens us to the Father's love. By understanding that love, we better understand how to love others. Prayer can be quiet thought in church or a repetitive, calming phrase called *centering*

161

prayer or the *Jesus prayer*. It can be meditation on the Scriptures or through guided imagery; it can involve the rosary, spontaneous group prayer, or any number of expressions.

We Catholics, especially if we're older, are familiar with the concept of penance. Penance strengthens our prayer lives and the goodness within us. It is our widow's mite of suffering offered to the Father. He adds it to Jesus' gift of the Eucharist for the purpose of furthering His plan. Soothing an insulting, angry spouse is one form of penance. Fasting is another one. The traditional Catholic fast is one meal, plus two light snacks that together don't equal a full meal.

The strength to live His way is also found in trust. We humans are tempted to rely on force, making marriage a power struggle instead of a love relationship.

Instead, we husbands must truly trust our wives. Each of us must understand: "Yes, she fails; she's human. But she wants to love me."

The best way to encourage her to want to love you more is to love her with everything you've got.

Wives, your husbands fail sometimes, too. They don't always love you the way you need to be loved. Sometimes they're selfish. But believe this, every one of you: he yearns to love you. The best way to teach him how to love you more is to pour out your love in total dedication, and believe he'll respond.

If we allow ourselves even a little laxity, we're being less than we can be. We're called to love each other as much as we can. That exuberant maximum will be different for each person. You might find yourself excelling in gentleness and forgiveness while your spouse grows in spontaneity and joy. Each of us is stronger in some graces, needing more prayer in others.

How to Grow a Lover

Some years ago, researchers decided to test the effect of affection on houseplants. They placed two sets of plants in separate parts of a greenhouse, making sure the physical conditions were exactly the same. The amounts of sunlight, water, and fertilizer were all controlled, as was the type of soil.

For one set of plants, they made life as miserable as possible. They constantly played harsh music, yelled, and insulted the poor things. To the other plants, they played soft, gentle music and offered constant praise.

The second set of plants blossomed incredibly, way beyond the capacity of the soil, fertilizer, sun, and water. The first set of plants withered and died.

The way to grow a husband is to talk gently and lovingly and in praise. The more criticism he receives, the more he will live out your prophecies.

Men, are you listening, too? The harsher you are with your wife, the more she will turn to attack you and the less love she will find within her grasp. She won't necessarily say, "I won't love because he's so cruel." She'll probably say instead, "He's right. I am not capable of loving. I am bad."

These statements are, in a twisted way, self-fulfilling prophecies:

"You don't care about me. All you care about is yourself."

"How could you *do* such a thing?"

"I don't know why I bother (. . . with you)."

"I forgot (. . . because you aren't important enough to make me remember)."

Our spouses are much more likely to become the kinds

of people we "speak" them to be than the kinds of people we're trying to make them. Pressure, punishment, and force simply do not work in a husband-wife relationship. We may achieve a Mexican stand-off but not a real union of love.

To some degree, we're all guilty. These kinds of mistakes happen, even if we aren't extraordinary scoundrels or suffering in bad relationships. Less than perfect conduct is present even in the best marriages.

If we're clever and we apply enough pressure, we could probably force our spouses to perform as we wish, at least sometimes. But their hearts won't be in it, and after all, aren't hearts what marriage is all about?

It's our responsibility to bolster the good self-images of our spouses. The better their self-images are, the better they'll respond to us. They'll be more capable of loving; freer from defensiveness, narrowness, and rejection.

If our lovers see themselves as inadequate in our eyes, they simply won't have the confidence to love. But if we're frequently telling them how much they mean to us, how much more joyful our lives are because of their presence, the more they'll pour out their love on us. There will be a tremendous increase in their capacity to love because we have expanded them with our praise.

You're Irresistible, Dear

"Words flow out of what fills the heart," Jesus told the Pharisees in Matthew 12:34. Out of those words a home is created. When you provide an environment of unconditional tenderness, your beloved becomes the kind of person who does fit your life. Like houseplants, spouses bloom when they believe they're so wonderful in your eyes that you just can't resist them.

If they receive love only when they perform correctly, they can never believe in the love. Even worse, they can never believe in themselves. When that love is constant, relentless, when it is absolutely, totally poured out, the rewards are great.

There is no man who is loved by a tender woman who does not discover riches in himself that he never believed were there. There is no woman who is loved by a gentle man who does not live way beyond her outward potential. Every bit of love you ever expressed throughout your marriage has been more than returned. Take a moment to think about it.

The Lord's way really does work. We're losing so much if we don't try it. We can't be slapdash about it, though. It won't work if we try a little of it for a little while. We really must make a commitment to love our spouses the way the Lord intends.

When you want to give up, remember this: You are instruments of His love. Husbands, the Lord has specifically chosen each of you to love this particular woman the way He wants her to be loved. Wives, you are each called by Jesus to touch, to heal, to console, and to bring this man to life the way He wants to do it Himself.

Do you see the wonder of it? This is an awesome commitment and a great honor. Jesus trusts you the way He trusted His disciples. He wants you to make His Kingdom come alive in the hearts of His people. Matrimony is a magnificent call to love totally and unreservedly.

Consider these questions privately:

When do I best increase my spouse's self-esteem? When do I wither my spouse by failing to love? What steps can I take to nourish my lover more?

What is holding me back from being a more perfect lover? Fear of hurt and rejection? Indignation? Fear of losing my "rights"?

Am I willing to incorporate prayer and/or penance into my life for the sake of my beloved? What, specifically, will I do?

Before we cover the next questions, let's review how to share. Remember to focus on your own feelings. These questions are meant to stimulate dialogue between you and to clear up misunderstandings. They are absolutely not a place to lay even the slightest blame. Don't, for instance, say, "I have trouble loving you when you're acting like a jerk, because that's when you make me the angriest." Do say something like "When we quarrel, I feel afraid that you'll stop loving me. I feel ashamed of myself, too. I'm afraid to share those feelings, so I cover them up with anger."

A warning: if you can add a "like" or "that" after "feel," it's a judgment, not a feeling.

Remember: use at least ten minutes to write and at least ten minutes to talk. Enjoy.

Share these questions with your spouse:

My dear, I know that sometimes I love you less than I am able. I want to be closer to you; I want to love you more. These are the feelings that hold me back . . .

My dear, I want to increase my life of prayer and/or

penance so I can love you more perfectly. I am thinking of doing the following . . . I would like you to support me by . . . Will you please . . . ?

What do I like best about you? What are your special goodnesses, the things that fill me with delight?

An exercise in happiness:

At least once a month in the next five months, find a way to tell your lover just how wonderful he or she is.

Some ideas for men:

- Bring home flowers or a small gift.
- Surprise her with a dinner out or perhaps brunch on Sunday.
- Spend an evening or a Saturday being completely present to her. Do anything she wants, providing you can share it together. A walk on the beach is great; reading books on the beach is not.

Some ideas for women:

- Dress for dinner with him. Pull out all the stops: full makeup, the works.
- Hide a love note under his pillow, in his lunch box or briefcase.
- Bake him a cake or grill him a steak, with all the fixings he likes.

Finally, let us invite God into our marriages:

Eternal Father, my prayer today is for freedom: freedom from my cage of resentment and anxiety. Please grant me the grace to love as bountifully as You do. Please free me from the fear of rejection and hopelessness; give me the greatness of heart to trust my spouse's goodness.

Thank you, Lord, for choosing me to be the one to love my wonderful husband (wife). Thank you for trusting in me and believing in my goodness. Please help me love my spouse the way You want to do it Yourself. Amen.

CHAPTER 7

BELOVED, I BELONG TO YOU

(LK. 15:11–20)

Jesus was very popular among the sinners and tax collectors, and one day, while they were crowding around him, the scribes and Pharisees began to complain. They grumbled, "This man welcomes sinners and even eats with them" (Lk. 15:2).

Evidently they thought their virtue made them better company at dinner and probably in heaven as well. Jesus, who didn't agree, told them a story.

This famous parable has probably prompted more elbow digging and finger pointing than any other passage of the Bible. Of course, we've heard the parable of the prodigal son many times before. This time, let's read it carefully and try, prayerfully, to see where we fit in, particularly in relation to our spouses.

There was a man who had two sons. The younger one said to his father, "Father, let me have the share of the estate that will come to me." So the father divided the property between them. A few days later, the younger son got together everything he had and left for a distant country where he squandered his money on a life of debauchery.

When he had spent it all, that country experienced a severe famine, and now he began to feel the pinch; so he hired himself out to one of the local inhabitants who put him on his farm to feed the pigs. And he would willingly have filled himself with the husks the pigs were eating but no one would let him have them. Then he came to his senses and said, "How many of my father's hired men have all the food they want and more, and here am I dying of hunger! I will leave this place and go to my father and say: Father, I have sinned against heaven and against you; I no longer deserve to be called your son; treat me as one of your hired men." So he left the place and went back to his father.

While he was still a long way off, his father saw him and was moved with pity. He ran to the boy, clasped him in his arms and kissed him. Then his son said, "Father, I have sinned against heaven and against you. I no longer deserve to be called your son." But the father said to his servants, "Quick! Bring out the best robe and put it on him; put a ring on his finger and sandals on his feet. Bring the calf we have been fattening, and kill it; we will celebrate by having a feast, because this son of mine was dead and has come back to life; he was lost and is found." And they began to celebrate.

Now the elder son was out in the fields, and on his way back, as he drew near the house, he could hear music and dancing. Calling one of the servants he asked what it was all about. The servant told him, "Your brother has come, and your father has killed the calf we had been fattening because he has got him back safe and sound." He was angry then and refused to go in, and his father came out and began to urge him to come in; but he retorted to his father, "All these years I have slaved for you and never once disobeyed any orders of yours, yet you never offered me so much as a kid for me to celebrate with my friends. But, for this son of yours, when he comes back after swallowing up your property—he and his loose women—you kill the calf we had been fattening."

The father said, "My son, you are with me always and all that I have is yours. But it was only right we should celebrate and rejoice, because your brother here was dead and has come to life; he was lost and is found."

Luke 15:11–32

The Pharisees probably listened to this parable feeling the warmth of charity and some righteous smugness. It was a wonderful story, but it didn't apply to *them*. It was a clever tale of God's forgiveness for sinners; forgiveness they—like the virtuous elder son—didn't need.

We all tend to think like the Pharisees, and that's not a good idea. When it came to spiritual growth, there was much more hope for the younger son than for his elder brother.

Let's try putting ourselves in the place of each character in the drama: the loving father, the indignant elder son, and the penitent younger one.

You don't have to pretend you're an aging farmer or a swinging single. Jesus meant this parable to be generously interpreted. For the purposes of this chapter, then, let's think of ourselves as the loving spouse, the indignant spouse, and the penitent one.

The Wounds of Marriage

Remember the old saying "You only hurt the one you love"? That's because the one you love is the only one who lets you get close enough to cause that hurt.

When we hurt, it's because we care. We want our loves to approve of us. We want them to be interested in what we have to say. We want them to take on our concerns, to find pleasure in our company, to treat our opinions with respect.

Rejection isn't ever pleasant, but we can shrug it off more readily if it doesn't come from the ones we love. We all like to impress others, but we aren't seriously hurt when we don't succeed.

Most of the time, we're pretty humble. We don't expect everyone to have a burning desire for our companionship. But when a husband or wife doesn't desire our company, day after day, night after night, we hurt. We hurt deeply.

When we love, our defenses are down. We don't want our words to be judged and analyzed by someone who is supposed to love us. After all, we trust our loves, so we speak spontaneously.

Spontaneous speech is a rare gift, and we don't usually share it. We're always personal with our spouses, though, so when we're faced with indifference, cruelness, or even anger, we're wide open to the pain.

That's why forgiveness is the single most essential blessing a husband or wife can ask from God.

The Gift of Trust

There's a tremendous vulnerability in the love relationship, and too often, we don't notice it. So often, we forget how fragile a gift our spouses are giving us.

Sometimes we don't forget it. We may even take advantage of it. A man who chooses the newspaper over his wife may say, "I'm not trying to hurt her. I'm just trying to unwind, and as hard as *I* work, I sure need to." A woman who gives her husband the cold shoulder may argue, "I'm not ignoring him. I'm just busy—doing *his* laundry."

We try to persuade ourselves that we're not deliberately hurting the other person. If we're honest with ourselves, though, we know better. Once we know our actions will pain our loves, we can't close our eyes and pretend innocence.

The best of us sometimes take advantage of this gift of trust. Don't be discouraged, though. Our goodness is not determined by our flaws, but by our willingness to change those flaws.

Let's Call Ourselves Leaders

Anytime we're tempted to justify our actions by watching our friends' marriages, we're headed for trouble. We can't be quitters who think marital pain is normal. Sure, there are unhappy marriages all around us, but that's because everyone around us has already thrown in the towel.

In the parable of the prodigal son, Jesus calls us to be leaders. He calls us to be happy—and to be brave enough to face our mistakes. We're dodging the issue if we say, "There's misunderstanding and pain in every love relationship. It's only natural. We'd be naive to expect anything else."

Why settle for a wounded, hurting relationship when we have a much better choice?

Remember, you are not just human. In 1 Peter 2:9,10, the apostle says, "You are a chosen race, a kingdom of priests, a holy nation, a people to be a personal possession to sing the praises of God who called you out of the darkness into his wonderful light. Once, you were a nonpeople and now you are the People of God . . ." Jesus Christ came to earth to free us all from the hopeless limitations of humanity. With God's grace, you can, indeed, have a truly loving relationship. It's your choice.

It's not a choice you should make next week or next year. It's a choice to make now. Hurry! Your family's happiness is at stake.

The lack of happiness in today's marriages is a life-threatening illness. If a husband was vomiting and feverish, and had a sharp pain on the lower right side of his abdomen, his wife wouldn't shrug her shoulders and say, "Oh, well. Must be appendicitis; that's pretty common. Most people get it sooner or later." Instead, she'd be frantic. She'd rush her husband to the hospital. She'd want to take the pain away—now. All we husbands would do the same. When our husbands or wives hurt from wounds we inflicted, though, we're much more relaxed.

We humans are much more likely to excuse our own defects, and much less likely to excuse our lovers' flaws.

174

There's a good rule of thumb we can all follow: when we find ourselves making excuses for our behavior, that's when our loves are feeling their greatest pain.

Sometimes we can't even see our own defects. Our society preaches self-centered hyperactivity; if we've been good listeners, we're too involved in our own ways of life to notice when we're hurting someone else.

To Love or Be Loved?

Many of us are familiar with the Greek myth of Narcissus, the man who loved himself more than anyone else. One day, he saw his reflection in a pool and fell violently, passionately in love. He tried to kiss himself, but naturally, that didn't work. He couldn't hug himself very well, either, and he was so disappointed, he finally died. Really, poor Narcissus could never have been happy. Even if he finally got that promotion, moved into the suburbs, and surrounded himself with expensive stereo equipment, he would have felt emptier and lonelier.

The truth is, we're only happy when we're focused on others, and we're miserably unhappy when we aren't. Often, we're hurt because we would much rather be loved than love. We take our spouse's goodness for granted and are constantly looking for more.

Again, that's not because we're bad people. It's because we've learned, when looking for happiness, to look the wrong way.

That natural impulse is a recipe for trouble. Love is supposed to pull us outward until we're taking the other person even more seriously than we do ourselves. As our love grows, we start to find our own well-being in our loves' well-being.

Marriage is not supposed to be a business deal in which each partner receives separate rewards for a joint effort. It's a call for both husband and wife to be totally absorbed in each other. It's a call to spend all our talents, our energy, enthusiasm, and responsiveness for one precious purchase: bringing true joy to our loves.

Yes, we fail. We're not awful people if we don't succeed, and we shouldn't expect perfection, but we do need to examine our goals.

If we think the purpose of marriage is to be loved, it will pain not only our partners but ourselves as well. Why? Because we're clinging to an illusion: that the more we are loved, the happier we are.

If we are experiencing hurt in our marriages, we need to find out why. We must go beyond the specific incident that triggered the pain: "He forgot our anniversary." "She doesn't care how hard I work."

We may be choosing to experience the pain. If, hidden in our hearts, we have a whole series of expectations for our partners and lists of our own rights, we're headed for a future filled with heartache.

Sin Is a Four-Letter Word

Physical pain is terrible. It's awful to contemplate, much less to experience, but emotional anguish is far worse.

With that in mind, ask yourselves, "What causes the most pain in this world?" Terrorism? Cancer? Prejudice?

No, sin does.

We honestly don't know what sin is. We think sin is an activity, perhaps a glamorous one; one that brings us pleasure, profit, or satisfaction, advancement or whatever else we find attractive. Masquerading as a seemingly innocent quest for "fairness," it can appear to be simply an act of stress reduction, a way of standing up for our rights or getting even.

We don't realize that pain is intimately connected with sin. If we could wipe out sin in a husband/wife relationship, we would eliminate 90 percent of that couple's emotional pain.

"We're sinners."

How does this expression make us feel?

Most likely, rather neutral. We're probably not too offended, although this statement is worse than any obscene phrase we could imagine.

Just stop and think about how callous we've become. If I were to fill this book with filthy words, you'd say, "How dare he use that kind of language on us? We didn't buy this book to be insulted."

It's a far more horrible insult to say that we're sinners. We should be cringing, wanting to deny it. Instead, it doesn't faze us in the least.

One hundred years ago, Father Damien, a priest in the leper colony on Molokai, Hawaii, became a leper himself. His parishioners were no longer the ill he tended. "We lepers," he called them proudly.

His public admission was admirable, but it didn't detract in the slightest from the deadliness of that disease.

Likewise, the admission that we're all sinners doesn't make that sinful condition less lethal. When we say, "We're sinners," we're really saying we are people who inflict pain. We are infectious with unhappiness; we make those around us suffer.

We're passive about sin because we don't recognize what it means to be a sinner. We Catholics have a certain prayer at mass: we confess to Almighty God and to our brothers and sisters that "I have sinned through my own fault in my thoughts and in my words, in what I have done, and in what I have failed to do." Whether Catholic or not, what goes on inside us when we say, "I have sinned"? Is it unfair to say: not much?

An admission of sin is of the greatest and most important seriousness. It's an opening of our hearts to those around us and, for Catholics, a necessary preliminary to receiving the Body and Blood of Christ. It's our opportunity for a true conversion experience. Do we realize this, or is our admission of sin merely a ritualistic straightening of our clothes, rather like brushing dust off our coats before we walk into church? For many of us, it's only a lighthearted "I'm a sinner, you're a sinner, all God's children are sinners." It's not unlike "I have red hair" or "I'm five pounds overweight."

We resist an awareness of our sinfulness because we don't want to go on any guilt trips. As a society, we're determined to avoid neurotic guilt, even to the point of ignoring our wrongs. It's easier to ignore those wrongs when we don't accept God's view of life. We may admit that, yes, in His eyes we've committed a sin, but we add that we're normal human beings and we're no worse than anyone else.

That excuse isn't worthy of all you tremendously good couples who are in the world today. Remember, we're called to be leaders, not sheep following the rest of society on a downhill road. Everyone else's sins don't excuse our own; they merely add to the world's problems.

I ask you to think and pray over the following question, because we all have to admit our flaws. Once we admit we are sinners, we can soar. Since we have such great potential, it would be terrible to be grounded.

Ask yourselves, "Do I really stand before God as a sinner and see the pain my sin is inflicting upon His people, especially my spouse? Or do I see it with this world's eyes and pass it off with a shoulder shrug?"

Honesty will give you the answer, and your goodness will tell you what to do.

Sin Is a Way of Life

We tend to cheapen sin. We say, "Sin is something I did that I shouldn't have done." When we're a bit more mature, we say, "Sin is something I should have done but didn't do." Either way, we view sin as an act, thought, or activity, or a neglect of the same.

We have to recognize that sin is a way of life.

A sin is not merely doing something that is bad in itself, nor is it merely a neutral action that is motivated by a sinful purpose.

Sin is a whole orientation toward life: "I am a sinner," not "I did sinful things." My sinful actions merely reflect where my heart lies.

When I say, "I am a sinner," I'm saying I'm committed to a way of life that is self-centered and unloving.

To many of us, that's a threatening truth. We want to deny it; to say, "I'm not that kind of woman"; "I'm not that kind of man. Most of my actions are good, or at least neutral. They're not bad." Again, we have to stop deluding ourselves. Sin isn't merely action.

Most of us do many good things: those we approve of.

Otherwise, we're neutral, and that's because we're neutral people. That's not virtue and that's not lack of sin.

We're living a sinful way of life when we're living for ourselves, our own satisfaction, and our own advancement. In sin, others fit best into our lives when they give us these things.

That's what it means to say, "I am a sinner." That's why most husbands and wives focus on being loved rather than on loving. We can perform all sorts of good actions sinfully if our attention is fundamentally on us.

In a marriage relationship, the basic choice is between you and me. We sin when we choose me over you. We do this in many subtle ways:

We don't say we're self-centered. We say we're independent. We stand on our own two feet.

We don't say we're indifferent to the needs of our spouses. We say there has to be give and take.

We don't say the other person is less important than we are; we say we have a lot of responsibilities and we can only do so much.

It's no wonder we say such things; it's the way we've been trained. We've all seen tests that measure marital happiness. These tests ask spouses whether they're satisfied in their marriages.

A real test should ask, "Is my spouse satisfied? What am I contributing to his or her satisfaction?"

"Beloved, I Belong to You"

Marriage is a commitment to belong, totally and fully, to that other person.

Most of us don't like that; we've adopted independent life-styles. We do nice things for the other person, but that isn't enough. That's exactly what we mean by a sinful way of life. Your husband didn't marry you to be fitted into your way of living. Your wife didn't give herself to you as one of your many responsibilities.

When you say "I confess" this Sunday, don't focus on whether you neglected her or whether you were nasty to him this week. Ask yourself, "Did I fully belong this week? Was I really married? Did I even intend to be?"

The problem is not that we fail sometimes. The problem is that we don't even try to belong. Our society teaches us to be ambitious. We should be ambitious, then, to fully belong to our spouses.

We also need to recognize that sin is never "out there." There is probably no such thing as sin in itself. There are only sinners. Sin is personal. Animals can't sin; they can only do horrible things. We can't sin when we're asleep or out of our minds. The deed does not make the sin; the person does.

Right now, you're probably wondering how you fit into all this. You may be admitting that sometimes you don't always do as well as a wife should, or that you don't always do the right, meaningful things as a husband.

Take it one step further; when we think that way, we're still isolating ourselves from our sin. We have to learn a new way of thinking, and it takes openness and a fair amount of courage. We have to let go of our defenses; we have to stop depersonalizing sin. We have to stop thinking it's outside us, like stained clothes or scaly skin. Only then can we begin the Lord's way of healing and growth.

The Prodigal Son

Aren't we horrified by the prodigal son's gall? He went to his father and said, "Okay, I'm old enough, I want to be independent. Give me my share."

Most of us wouldn't be as generous as his father; we'd put that brat in his place. "Share?" we'd ask. "What do you mean your share?"

We're indignant that he could have been so greedy and cold-blooded. Our feelings are right. His heartless demand for money was much more sinful than the way he spent it.

We think the sleeping around, the drinking, and the reckless spending were the younger son's sins. They weren't. The sin had already been committed. Those activities were merely expressions of the life-style he had chosen to live; a life-style in which he had divorced himself from his father. Demanding his share of the estate was more than rude. It was a statement: "I no longer belong to you." In effect, he was saying, "I want to live my own way. I want control of my life; you and your desires don't influence me." That's when he decided to be a sinner.

The relationship between father and son is the most important part of this parable. The debauchery is a very small part of the story, like the famine and the degradation of starving while feeding the pigs. They're mentioned in order to show how harmful sin is.

The prodigal son probably could have said, "Look, I don't have anything against the old man. I'm not doing these things because I dislike him, much less hate him. I just want my due. I don't want to live on a farm all my life; I have other plans."

Put that in your relationship. Have you ever really felt the sinner with your wife, with your husband? We limit sin in a marriage to adultery, wife beating, and desertion. Most of us find it easy to refrain from those.

When someone tells me, "I haven't committed adultery," I'm tempted to answer, "When was the last time you had a chance?" Often, our virtue is lack of opportunity. Adultery isn't merely sleeping in someone else's bed.

Adultery happens when you don't enjoy the bed you're in.

Many good husbands and wives would never look at another man or touch another woman, but their sexual response to each other is dutiful, grudging, or patient. That's infidelity.

In other words, infidelity is not the actual act of intercourse with the other woman. It's the severing of relationship with your wife. It's the putting her out of your life. You don't need a mistress to commit adultery; you do it alone.

That's because, like the prodigal son's debauchery, an act of adultery isn't the primary sin. It's the expression of a sin that's already been committed.

If you're really involved with your wife or husband, physical adultery is unthinkable. You won't have your mind on it; if the opportunity comes up, you won't be interested. Your heart's already taken.

It's much more difficult not to live adulterously, now that we know where adultery really begins. Many of us call ourselves married, but we're really "married singles." That means we don't fully belong to our loves. We just eliminate certain activities like dating others, staying out all night with the boys, or buying extravagances like furs or sports cars. We're living a single way of life with occasional limitations.

Let's Stamp Out Spouse Abuse

Like adultery, spouse abuse isn't as obvious as it seems.

A husband may not be innocent, even if he's never touched his wife or even shouted at her. Emotional pain is a subtle, terrible thing.

Do you husbands listen, really listen to your wives? You must do it all the time, not just when she's talking about something interesting. When you stood at the altar, you didn't pledge to listen to her topics. You promised to listen to *her*.

The average wife suffers more pain because of her husband's listening habits than from any other factor. The emotional pain of being ignored is as real as a migraine headache. The pain recurs again and again; it becomes a regular part of her life. We men can't say, "Well, that's the way I am. She'll have to get used to it," any more than we'd say, "Those migraine headaches are tough, but then, life is tough. She'll just have to suffer."

Men aren't the only ones who inflict emotional pain. Wives, unfortunately, can match their husbands blow for blow.

Twelve million husbands in the United States have been physically beaten by their wives. Many more husbands have been tongue-lashed, and the tongue is a sharper weapon than any fist, pot, or rolling pin.

When I say this to an audience, the women will tell me, "If you were married to my husband, Chuck, you'd do it too." But I didn't choose to marry those men. They did. Every wife has promised to love her husband without fail until death parts him from her.

Exasperation is normal; we're good people, even when we fall into that trap. Again, remember the prodigal son. Like adultery, tongue-lashing isn't the real sin. The real sin is that we haven't really decided to be married. We're living together with benefit of clergy, but that's not marriage.

Tongue-lashing happens because we store up hurts and grudges. Then we explode. We don't feel any particular obligation to hold ourselves back. After all, we think, we have rights in this family. It's a shame, but tongue-lashing is what works. What else can we do?

If you're thinking like that, you're asking the wrong question. Don't wonder if your anger is justified. Ask yourself—ask your husband!—is he afraid of your tongue?

Cast off the right to vent your anger on your love. Don't say, "Well, I know it's not the nicest way to act. I wouldn't do it all the time, but I can only take so much." In those thoughts, the focus is on yourself, not on your love.

Whether you're examining your listening habits, your anger, or any other flaw, don't let yourself be deluded into saying, "Well, I don't do it that often. I'm not like you-know-who." Live for yourself and your own family. Living next door to the neighborhood ogre doesn't make your household any happier. We shouldn't compare ourselves to our spouses, either. Our spouses could be the greatest sinners in the world, but that doesn't reduce our sin in the slightest.

Your Love Is Your Life

Husbands, do you really belong to your wives? We're not talking about whether you love her, whether you're nice or do all the right things by her. Those are good beginnings, but have you really put yourself in her hands?

The issue is one of trust. Do you really believe she loves you even more than you love yourself? That's what marriage is all about. As anniversaries go by, you should become two in one flesh. You should be less and less yourself.

That's a great challenge Jesus gives us, and it's in startling disagreement with the lessons of our me-first society. It's a challenge that asks you to give your all. It isn't enough for two independent souls to live side by side, smoothing out each other's rough edges.

When you're really married, you're no longer running your life. There are two of you inside, and you can no more ignore the needs and desires of your love than you can ignore yourself.

Very frequently, good wives will say, "My husband is my life." That's a great sentiment, but is it really true? Or is it something romantic to say when you're feeling very close to him?

Of course, that perfect oneness is an ideal; most of us probably won't reach it in a lifetime, so don't feel discouraged if you haven't accomplished it. Instead, begin with a question: Do you really want your husband to be your way of life?

Your answer is visible in ways you might not imagine. For example, if a stranger walked into your home, would he know there was a man living in the house, or would it exclusively show a woman's touch? Maybe your husband's picture is on the mantel, but does that mean he lives there? He might be somewhere overseas.

Maybe he likes it that way, or he doesn't care. On the other hand, maybe he really does care, but he has given the house to you in order to make you happy.

Our homes mirror our married singlehood. Over the years, in many marriages, the home becomes the woman's possession, purchased for her by her husband. That's a strong, sad statement of where he fits in to her life.

It's also a statement of where she fits in to his life. In many cases, he doesn't want to be any more married than she does. He assumes his wife is content with the style of life he has created for her. In the meanwhile, he's free to pursue his own goals, whether around the house also, or out somewhere else. Then we find the irony of good, loving people who yearn to be close to each other, held apart by their own possessions.

Have you really decided to get married, or are you taking your portion of the marriage and not living riotously? Remember, riotous living was not the prodigal son's sin. Refusing the relationship was his sin. Had he been married, he would have run to the store for his wife at midnight and may have even pitched in with the chores, but he would have wanted to live his own life.

A Personal Savior? Who Needs Him?

In many ways, we're troopers. We find the courage and the strength to face two-career stresses, sickness, unemployment, and the trauma of our children seeking refuge from their own loneliness in sexual relationships and drugs. When it comes to spiritual challenge, though, many of us look the other way.

Many of us are simply not facing the truth that we are sinners. That's not mere blindness. It's a festering wound that spreads poison through the whole body. If we're not sinners, we don't need a savior. We lose our relationship with Jesus. He becomes a nice guy to us; a prophet or a wonder person who lived a long time ago and put down an idealistic way of life. Gee, we think, if everybody lived it, we'd all be happy. But we don't really need a personal savior until we can say, "I am a sinner."

Many of us approach Jesus from the wrong direction. We start by looking at Him and seeing what a wonderful person He is; how kind and sweet and loving. Then He identifies himself as a savior, our personal savior. We don't feel the need for a personal savior, but since He says so, we agree. We're along for the ride, but we don't feel much need for salvation because we don't sense our own sinfulness.

Instead, we must start from a new direction. We must see our own desperate need for a savior. Then Jesus will fit into our lives entirely differently. We'll have a yearning for Him, a burning desire instead of a detached interest.

How Much Love Is Enough?

No matter how good you are, you must focus on your own successes and failures if you want your marriage to grow in love and beauty. It's a constant temptation to look toward your spouse instead: to test the waters, to see if he's up to this kind of relationship, if she's responding the way you think she should, or whether she's even worthy of it. Sometimes we all fear that our goodness will bounce off our loves like water off rocks. Then we'll be left alone, with nothing but stark and cynical reality.

Of course, behind all those fears is the unspoken judgment that we're better people than our spouses are. That isn't a good way to think.

Ask yourselves this question: "Am I truly willing to be a full-fledged husband?" "Am I truly willing to be a full-fledged wife?" You mustn't decide what that means by watching your friends and neighbors, no matter how well intentioned they may be. You must make your decision in accordance with your beloved's needs and your vocation from God Himself.

Ask yourself, "Am I willing to accept a life of total love, not of being loved but loving?" If the answer is "yes," then look at yourself clearly. All of us are good, tremendously good, people, yet we could all honestly say, "How can I treat her this way?" "What have I been doing to him? I truly am a sinner. Why, I haven't been married at all. I've been doing married things, a lot of them, the right ones and very well, but I've been expecting rewards. I've been paying entirely too much attention to *me*."

That's when we truly become aware not that we have sinned, but that we are sinners.

When the prodigal son chose to be a sinner, to breach his relationship with his father, he was young and single. He used harlots as his sin of choice.

We might choose a job instead of a full love relationship. We might choose our children instead, or the television, a book or a hobby. It isn't riotous living, but it's the product of sin just the same.

Now, there's nothing wrong with doing well at your job. There's nothing wrong with being a good parent, being well read or talented. But don't be an "unwed" mother or father. Don't be married to the boss; be married to this lover you have chosen.

The Joys of Hitting Rock Bottom

If we're to make the prodigal son's final choice of love over self-interest, we must first become disillusioned with ourselves.

The prodigal son hit rock bottom. Then, the parable says, he "came to his senses." It didn't say he recognized debauchery was wrong. He didn't exclaim, "Boy, did I spend a lot of money on nothing," or "Gee, getting drunk isn't that great, after all." The parable says, simply and powerfully, that he came to his senses.

Then Scripture tells us what coming to his senses means. Immediately he said, "I will leave this place and go to my father." When he came to his senses, he realized who he was: his father's son.

A married man doesn't come to his senses as a male adult. He comes to his senses as a husband. He says, "I will go to her." When a wife comes to her senses, she says, "I will go to him."

You see, when we come to our senses, we do more than admit we ought to do better or we've been wrong. This coming to our senses concentrates on the other person, because our spouses are who we *are*. The prodigal was his father's son. You are your wife's husband; your husband's wife.

We all need to understand that our identities come from our loved ones. There is no such thing as a full, independent life with relationships on the side. Because we are so intimately defined by our relationships, our coming to our senses makes us look outside ourselves. It makes you, a lover, look to your wife or husband.

We all have selfish impulses. We hide them behind facades of sophistication or worldly wisdom. I'm going to outline a few below. In the stark contrast of black print on white pages, they'll look horrible. Mean. But we all need to look. Remember, admitting our sins gives us a true feeling of freedom. It's even uplifting. Why? Because it's that necessary first step to becoming a better person.

Hopeless popular wisdom urges us to think these thoughts:

"I'm not getting enough from this marriage. Why should I stay with you?"

"You're not the person I thought you were. You aren't

living up to my expectations. I have plans and dreams, and you're holding me back."

"Darling, I love you so much. But you have to love me, too."

"I'm not going to love you unless you love me. I'll measure out my love."

Or, in a nutshell, "This marriage is about my satisfaction. I married you for my own pleasure, and pleasure is what I expect."

The urge to excuse ourselves for this is almost irresistible. We want to say, "Oh, no, that's not really the way it is, because I give. I know I have to give, but he has to give too; she has to pull her load."

Again, comparisons only defeat our goal. The prodigal son didn't give his father game points for goodness or generosity. He didn't think about how much he owed his father. He simply faced the truth: he didn't belong to his father any more because he hadn't wanted to.

This parable wasn't a lesson in fairness. It was a lesson in recognition. When the prodigal left home, he stopped being a son, not because his father didn't want him, and not because his father deserved a better son. The breach was his own personal choice.

All of us have faced that choice. How have we chosen? Are we married, really married, or are we single? Do we live as lovers, as husbands or wives? Or do we live as we wish, earnestly hoping our spouses can accept our decisions?

Consider these questions privately:

What thoughts and attitudes of mine keep me from living as a lover: a husband or a wife?

How does my marriage fit my life-style? What changes must I make so my life-style will fit my marriage?

Do I really believe I am a sinner? Why or why not?

Share these with your spouse:

What dream has this chapter inspired in me? (Be as idealistic as you choose.) How can you, my love, and I make this dream come true?

"Thank you, dear." Spend ten minutes writing a simple letter to your love, a letter of thanks for that delicate gift of trust. For instance, does she trust you to care about her problems? Does he let down his mask of masculine toughness to be tender during lovemaking? (Remember, focus on your own feelings. Be respectful; never judge your spouse.)

Finally, let us invite God into our marriages:

Dear Lord, let me stop dwelling within myself and live instead in relationship with my beloved spouse.

Let me be grateful for that fragile gift he (she) has given me: his (her) trust. Let me treat it with gentleness and return it in full measure.

Let me forgive my lover's wrongs and ask forgiveness for mine.

Like the prodigal son, let me be open to my sinfulness and yearn for Your presence in my life. And like the prodigal, help me realize that we are born to be lovers, not lonely, loveless individuals.

Give me healing and the grace to grow in you. Amen.

Chapter 8

I No Longer Deserve to Be Called Your Spouse

(Lk. 15:20–32)

Jesus spoke in parables, both for the disciples of His time and for those of the future. He expects us to apply His lessons to our own lives. For us, the parable of the prodigal son might become the parable of the prodigal spouse:

There was a woman who had a husband. They had been married for more than twenty years when he said to her, "Sorry, dear, but it's time for me to find myself. Let me have the share of our property that will come to me. Sure, I'll put the kids through college. But I'm forty years old and I want to live a little before it's too late. Besides, my psychologist says these urges are normal for a man in the change of life." A few days later, he got together everything he had and left for the coast, where he lived in a beach cottage with a buxom young blonde.

The woman's neighbors were scandalized. They felt sorry for her. Joe, who was working on his car, shook his head, then went back to work. Mary cooked a fine dinner for her, and the two women had a long talk. Mary showed off her new living room furniture and the kids' athletic trophies. Joe wasn't there; he had to work overtime, Mary said. They had too many bills to pay.

A year later, the woman's husband came back. While he was still in the driveway, she saw him and was moved to tears. She ran to him, clasped him in her arms, and kissed him. They went to the best restaurant in town and began to celebrate.

Mary and Joe couldn't believe their eyes. They sent a mutual friend over to investigate. The friend told them, "You can't imagine the scene at that house. Her husband has come home, and they're acting like a couple of kids."

The news made both Joe and Mary angry. "He treated her like dirt," they said. "She's nothing but a doormat. She ought to give him a piece of her mind, then throw the bum out."

As time went on, the woman and her husband didn't do much yard work. They usually stayed inside, and Joe and Mary could hear laughter and sounds of merriment. When they did come out, they had their arms around each other. They both seemed happy. It was downright indecent, somehow.

Their foolishness made Joe even angrier than before, especially when Mary started hanging around in the garage and interrupting his work. "What's your problem?" he said finally. "Don't you have anything to do?"

"I thought you might like to talk to me. Maybe we could go out together."

"Hey," he said, "that's a great idea. Can't do it tonight, though. Got a poker game."

"Tomorrow?" Mary asked.

Joe rolled his eyes. "I was planning to fix the bathtub; you knew that. Look, let's do it next Saturday."

"Oh, we can't do it then. Next week's the garden show."

"Well, find us a time, okay?" Joe crawled back under the car.

Mary went back into her shiny-clean kitchen. Something was wrong; she didn't know what. "I couldn't ask for more," she told herself. "Joe never looks at another woman; he's always home on time and he doesn't drink. We've raised a family together, bought this lovely house. So why do I feel so sad?"

The reason, of course, was that she wasn't living for Joe, any more than he was living for her. Our modern society would understand. After all, Joe and Mary were each entitled to realize their potential. But our secular experts cannot explain the wrenching emptiness that results when we choose ambition over love.

Suppose Joe and Mary wanted to reconcile. How would they do it? They might be tempted to catalog a list of sins: "I worked on the car when you wanted to talk"; "I let you work overtime so I could have a nice house."

195

It would be a good and noble effort, but it wouldn't even touch their real problem. Their sin was more than a grocery list of mistakes. Their sin was choosing self-centered ways of life.

They—and we—should look to the prodigal son. In that parable, Jesus gave us an ideal example of reconciliation.

When the prodigal wanted to reconcile, he said, "Father, I have sinned against heaven and against you; I no longer deserve to be called your son." He didn't say, "Let me tell you all the things I've done," or "You shouldn't have anything to do with me because I've been such a rotten boy."

He said only, "I no longer deserve to be called your son." He knew that his breach of relationship was more serious than his sleeping around, his drunkenness, or his carelessness with money.

Fairness: That Pagan Standard

In sin, we deny who we are by denying the loves in our lives. We silently say, "I'm not your husband, I'm me." "I'm not your wife, I'm my own woman." This declaration usually shows up in ordinary ways, not spectacular ones.

Most of us are petty sinners. It takes talent to be a big-league sinner. We don't go downtown and get outrageously drunk, at least not usually. Most of us don't lock our wives in the basement, call on the devil, or whatever seems to make good movie material. Instead, we say, "Don't I have any rights in this marriage?" or "That's not fair. When am I going to get something out of this?"

It's all the normal, everyday sinfulness that says, "You're a man who's supposed to make me happy," or

"You're not flesh of my flesh. You're here because I like what you do for me."

Remember, fairness is a pagan standard. It has nothing to do with God.

How often do we structure our marriages in terms of fairness? We say marriage is a 50–50 proposition. That sounds like an ideal compromise, but it's not God-centered and it simply doesn't work. What happens if that perfect balance slips a little? If it's 51–49, our favor, that probably feels all right to us. But what if it's 60–40? Do we think it's about time we got our share, or do we begin to feel a little guilty? What if the scale tips to 70–30, and we're giving the seventy? Do we say, "It's all right; we're just having a rough time right now"? Or is it time to put a foot down?

If we want to become real husbands and wives, we must come to our senses. We must reconcile with each other. We shouldn't say merely, "I'm sorry I nag you," or "I'm sorry I close up." These are the expressions of sin, not the sin itself.

They're also easy to confess. Instead, we must be honest and trusting, both with ourselves and our lovers. We must say, "I am no longer worthy to be called your husband"; "I am no longer worthy to be called your wife."

Those are strong statements, but we need strong statements when we're speaking of sin. Sin is not a little petty thing; it's not a normal, everyday pastime. Sin is terribly serious, and we have to challenge it face-to-face. As long as we resist saying, "I'm not worthy to be called your spouse," we're refusing to come to our senses as sinners.

Someone has done a great public relations job on sin. We think if it isn't fun, it can't be sinful. Since we aren't having a good time, we must be virtuous. Right?

Growing Closer in Love

"I am no longer worthy to be called your wife (husband)."

"Why would I want to say that?" you may ask.

Because you must come to your senses if you want to grow closer to your spouse. Loyalty to the fairness doctrine will hold you back. "Sure, I fail to love," you might say, "but he fails too"; "She fails, and her failings are worse than mine."

Now you're both living a sinful way of life—and you're matching sins. See how fairness backfires? We simply can't use it as a life-style because it means we must judge our lovers.

When we're living in relationship, we must look at who we are. I'm my father's son whether or not he's a good father. I'm my brother's brother whether or not he deserves it. Besides, isn't it arrogant to say whether someone deserves my love? Who am I to judge? It also wastes time. My whole way of life should be to love her, to love him.

But It's My Life, Isn't It?

We must recognize that small flaws aren't that important. We don't fail to live God's plan because we shout, get angry, pout in silence, or any of our normal, everyday little sins. We must recognize something much deeper: "I'm living a single way of life in our marriage."

Sometimes selfishness is more subtle than we think. Yes, we come home every night, and yes, we have meals together. Sure, we talk with each other and do all the husbandly and wifely things that we should, but we may still be living as if we're single. Maybe it's so deeply ingrained, we don't notice it. We think, "She fits me like a glove"; "He's just what I need."

That's a denial of our relationship; it says we're separate but equal partners in a businesslike arrangement. That's not answering the Lord's call to unity.

Sin happens when we make our loves accept our terms on companionship, sex, or anything else we have to give:

"Sorry, dear, I just don't feel like it tonight."

"I've had a hard day. How about tomorrow?"

If we speak this way, we're responding to our moods, not to our lovers. This attitude will grow like a weed. If we don't pull it by the roots, we'll find ourselves measuring our loves' needs and desires, using our own moods as a yardstick.

These statements draw some strong reactions, especially in an audience.

"That sounds very nice," people will tell me. "In fact, it would be beautiful. But, look, we're human. We have to have some joy in life, too. If I behave like that, he'll walk all over me." "She'll just grab everything she wants."

There's a difference between a doormat and a lover. A doormat lies on the floor because that's its job. It isn't there because it loves you. Jesus was a perfect lover. Was he a doormat?

Keeping Score

Have you seen one of those old-fashioned billiard rooms? There are wires above the table, and you can move a marker for every point you score. If one of these would be a good idea in your house, you and your spouse are probably in a great deal of pain.

You weren't called to the sacrament of Matrimony to be happy. You were called to make him happy, to make her happy. Let's be competitive about that instead.

Sometimes we judge the success of a marriage by the level of unhappiness. We lie to ourselves and console each other, saying we're not doing too badly. We have carefully rationed interludes of romance: birthdays, anniversaries, and the like. Forget all that; it's organized misery.

The only way we should be single is in recognition of our sins. Even then, we must be thinking of how our sins harm our lovers. What do our sins reveal about our love relationships?

We must come to our senses and say, "I am a sinner." We can't pretend our sins don't exist. The only way to erase sin is to seek forgiveness.

The prodigal son didn't say, "It's normal for young men to sow their wild oats." He didn't say, "Every man likes women," or "All guys like a drink every now and then." He didn't theorize, "Money is only money." Instead, he came to his senses and said, "I no longer deserve to be called your son."

Now, most of us haven't sinned as spectacularly as the prodigal son. Again, that's not the point. We shouldn't say, "I don't deserve to be called your wife because of what I've done." Instead, we should realize, "I don't deserve to be called your wife because I have not *been* your wife, and because I have not allowed you to be my husband."

Deeds don't make the sin. The denial of belonging makes the sin. Sin is the keeping of ourselves to ourselves, whether it's expressed in reprehensible actions or in perfectly normal ones that may even be quite praiseworthy. "I no longer deserve to be called your husband." That may be hard to say. We might disagree: "I always support her, I don't drink up the paycheck, I don't sleep around." But have we been part of her heart?

We must say, "I no longer deserve to be called your husband because I haven't been living for you. I've been living with myself, and you're nearby. I have taken my share of the marriage and squandered it."

Sin Is Reasonable

Saying no in sex is adultery. On your wedding day, you said your body wasn't yours anymore; it belonged to your beloved. Later on, you can't change your mind.

St. Paul states very clearly in his first letter to the Corinthians that a husband's body belongs to his wife and a wife's body belongs to her husband. In 1 Corinthians 7:3, 4, he says, "The husband must give to his wife what she has a right to expect, and so too the wife to her husband. The wife does not have authority over her own body, but the husband does; and in the same way, the husband does not have authority over his own body, but the wife does."

Yet we tend to think it's normal to deny sex to our lovers. We don't realize it's a form of theft.

We simply must stop thinking that marriage is like living with a roommate. Marriage is a real integration. It is truly becoming one in mind, heart, and body.

Again, that isn't reasonable in the world's eyes, but love doesn't have anything to do with reason. Reason can be depressing; it can lower our standards and tell us not to yearn for more love than our neighbors have.

With today's economy and its increased emphasis on careers and materialism, both husbands and wives are finding themselves too exhausted, too stressed, and even too busy to physically love each other. We'd rather fill out reports or drive the kids to scouts than make passionate love.

Doesn't that sound bizarre?

Go make love. It'll keep you out of trouble. The goodness of a passionate relationship spills over onto your friends, your neighbors, and especially your family.

A passionate love relationship, for instance, fosters patience. When you're passionate toward each other and your son misbehaves, you'll say, "Ah, isn't that cute? He's just like this father."

When you're not passionate toward each other, you'll shout, "You little brat! You're just like your *father*."

Marriage is more than a piece of paper you signed one, ten, or fifty years ago. It's a sacrament, and your love, including physical love, is sacramental.

I think priests and pastors should stand at the church doors every Sunday and ask each incoming couple this question: where do you score this morning on passion, on a scale of one to ten? If the couple scores lower than eight, their pastors should send them home to bring that number up.

Casting Out Delusions

"I am a sinner. I no longer deserve to be called your wife"; "I no longer deserve to be called your husband."

Please consider saying those words. It would be a tremendous gift to your beloved and a real infusion of grace in your marriage. I'm not asking you to say you're a horrible person. The horror isn't your honesty about your faults, but our delusion that sin is not part of our lives.

What happens, for instance, when things blow up between you? You could declare a silent mutual agreement not to fight anymore. Then the house is quiet, but the trouble hasn't quite gone away. Perhaps you decide you're getting nowhere and resolve not to bring the issue up again. Again, you've solved nothing, but you've closed off another area to each other.

Are you the family peacemaker? When I hear of a peacemaker, I always want to know who starts the wars. Frequently the peacemaker does.

Am I Sorry? Or Am I Married?

What do you mean when you say, "I'm sorry"? It usually means, "I did something rather bad." "I shouldn't have lost my temper." "I should have remembered you on our anniversary." "I shouldn't have gotten home so late for supper."

"I'm sorry" means "I know my action was inappropriate. It wasn't worthy of a good person like me." It's a very self-centered awareness.

"I'm sorry" can mean other things as well. It might mean, "You're very angry about what I did. I can't understand why; I don't think it was that bad. But you're not going to get over it until I say I'm sorry, so I'll say I'm sorry and get it over with." In this case, I really do want to reconcile, but I'm not admitting I'm wrong.

Or maybe "I'm sorry" means, "Gee, you're hurt and I don't like to see you hurt. I'm not hung up about saying

I'm sorry, so if it makes you feel better, I'll say it." It's a remedy, like bringing you chicken broth when you're sick.

"I'm sorry" is a request. We're really asking our loves to say, "Ah, that's all right; forget it. I do things like that too."

That's why when we say, "I'm sorry," we're selling ourselves short. We're not facing the truth that we denied our relationship. We're only facing the symptom: what we did. If the prodigal son had behaved this way, he would have said, "It's not worthy of me to be sleeping around, so I won't do it anymore." That doesn't touch his sin, does it? His sin is against his relationship with his father. The prodigal could have stopped sleeping around and drinking; he could have worked very hard, earned back all the money he squandered, and sent it home to his father, and still he would not have come to his senses.

When we say, "I'm sorry," we're avoiding both the Gospel story and our own identities: those of husband or wife, not just man or woman. Denying relationship is like sticking our heads in the sand; it doesn't cause the truth to go away. Our very natures have been changed because we belong to our loves.

No Excuses, Please

When our loves tell us, "I'm sorry," and we answer, "Well, that's all right," we're really saying, "Okay, let's be friends—until this happens again."

We have memory rights when we excuse that way; we're allowed to revive the old hurts whenever appropriate. This way, we can protect ourselves. We don't have to trust as much because, after all, our loves let us down before.

Most husbands and wives excuse instead of forgiving. It's the normal thing to do. It's also safe. Excusing isn't personal; it isn't open. I can almost hear an undercurrent of thoughts: "Well, she and I are both sincere and we should get back together again anyway. Maybe next time, I'll be the one who has to say I'm sorry, so I might as well be gracious about it." In the back of our mind, we're waiting to see if he's learned a lesson, if she's gotten the point—and whether things are going to change around here.

Excusing is too shallow an option for two good lovers. Instead, we must forgive and seek forgiveness. The prodigal son said, "I will go to my father and say: Father, I have sinned against heaven and against you; I no longer deserve to be called your son; treat me as one of your hired men." He put himself completely in his father's hands. He publicly acknowledged the breach of relationship. He didn't say, "I'll pay you back the money I wasted." He didn't invite his father to excuse him.

He knew better. He knew that "I'm sorry" so often means "I've had enough of our fighting. I'm hurting too much for any more of it, so let's make up."

When we say, "I'm sorry," we appear to be the heroes, but that isn't really true. We're looking for something: for peace in the home or for our lovers to be nice to us again.

The prodigal son saw through all of it. He simply said, "It's over. I'm not worthy to be called your son. Treat me like a hired hand."

That's what it's like to come to our senses. Ordinarily we wouldn't see the need for it unless we'd dealt with a great trauma like physical adultery or beating. That's where we're wrong. The trauma of sin surrounds us every day.

Sin: It's Not What It's Cracked Up to Be

Most evil isn't glamorous. It's banal: trite, everyday, and all too common. Adolf Eichmann, for instance, lived quietly in Argentina for more than a decade. His neighbors probably never dreamed that this quizzical, cynical, almost kindly-looking man would someday be hung as a mass murderer, condemned for the deaths of millions of Jews in Nazi Germany and occupied countries.

Eichmann looked as ordinary as you or I do. He could sit beside you at work or in the next pew at church and you'd never notice him. That's a tragedy.

Take that idea one step further: Imagine yourself living next door to such a criminal, thinking, "These days, everyone's living differently than our parents did. Nice homes, nice cars; busy, busy, busy. I'm not sure I agree, but my neighbors seem happy enough. Well, it must be all right, because there's nothing wrong with them."

As a society, we're obsessed with the desire to be like those around us. Why? Because watching others absolves us of having to try harder than they do. If all our friends are getting divorced, we reason that it must somehow be all right. If they watch television every night or throw dishes at each other, we can decide that's normal, too.

Worst of all, we decide it's normal to be independent from our loves. How could it be terribly wrong when no one even notices? No one points and says, "Aren't they awful?" Of course, no one pointed to Eichmann, either.

That's why each of us must come to our senses, whether or not our family and friends agree. We must do this sincerely and with thought.

Right now, we aren't focusing on the petty little defects that creep up, like forgetting to set the table or run to the store. We're focusing on bigger sins, like hurting comments; we know exactly how much they hurt, and that's why we make them. Perhaps we're fighting and she's winning, so we think, "I'll knock her off her horse." Maybe he inflicted some pain and we want to hurt him back so he'll know how it feels.

These sins can be quiet sins as well. How about when we dive into the newspaper as soon as we come home from work? Our lovers plead with us to talk, so we put down the paper—slowly—and make sure we don't sound enthused. "Yes?" we groan. If we do it well enough, they'll take the hint and go away.

Now, one night of that isn't bad, but if that's a pattern, that's evil. So is the control that some of us exercise through sex. No human being should control another one.

Thou Shalt Not Behave Like Everyone Else

"But everyone does it." The answer comes automatically. We don't let our children fool us with that one, but without realizing it, we use it ourselves: Other people work overtime. Other people don't date after marriage; they stay home like old married couples are supposed to. Other people don't hold hands and they don't feel too rotten when they insult each other in a fight.

Now, why did Jesus come to earth? He came to change everyone. There's no Gospel passage that says, "Thou shalt do as everyone else does." Nor did He say that when we appeared before Him in heaven, He'd reward us because "I was hungry, and you behaved like everyone else."

We're called to a better goal. Everyone else doesn't recognize that we're called to be higher than a blind average. Everyone else doesn't recognize sin. They think sin is fun; sin is the normal human condition; sin is to be expected.

No, it isn't. Sin is why Jesus came to die on the cross. God thinks sin was serious enough to merit the suffering and death of His only Son. He didn't just shrug His shoulders and say, "So this man didn't listen to his wife. What husband does?"

On Good Friday or when we see a cross, we know Jesus died for sinners. Other sinners, primarily. Big-time sinners. We think of murderers. There really aren't many murderers in this world, but there are legions of men who are not fathers to their children. That's why Jesus died. There are women who think marriage is a woman's privilege; they do nice things for their husbands because it pleases them and keeps the guy pacified. That's why Jesus came to die. Countless wives shout at their husbands. That's the reason for the cross. A lot of husbands aren't really interested in their wives. They'd do anything for their wives except listen to them. That's why Jesus was crucified.

When Jesus said, "Father, forgive them; they do not know what they are doing" (Lk. 23:34), he was speaking of us and our petty little sins, not just the Hitlers and the Herods of this world.

It's hardest to change our behavior when we feel justified; in other words, when we're right.

Rightness is another reason Jesus came to earth. Being right kills a love relationship. Rightness doesn't justify inflicting hurt. The prodigal son didn't say, "After all, Father, I only took what was coming to me. It's my business how I spent it." He said, "I will go to my father and say: Father, I have sinned against heaven and against you; I no longer deserve to be called your son."

Apply that to yourselves: "I will go to my wife and say, 'I no longer deserve to be married to you.' " When you decide to do this, you have recognized that you are living a sinful life-style, not merely doing sinful things.

Let's Hurry to Forgive

The parable of the prodigal son continues, "So he left the place and went back to his father." He didn't think about it; he didn't congratulate himself on his conversion. He simply went.

His father was standing a long way off, looking, hoping, yearning. We don't hear a single word of grumbling in this parable. The father didn't say, or even think, "I hope my kid gets straightened out. I hope he comes to his senses and knows what he's done to me."

A husband and wife must have that same yearning to embrace. We must also be looking from a long way off, watching and hoping for that first sign that our spouses are seeking forgiveness. When our loves try to reconcile, we so often make them go through their paces: "I want her to realize this is serious"; "I want to make sure he knows how much he hurt me."

The prodigal's father cast all that aside. The parable says, "While he was still a long way off, his father saw him and was moved with pity. He ran to the boy, clasped him in his arms and kissed him." At the first sign of his son, the father was overwhelmed with eagerness. He hurried to reach his son and proclaim their relationship again. He didn't test the waters; the slightest sign that his son was responsive again was enough.

Do we do likewise, or do we cling to our hurts and our righteousness? We test our loves' sincerity, thinking, "He has to earn his way back. She has to prove she's reformed." That's not forgiveness.

The father didn't exact any fee from his son. The father was simply drawing him in with love, hoping against hope they could reconcile, because he wanted to be close to that boy.

Even though the boy saw his father's openness, he didn't feel extremely sure because he was so aware of his sinfulness. He insisted on saying what he'd come to say: "Father, I have sinned against heaven and against you. I no longer deserve to be called your son."

But his father ignored the past. He hugged that boy and leaped up and down for joy. He shouted, "Come on, everyone, get him a robe, get him a ring, put sandals on his feet, kill the best beef on the farm. Let's have a party!"

He wasn't rejoicing because his son was going to change or because he was penitent. The father rejoiced simply because he could touch him. When our loves seek our forgiveness, our response must be the same. It can in no way, shape, or form be judgmental, nor can there be any superiority.

The Memory Weapon

When our loves seek forgiveness, we must pledge to wipe out the memory of their wrongs. As long as we remember those wrongs, we have not yet forgiven. We may act very manfully. We may be virtuous enough never to bring them up, but they poison our love, even if only through intermittent flare-ups. When our loves ask for forgiveness, our response in joy is to reaffirm our relationship by saying, "My beloved wife . . ." or "My beloved husband . . ." What we remember from now on is his humility, her goodness.

This is a key point. Too often, we give ourselves great credit for being long-suffering. We're long-suffering, though, because we have such long memories.

If you want to know just how forgiving you are, ask yourselves, "What do I remember?" Do we remember our own goodness in forgiving so graciously, or do we recall with wonder our loves' humility?

Do we recall the sin? If we recall the sin, our spouses can never be touched by the forgiveness. We could fool ourselves and say, "Well, I'm not holding it against him"; "I'm not using it against her." If we're keeping it alive in memory, though, it's more important than our relationship.

Remembering our loves' sin is more than ungenerous. It's wrong. When we refuse to forget, the question becomes not "What has my love done?" but "What am I doing?" Unless we're ready to forget that failing, we have to seek forgiveness for holding the memory.

We're called to give this total forgiveness, not the lukewarm excuses and apologies that seem to satisfy others. We are called to remember the sinner's seeking of reconciliation, not the sin. The prodigal's father illustrates this beautifully. He didn't ask, "Did you spend all that money?" He didn't add, "Are you going to be a good boy now? Are you going to settle down? Did you learn a lesson?" He didn't even hint as much.

The father did say, "This son of mine was dead and has

come back to life." With that statement, he wiped out the boy's denial and reestablished their relationship. He recreated the boy's identity. A truly forgiving wife or husband says the same: "Yes, dear, you are my spouse. I could never let you go. I'm so glad to have you back. I want you so much, my whole life centers around you. I will celebrate having you again."

That celebration marks not your love's sin but your renewed belonging. It rejoices: "How good you are in wanting to belong to me. I thought I had lost you. I thought I could never hold you like this again. I thought my life would always be so empty, so incomplete, so disjointed. But you are my husband (wife). You're so wonderful, I'm so lucky to have you. My heart is pounding for joy. I'm delighted in who you are to me, and I'm so glad that I'm able to show it. Come, let us be merry, let everyone know: not that I who have been offended have finally been justified, but that you are so good, and my belonging to you is precious to me. I will always remember you coming into my arms again."

When we forgive like this, we follow Jesus' teaching and become true lovers.

Have You Heard the One About . . . ?

When we hear the Gospel, we listen to the first line or two to see if it's new. If it's not, we tune out. "I've heard that one before," we think. But there isn't a single verse of Scripture that tells us merely to listen to the Gospel. We're supposed to live the Gospel. That's the way we preach it.

I don't think we're bored with the prodigal son, though. This parable prompts us to say, "Jesus really knows how to say things, doesn't He?" We think of a few prodigals we know and hope our husbands are listening; that our wives get the point. We don't really apply it to ourselves. We don't realize the Lord is moving within us, seeking to teach us through this story.

Perhaps we mentally cast ourselves in the role of the son who stayed. The Lord really blasted him, so we don't want to say it out loud, but secretly we're behind him all the way.

The older boy wasn't all that gracious, but we have real empathy for his position. The prodigal had fun. It might be sin, but it was good sin. His dutiful brother was just hanging around, waiting for his father to die and leave him the farm.

We shouldn't feel so sorry for the second son. He had no more relationship with his father than his brother did. Both boys were sinners. Both boys were living their own ways of life, centered around themselves. One of them expressed it in a spectacular way by going to a far-off country and doing all sorts of extravagant things. The other boy looked good on the outside, but where was he in relationship with his father?

Obviously, not very close. Otherwise he could never have acted as he did. He never shared his father's pain over the other boy's absence.

If the older son had been in relationship with his father, he would have known what the younger boy meant to his father and he would have rejoiced for his father's sake. But he was thinking only of himself for all those years when his brother was gone.

The second son had equal need to go to his father for forgiveness. He might have said, "I am no longer worthy to be called your son, not because I live riotously but be-

213

cause I don't understand you. I'm not part of your heart; otherwise I could not be so cold and indifferent, so wrapped up in myself."

Sin Can Be Subtle

There are plenty of second sons in our marriages. Maybe our spouses do more "bad" things, but we are equally guilty of failing to love. If we've realized this, we can go to our spouses and say, "My beloved, I am no longer worthy to be called your spouse, not because I've done anything, but because I haven't belonged to you. I belong to myself. I haven't been responding to you, my dear. I've really been responding to my own integrity and sense of self-dignity."

Can you imagine the joyful response the second son would have received if he had reconciled with his father? Remember, this father never gave any grudging replies like "Oh, it's all right," or "I'm glad that's over." When his younger son came to him, he merely reaffirmed the relationship. That's true forgiveness.

Accepting Forgiveness

We should be eager to seek such forgiveness ourselves. First, of course, we must search inside for our sins. One area we all overlook is the one I just mentioned: our memories of our spouses' failings. This is so important, I'm going to repeat it: These memories become our own failing; that of coldheartedness. If we are guilty of this, we must say, "My beloved, I have been remembering your failings. I am no longer worthy to be called your wife (husband)."

It isn't easy to accept our spouses' forgiveness. It's easier to keep concentrating on ourselves. Even after we've been forgiven, it's normal to wish we could make up for the hurt. Don't do that.

After your love forgives you, you must simply rejoice at being accepted back. You should concentrate on your love's acceptance, rather than on the sins you've committed. Focusing on your sins may be virtuously self-punishing, but it's also self-centered. Besides, you can never really make up for the pain you caused. Exactly how many compliments would you have to deliver in order to erase an insult?

You can avoid this self-defeating trap by welcoming the goodness of your lover. The more you can concentrate on how good she is, how forgiving he is, the more you'll be able to accept that forgiveness. If you look to yourself and try to make up for the past, you'll prevent your own healing. Furthermore, scorekeeping is a subtle method of avoiding relationship. It's a way of canceling sin, not admitting it as a way of life and accepting your lover's goodness. That's called a false motivation.

Often, we don't live in relationship with our loves because we think "husband" and "wife" are job descriptions, like "homemaker" or "diplomat." That's not true.

Being a wife is not an occupation, it's a relationship with another human being. You can do all the wifely things in the world, but you aren't wives at all without your husbands.

Men, the same applies to you. You may live faithfully with one woman throughout your life, but that doesn't make you a husband.

215

It doesn't matter how many children you have by each other or how long you've lived in the same house. Only your choice of each other on a daily basis makes you husband and wife. So does a constant seeking of forgiveness, because we are sinners. We will continue to be sinners, even after we are reconciled. Marriage is a constant offering of forgiveness as well.

You Forgive Me? What Did I Do?

You can't offer forgiveness to someone who doesn't ask for it. The father couldn't search out the youngest son and say, "You're forgiven." He didn't know he'd sinned. The father couldn't say, "I forgive you" to the oldest son because that boy was even less convinced he was a sinner. Likewise, you can't go to your spouses and say, "You are forgiven." They'll ask, "What for?" But when forgiveness is sought, it has to be given generously, as the Lord teaches us.

Jesus said, "Do not judge, and you will not be judged; do not condemn, and you will not be condemned; forgive, and you will be forgiven. Give, and there will be gifts for you: a full measure, pressed down, shaken together, and overflowing, will be poured into your lap; because the standard you use will be the standard used for you" (Lk. 6:37, 38).

Ask yourselves: "Can I stand before my heavenly Father and say, "Father, I ask nothing more than the forgiveness I have given my spouse"? Don't worry about whether you forgive your friends, the parish priest, or your children. Concentrate on your spouse; that's where it all begins.

We should see that passage of Scripture as an urgent call, not a heavenly threat. How can our husbands and wives believe God forgives them if we don't?

"Well, he knows God is better than I am"; "If she thinks God is like me, she's in trouble."

That's an intellectual argument, and no matter how earnestly you insist on it, it will never touch your love's heart. We must all experience forgiveness in human terms.

He's Depending On Us

We simply have no idea how important we are in God's plan.

Jesus' words to our spouses are only as believable as we are. He has placed Himself in our hands. We really are the body of Jesus; that's not just a nice theological notion. We have been called to express Him, His view of life and His way of living. We do this by the way we live. Specifically we do this by the way we live with our husbands and wives.

The Lord says forgiveness is part of the Kingdom of Heaven. When my beloved experiences that goodness within me, the Kingdom of Heaven becomes real to him or her. It's much like teaching our children that Holy Communion is a meal with Jesus. How can we do that unless they're experiencing a family supper?

How can you believe in the overwhelming mercy of our Father if your wife is not merciful, if your husband is not compassionate?

The believability of God and God's way of life is in your hands. Please, search within yourselves to discover how you are a sinner with your wife, with your husband.

Why not make today the day you do this? Then spend some real time with each other and seek forgiveness, regardless of whether your spouse seeks forgiveness, too.

Beloved, I Have Sinned Against God and Against You

You may be thinking, "How can anyone ask us to do that? How can someone just presume we're in sin and need to be forgiven?"

That very question indicates that we're in the position of the older son. We think because we've been doing the right things, we don't have any sin. We're fooling ourselves. We know that someday we will stand before our Father and say, "I am a sinner."

We sin much more against our husbands and wives than against anyone else on earth. That's because we have more opportunities. It's not simply because we live with each other, but because our loves are more open to us and seek more love from us than from anyone else.

It's not presumptuous or unreasonable to say that each of us as husband or wife really needs to seek forgiveness, not just in the sense of "Well, I have little defects. I suppose I could say I'm sorry for those," but in the sense of "I am a sinner before God and man. I am not worthy to be called your husband"; "I am not worthy to be called your wife because of my whole attitude; because of my whole lack of belonging; because I have lived my own way instead of putting myself in your hands."

Maybe you're willing but cautious. You're tempted to tell your spouse, "Okay, I'll go first, you go second."

Don't; you're not ready.

If you're really conscious that you're a sinner, you're completely unconscious of your spouse as a sinner. It works in reverse as well: The more conscious you are of your spouse's sin, the less conscious you are of your own. If you're still focusing on your spouse's sin, you are in no state to seek forgiveness, and maybe you should say that. You could say, "Help me, beloved. Let us go to the Lord together to soften the hardness of my heart. How could I be so indifferent to my own sins and so conscious of yours?"

This is a wonderful opportunity to discover each other; to come to your senses. As soon as you finish this chapter, go to your beloved and say, "My dear, my beloved, I have sinned against heaven and against you." Then specify the ways. General confessions aren't much help.

You should describe the specific ways you've established your independent life-style; how you've shown your indifference; how you've chosen self over your beloved; how you really haven't been married.

Think of this: your love has gone a long, long way to be your husband or wife. It doesn't matter whether or not your love is a sinner.

If I'm a sinner, I need forgiveness. Maybe someone else needs forgiveness, too, but if I need forgiveness, that's where I must concentrate. The more I recognize I am a sinner, the more unworthy I become in my own eyes and the less conscious I become of my spouse's growth—or lack of growth—toward God. I need forgiveness. I need to belong again. I need to come to my senses; I need that awakening to be truly recognized, not only by myself, but by that person I have pledged myself to.

All too often, we'll ask for forgiveness, then add, "Now

219

it's your turn. What? You're not going to say anything? Well, I take mine back."

We must seek a healing, not a trade-off. This is not an event where we come together to confess to each other. Here, each of us must come to his senses alone.

Go ask forgiveness of each other, not next week or next fight; do it right now. This reconciliation can be a real moment of grace. It can be a profound occasion for love. Read the questions below and search inside yourself to discover how you have sinned against God and against your spouse. Pray together for the grace to seek forgiveness and to freely forgive. Then close this book and enjoy.

How have I sinned against God and against my beloved husband or wife?

- Have I believed the purpose of my marriage is to make my lover happy? Or have I thought this marriage is for my happiness instead?
- Have I been living my own life-style, expecting my spouse to fit my demands?
- Am I sensitive to my spouse's hurts and needs? Or do I react only to myself?
- Have I kept my lover out of my heart, not allowing my husband, my wife, to truly be part of me?
- Have I withheld my attention and approval?
- Have I withheld my body?
- Have I yielded to the temptation to hurt with words?
- Have I insisted I was right instead of working toward a solution in love?
- Have I insisted on fairness in our marriage instead of unbounded love?

- Am I more conscious of my love's sins than I am my own? Have I refused to forget my love's failings? Do I keep them alive in my heart to use as weapons?
- Have I been imitating the life-styles of "everyone else" instead of imitating Christ?
- Have I made our family meals a real time of sharing? Do I show my love for our children?

A prayer for grace:

Lord, let me truly come to an understanding of my own sinfulness. Help me see myself as I really am, not hidden behind a mask of pride, fear, and self-interest.

I want to ask my spouse to forgive me for denying our relationship, for not living as a lover. Give me courage; help me to be sincere.

Help me to not expect my spouse to ask for forgiveness in return. Give me the grace to understand that each person grows at different rates. Let me wait lovingly and patiently until my spouse is ready.

Should my spouse ask forgiveness of me, help me to give it wholeheartedly. Let my love's failings be wiped forever from my mind so we can live together in joy.

Thank you for the wonderful goodness of my spouse. Let us both rejoice in Your gift of healing; let us always see each other through Your generous and all-forgiving eyes.

Be with us as we celebrate Your love for us and our love for each other. Amen.

The reconciliation:

Your own words might be similar to this:

"My beloved, I have sinned against God and against

you. I can see how wrong, how selfish, I've been. I've been living with myself, not with you, dear . . . (Add specifics.)

"My sin has isolated me from your love, and I can see how lonely I've made both of us. I want to truly live as your husband (wife). I love you so much. Please forgive me."

When your spouse seeks forgiveness, your response might be similar to this:

"I forgive you, my beloved. You are such a good, loving person. I thank God for giving you to me and for bringing us closer to each other right now.

"I want to belong to you, too. I love you so much; you are the most important treasure I have. I'm so glad I have you, because my life would be empty if you weren't here. I want to celebrate, to tell everyone how wonderful you are and how much you mean to me. I will always remember your goodness and love in coming to me today. I will never forget it."

EMPOWERMENT

CHAPTER 9

MY TALENT IS LOVING YOU

(MT. 25:14–30)

We should feel indebted to the scribes and Pharisees. They provoked Jesus to some marvelous retorts. These were more than snappy comebacks, though. They were lessons. Although they were uncompromising, we should take heart in the knowledge that our Lord's mind was also on his beloved disciples. He wasn't condemning us, but asking us to be our best selves. He was explaining that His Father has filled us with goodness, and if we will spend that goodness on others, it will grow in us beyond measure.

After one fierce debate with the Pharisees, Jesus sat on the Mount of Olives and told His disciples about the Kingdom of Heaven:

It is like a man about to go abroad who summoned his servants and entrusted his property to them. To one he gave five talents, to another two, to a third one, each in proportion to his ability. Then he set out on his journey. The man who had received the five talents promptly went and traded with them and made five more. The man who had received two made two more in the same way. But the man who had received one went off and dug a hole in the ground and hid his master's money. Now a long time afterwards, the master of those servants came back and went through his accounts with them. The man who had received the five talents came forward bringing five more. "Sir," he said, "you entrusted me with five talents; here are five more that I have made." His master said to him, "Well done, good and trustworthy servant; you have shown you are trustworthy in small things; I will trust you with greater; come and join in your master's happiness." Next the man with the two talents came forward. "Sir," he said, "you entrusted me with two talents; here are two more that I have made." His master said to him, "Well done, good and trustworthy servant; you have shown you are trustworthy in small things; I will trust you with greater; come and join in your master's happiness." Last came forward the man who had the single talent. "Sir," said he, "I had heard you were a hard man, reaping where you had not sown and gathering where you had not scattered; so I was afraid, and I went off and hid your talent in the ground. Here it is; it was yours, you have it back." But his master answered him, "You wicked and lazy servant! So you knew that I reap where I have not sown and gather where I have not scattered? Well then, you should have deposited my money with the bankers, and on my return I would have got my money back with interest. So now, take the talent from him and give it to the man who has the ten talents. For to everyone who has will be given more, and he will have more than enough; but anyone who has not, will be deprived even of what he has. As for this good-for-nothing servant, throw him into the darkness outside, where there will be weeping and grinding of teeth."

Matthew 25:14–30

How Talented Am I?

God Himself has given us our talents. He generously asks us to use these investments for His people's sake; most specifically, for those people we have chosen to marry.

First, of course, we must realize what capabilities, skills, and graces Almighty God has given each of us, specifically as husbands and wives.

Too often, we behave like the man who buried his treasure in the ground. We may not think we're doing that, but we still say:

"But I'm not that good."

"I can't do that."

"I'm not like other women" or "I'm not like other men."

"Talent?" some of us may say. "My talent is in accounting, or finance, or . . ." We say this with some pride, but also in despair. Many of us don't believe we have a special talent to love, to be generous or tender or forgiving. Oh, we can summon that behavior if we try hard enough, but it's work. It isn't our "talent."

Guess what. You don't have to put yourselves down anymore. Cast it aside. When it comes to talent at loving, each of you is an Olympic-weight champion. Some of you have bigger, more developed muscles than others, true; but that's because some of you have been in the gym. In each of you is a gold medal. Our Father put it there.

It we want to live as a whole, healed people, we must recognize that God has given each of us a marvelous capability to love our spouses.

In 1 Corinthians, St. Paul tells us that, yes indeed, we can do it. The culture of Corinth was, ironically, much like ours: It was a Greek seaport, a melting pot of philosophies and religions, and a well-known center of vice. Greece was quite proud of its intellectual strength, and that pride smothered the wisdom of the heart. Sexual mores were free and easy, and the young Christians were harassed for their religious beliefs.

To the Corinthians, Paul wrote, "None of the trials which have come upon you is more than a human being can stand. You can trust that God will not let you be put to the test beyond your strength, but with any trial will also provide a way out by enabling you to put up with it" (1 Co. 10:13).

Why Me?

Let's look at our resources from our spouses' point of view. Sometimes we're not good judges when it comes to ourselves.

Wives, ask yourselves, "Why did my husband choose me? What did he see in me that caused him to want to spend his life with me?"

Husbands, think: Why did your wife give herself to you? Why did she decide that a relationship with you should be the central core of her life?

Some of you will be saying, "Oh, I suppose I could name a few things, but after all, we were awfully young. I was kind of pretty then," or "I was the football quarterback."

Now, stop insulting yourself. Your lover wasn't that naive. Your spouse saw good qualities in you and was so breathtaken by that goodness that he or she promised to live with you until death. You don't make promises like that for a pretty face or big biceps. Your good qualities were given to you by God Himself, and they were spectacular enough to prompt someone to love and marry you.

Wives, what is inside you, as a person, that caused your husband to say, "Will you be mine?" Start thinking of the words he's said over the years, especially the ones you don't believe.

Husbands, you too should think of the words she's said in the past, ones that you just pass off.

Do you know why we pass off compliments? One reason, certainly, is that we've never been taught to think kindly of ourselves. In this culture, criticism is often the only acceptable opinion of self. Heaven forbid we should be bigheaded or fail to notice some little flaw.

Compliments are also challenges, and frightening ones at that. If a husband accepts his wife's compliment that he's a very gentle man, he'll have to live up to it. If a wife accepts a husband's compliment that she's sexy, she'll have to respond to him sexily. For some women, this isn't easy. They back away, saying, "I'd much rather be a frump."

Even though it destroys us inside, we find it easier to

say, "No, I'm really not gentle (considerate/funny/ beautiful/sexy). I just was this time."

I'm Good—But Someone Else Is Better

Someone else is always better in one area or another. We humans, with our unerring eye for self-insult, always find those people and put them in the spotlight.

"She's so patient. Compared to her, I'm a shrew."

"He's such a wonderful person. He must be closer to God than I am."

How destructive to think that way. God doesn't say, "Oh, yeah, I created Anne. She sure can scream. And as for George, he never prays to me. Where's his gratitude?" Instead, our Father just loves us.

It simply doesn't matter how we rate compared to others. We're missing the Lord's lesson if we say, "Well, I'm not as good as my mother was with my father," or "I'm not as good as the guy down the block."

The Lord has indeed invested in us. We don't have to win a Nobel prize to be wealthy, either. Earthshaking talents often look normal, even humdrum.

How about the gift of time? We have time; maybe not as much as we'd like, but we do have it. We each have a certain number of hours per day to spend as we will. There is lunchtime and coffee break time. There is diddle time, unwind-from-the-day time, and recreation time. For some of us, there's even complain-about-how-little-time-we-have time.

We also have double time; that is, when we're doing chores we don't have to think about. Laundry is one example; taking out the trash is another. They keep our hands busy, but our minds are free to think, to rest, or to share with our mates.

We need to realize that the Lord calls us to efficiency. Now, I'm not speaking of the expert and sometimes dehumanizing time-management techniques that use everything from flow charts to snubs. Nor am I talking about emergency measures, like quitting our jobs or letting the kids get encrusted with dirt.

I'm merely referring to the precious time we waste. Think for a moment; how many of those moments you call "your own" are your lover's, and how many belong to you?

Too often, we'll measure our marriages against an ideal relationship. The result is wishful thinking, feelings of inferiority, and despair. The Lord didn't ask for such comparisons. In the parable of the talents, He didn't differentiate between the servant with five talents and the servant with two. All that mattered was his stewardship: did the man really use his talents to the full? Both men received the same reward.

So, wives, examine an ordinary day. How much did you think about your lover today?

Sometimes you think about him, all right: "Boy, when he gets home . . ." That's not thinking about him, that's thinking at him.

Husbands, how much did you think about your lover today? With affection and eagerness, that is? "If I don't call, she'll kill me when I get home" doesn't count. That's not thinking about her; it's self-preservation.

Perhaps we call our mates to ask what's in the mail, what our friends had to say, and so on. Our mouths are moving, but we aren't really talking to each other. We're being safe, comforting ourselves with an amicable relationship. We're partners, we think.

Let's be lovers. Let's use our time during the day to plan how we'll be more effective with each other that night.

Time Costs More than Money

When we do come together, do we value that time as our most precious commodity?

Money is obviously a real problem in any human relationship. None of us seems to have enough; it's a cause for concern, and I'm not saying it shouldn't be. But how many hours do we spend worrying about the disposal of our income? Now, how many hours do we spend worrying about our lack of time together? We probably spend considerably less time saying, "Dear, when are we going to sit down and talk tonight?" and much more time saying, "What are we going to do about the orthodontist?" or "Dear, how much is in your wallet?"

We all know people who just can't handle money. Some of us are that way ourselves. These people get in terrible binds because the money just seeps away from them. Most of us are like that when it comes to time, not because we lack natural talent but because we lack attention, self-discipline, and even knowledge. Many of us don't realize how many wonderful things our time can buy.

It's much more important to budget your time than your dollars. Get out paper and pencil; write it all down. How much time do you have on an average day? How much of that time is used productively? How much of it is spent sitting on the divan, dreading to do the chores? How much time is spent pursuing hobbies and commitments you "ought" to love, but in reality make you feel weary and burdened? What are your weekends like?

Weekends are a national tragedy. They're when we're together the most, but do the least well with each other. That's not because we "need our space," because "even the best people get on each other's nerves," or anything like that. Those are nonsense; they're sophisticated ideas that mask blank, utter hopelessness.

The real answer is painfully simple. We don't do well with each other on weekends because we cram them full of "family" activities that aren't family activities at all. They're merely entertainments the family attends, such as the amusement park, the beach, a swimming party, or what have you. No wonder our weekends aren't warm and peaceful and happy. We spend our precious hours rushing from entertainment to delight and wondering if we're having fun yet.

We may rub shoulders and nerves all weekend, but we don't specifically plan how to be with each other as persons.

"We'll rush through lunch," we decide, "so we can get to the park (the children's game/whatever). And then we just have time to . . ."

Don't let that meal slip by. It's a wonderful opportunity to really be present to each other. It will be, that is, if we allow it to be.

My Time Is Your Time

How many of our evening chores could have been done earlier in the day? Do we spend our valuable time together reading the mail, paying the bills, or writing the grocery list?

Why did we postpone these chores? Is the delay worth the time we had to waste to get it?

We procrastinate for many reasons. Maybe we hate to do a certain chore: cleaning the refrigerator or doing the taxes. We decide, "I'll do it tonight. At least I'll have some company." Maybe we prefer the comfort of the home for a particularly nasty task; balancing the checkbook, perhaps. But we could do the checkbook at lunch instead of on our lovers' time.

We have to stop squandering the time the Lord gives us to spend with each other. There isn't that much of it. We're probably awake about sixteen hours a day, but we only have between four and six hours with our spouses.

How much of that time is poured into dry ground because we haven't thought ahead and put each other first? Time is critical if we're going to use our God-given talents for our lovers' well-being.

All too often, though, we think, "How am I going to spend *my* time?" Sometimes, even time with our lovers is spent for our own sake.

A woman might say, nicely this time, "I can't wait for him to get home . . ." She's certainly enthused, but she still might be thinking of herself. Does she finish the sentence, ". . . so I can give him a big hug and tell him how much I love him," or does she say, ". . . so I can get back to work," or ". . . so he can take these darned kids"? If so, she isn't eager for his sake.

Our men's gestures may also be self-motivated. Many men will say, "Look, honey. I know you're upset. Let's go out tomorrow. It'll be a nice evening; we'll spend some time together . . ." What's the unspoken finish? Is it ". . . because you've been looking so unhappy and I want to see you smile," or ". . . because when you get a break, I get a break too"?

In the latter example, the husband isn't loving her; he's

placating her. Now, his actions aren't motivated by a bad heart. He might be sincerely generous and take her out for a nice evening, indeed. He isn't doing it because he wants to spend time with her, though. He's doing it because he wants a peaceful home for a few days.

Now, most of us have mixed motivations. We're not wholly selfish. We're good people, but we're not perfect. Each of us should see where we can stretch our capacity to love.

The Fifteen-Minute Lover

We need to reevaluate our time in minutes, not in hours. How many hours' worth of minutes do we throw away every day?

Pennies are practically worthless these days. Some stores even set them out in bowls, with a sign: "If you need one, take one. If you have an extra, put it in." No one values them, but if you save them up, they become dollars.

We treat our minutes with the same indifference. How about the fifteen minutes just before supper? That's often the husband's time to sneak off toward the paper. Why not? He's just going to be under her feet anyway, he thinks. She probably agrees.

But when you add fifteen minutes here, fifteen minutes there, and fifteen minutes somewhere else, you've counted almost an hour of the evening.

Let's look at what we're throwing away, beginning with that fifteen minutes before supper. We wives busy ourselves with the meal while our husbands disappear. After supper, there's twenty minutes more before our favorite show, the volunteer meeting, the kids' sports or music lessons. There's no point in getting into anything then, so we just kill time. We may chat with each other, but there's no real communication. Afterward, it's almost bedtime. The whole evening has been lost, as far as loving each other is concerned.

We must decide to prioritize our time for each other. That doesn't mean adopting a rigid schedule: "Seven o'clock's our time together, son, so run along. We'll set that broken arm at seven-thirty."

We should value our time, though, the way we do our money. You remember the old cliché "Time is money." Businesses succeed or fail because they follow that principle. Time is also love. If a business used "Time is money" as earnestly as we use "Time is love," would that business be among the Fortune 500 or would it be bankrupt?

What Are My Talents?

Now, let's take a moment to write down those talents Almighty God has given us for the sake of our spouses. Each of us will have different talents, but all of us will have long lists.

If your list is small, don't feel discouraged. You're not graceless, just new to this kind of thought. The truth is, you don't know your own worth.

Do you have the knack of cheering up your wife when she's down? Do you make your husband feel that home is a refuge from the pressures of the world? Do you understand her dreams, the wishes of his heart? Don't forget the invisible graces: those that begin with "not." You may be free from jealousy, for instance, or you may be a person who doesn't get stressed too easily.

After you've thought of your special talents—and you

should be adding to the list as we go on—we'll explore the more general ones.

My Talent Is Tenderness

How do you spend your tenderness?

Some of you men may have raised your eyebrows. "Tenderness? That's my wife's department."

Maybe you only have one share of tenderness and she has five. That's all right. We're not asking how you spend five; we're asking how you spend one. Besides, we're in the midst here of a great masculine excuse. When something challenges us to be personal, we throw up a barrier and say, "Hey, that's great; for women, that is. Now let's talk about a man's subject, like courage."

You have tenderness. Furthermore, your tenderness is one of the reasons your wife loves you.

Wives, we must be careful not to use the same argument: "I'm much more tender than he is, so I can sit back and relax now. I don't need to improve."

Are you sure? You may be spending five shares of tenderness, but you have fifty. Don't ask whether you're giving more tenderness than he is. Ask whether you're giving the level of tenderness the Lord has invested in you.

How tender is your relationship with each other? Now, don't compare it with any other couple; compare it with your own capabilities.

How tender are you right now? Maybe this isn't a time that calls for tenderness, but that's all right. The Lord didn't say, "Invest the money when the opportunity arises." He said, "Invest the money." Furthermore, when you do invest, you get the interest, and the Lord pays much better than the national prime lending rate. His return is a hundredfold.

Our lovers married us in a spirit of hope. Men, our wives didn't sit down with a checklist and say, "Hmm. He's a little too busy with his work, likes to spend too much time on the car, can be grumpy when he's over-scheduled. But I suppose he's worth the price." At least, I hope they didn't do that. Instead, they said, "This man is so wonderful. I just know he'll always understand me. He'll hold me and love me and I won't ever be lonely again." Wives, your husbands did the same thing. They didn't cold-bloodedly say, "This is what I'm getting. Yup, I have my eyes wide open; I know she'll never be any better." They said, "I love her. I can't live without her. She makes my life complete."

Just Give What You Have

Women take some teasing for being bargain-hungry. They'll retort that you shouldn't let a man loose in the supermarket. Why? Because he just responds to impulse.

Isn't that what we all do at home? That is, except for special occasions when we create the environment: anniversaries and birthdays, for example. We work hard to make them happy times, and that's why they are.

Father's Day is a perfect example of how we can create an atmosphere, be it good or bad. On Father's Day we often send an unspoken message that says, "Our hearts aren't really in this. But we had one of these celebrations for Mother, and we'd feel terrible if we weren't fair to Dad."

Now, I'm not blaming the wives. This atmosphere is a joint effort, caused partly because the man won't cooperate. "Don't bother," he grumbles, perhaps silently. "Don't bother me. Give me a tie."

So often in our home, we're focused on things instead of people:

"I have to get supper ready."

"I have to get the kids to bed."

"I'm about to collapse. I've had an awful day and I just want to sit down and unwind."

When we don't think much about each other, we react to one another instead of responding. Suppose you went home after work or greeted your spouse at the door with a different attitude: a determination to give every bit of tenderness you have tonight. You may not have all that much. That's all right; just give what you have. Wouldn't it be wonderful?

Do we ever really resolve to be tender, not because she deserves it but because she's herself; not because it's his birthday but because I have this tenderness to spend?

How thoroughly do we examine what we've given, and how frequently do we focus on what we're getting? Especially when pain's involved, it's easy to measure out the first by weighing the second.

A woman, for instance, might think, "He isn't very tender, so I don't have to be tender with him. Even if I was, he wouldn't understand it."

But maybe he isn't tender because he hasn't experienced much tenderness.

Cosmic Little Everyday Talents

Your talents aren't all of cosmic importance, like tenderness and time. They could be small but powerful, like a sense of humor.

How many women keep everyone in stitches when they're out for lunch? Yet they never exercise that talent at home. How many men can be the life of the party or a delight for every other person in the office? His friends think he's so interesting, so alive and funny, but at home he's dull and silent; he saves his best for outside the house.

Now, part of it, in all honesty, is the partner's response. Too often, a wife will groan, "You're not going to tell one of your jokes, are you?" Meanwhile, everyone else is saying, "Tell that story again. I want to hear it." He does—when his wife isn't around.

How many husbands really encourage their wives to let themselves go, and how many roll their eyes and say, "She's kind of flaky, but that's my girl."

The Lord didn't say, "If your five talents will make money, invest them. But if you're afraid they won't get a return, you don't have to bother."

He said, "Use them." Do you invest your sense of humor?

If It Doesn't Earn Money, It Can't Be Talent

Do you ever smother your God-given talents? You could have natural talent for woodworking, ceramics, flower decoration, or any number of skills you don't pursue.

Too many of us have bought into a cash flow mentality that says, "If no one will pay you for it, it must be worthless." Some of today's greatest art forms were begun by people who were merely trying to have fun while using their natural talents. Madrigal singing was once an after-dinner entertainment where everyone joined in. In order to sing at a party now, you have to be a professional or people will think you're drunk.

We Americans no longer dance, paint, or build if we think we aren't "good." Even our children are becoming afraid to draw. They're self-conscious because their work isn't as professional as the designs in their comic books.

That's nonsense; dangerous, stifling nonsense.

Every one of us has talents that go unused. "I'd love to do that," we tell ourselves. "Too bad I couldn't make a living at it."

Evidently the Lord didn't think we needed regular income before He gave us a loan. Why can't we use it?

"Because no one would appreciate it."

He didn't say we should wait for others' approval. He said we should use the gifts He gave us.

Let's examine ourselves. What talents do we have? What would we do well, if only we had the time? What do other people seem to like about us? What do we think is fun?

Maybe your talent is writing poetry.

"Yes, but I could never get it published."

Don't worry about that; write for your spouse, your beloved.

Perhaps you're a very intelligent person. You do a great deal of reading and you're really quite knowledgeable. How much of your knowledge do you share with your beloved and how much do you save for someone who will understand?

Again, what talents are you suppressing? Do you even realize you're doing this?

Children can give us some good eye-openers about our hidden values. In some of the nicer housing developments, you rarely see grade school kids playing outside. They don't realize it, but they're too professional to throw an old, worn-out ball with the kids across the street. So often, unless they have a uniform and an organized league, they don't play.

We're like those kids. Why are our talents worth less if we spend them on our spouses and children?

Let's forget how much we're "not worth" and start spending ourselves.

In order to do so, we must take another look at our expenditures of time. By the way, don't be comforted because everyone else is wasting time, too. Let's just ask ourselves: how much of our time is spent doing things that are not only unnecessary but also harmful?

Again, children give a sterling example of how our best efforts can be misguided. As I mentioned earlier, we spend a lot of time chauffeuring them from activity to activity. That's bad for them. It really is, not because they don't develop their leg muscles, but because the places they're going to are harmful.

Dance class, scouts, sports, and music lessons all round out our children's education—and encourage them to be independent, unloving people. By keeping our kids in constantly moving cars, going from "experience" to "experience," we're teaching them a strong lesson about values in our society and in our homes. We're telling them these experiences are more important than the people in their lives. We're making them value things over people.

Ten or fifteen years later, when our efforts bear fruit, we'll ask what happened. We'll wonder why they refuse marriages or children of their own, why they get divorced, why they never call, why they never have time for anyone, why they seem lonely and don't know how to escape. Why? Because they were good students when they were young.

When we fill our children's evenings with activities, we're institutionalizing them. We're turning the home into a taxi stand and building up a peer group mentality. Has anyone noticed? Today, kids are socializing with one another at age nine the way we did when we were fifteen. They don't have even an older child's knowledge of how to stay out of trouble.

This chauffeured culture isn't any healthier for Mom and Dad. We shouldn't have time to chauffeur our kids. We should be too busy creating a home and family to spend that much time in the car.

Sex Is a Talent, Too

This section will probably provoke more confusion and hard feelings than any other, among both men and women. Some of us don't realize our sexuality is a God-given talent. Others wish our spouses would wake up to that fact. I honestly believe most couples fail to invest their sexual talents far more than they fail to be tender, forgiving, or generous.

When most of us ask, "How well do I use my sexual talents?" we think of frequency. We reduce sex to intercourse, and that's a problem.

If we believe that a husband and wife must communicate intimately with each other on a daily basis—and I strongly support that statement—it must include physical intimacy as well as verbal. They must set aside time, and I don't mean at eleven-thirty or twelve at night, when they are free to experience each other physically. Whether that is expressed ultimately in intercourse is not the point.

If a couple does take time to physically experience each other, intercourse will probably happen more frequently. One reason it doesn't happen is that it's unavailable. We're too busy.

God did, indeed, give us sex as a resource. Are we spending it or are we hiding it in the ground?

Again, don't compare yourselves with others. Surveys may be interesting, but they don't mean a thing to you as a couple. So what if you do—or don't—match everyone of your age and income and educational background? What matters is whether you're using your full capacity for sexual experience of each other.

Don't ask, "Are we getting enough?" The question is, "Do we have any left?" Don't ask yourself if you're meeting your desires or whether you're satisfying each other physically. Ask yourself whether you're giving each other all your sexuality.

Again, I'm not speaking of frequency but of passion. Physical communication is like verbal: it can be intimate or superficial. A couple may talk to each other every night, but perhaps they're just chattering. Are you making love, or are you engaging in sexual chatter?

Some of you will say, "What we have is quality rather than quantity." Quality is good, but this can be a means of avoiding each other. If you applied this phrase to conversation, it could create a pretty chilly relationship: "Find a significant topic, dear, and I'll talk to you." That's destructive. It's withholding ourselves, whether in verbal or physical intimacy.

We really aren't spending the sexual investment God gave us. We bury it in the ground, almost literally.

When you were married, you gave your bodies to each other so you could be healed of your hurts and aloneness.

Remember St. Paul's passage from 1 Corinthians: "The wife does not have authority over her own body, but the husband does; and in the same way, the husband does not have authority over his own body, but the wife does. You must not deprive each other . . ." (1 Co. 7:4, 5).

If a husband has to say to himself, "I wonder if she's in the mood tonight," her body is not his. If a wife has to figure out ways to seduce him, his body is not hers.

Again, I want to emphasize that we're not just talking about the completed act.

Why don't you set aside fifteen minutes to half an hour each day for physical intimacy? Perhaps from eight o'clock to eight-fifteen or eight-thirty, just to go into your room and experience each other skin to skin. Now, maybe "nothing will happen." Isn't that a terrible statement? All sorts of things can happen: in awareness, in sensitivity and tenderness. Yet we seem to think if we merely grow in love, our lovemaking has failed. We've fallen into this awful trap of all or nothing.

The Lord didn't give us sex that way. Sex should be a daily experience for husbands and wives.

Praise Is a Free Gift

To fully invest our sexuality, we should use all the resources at our disposal. Again, compliments are a powerful one.

Even if we think we don't notice details, we're probably better at it than we suppose. Do we turn our observations into compliments, or do we keep them hidden from our loves?

Do we note only the negative things? Some of us have been taught that it's "discerning" to see flaws, but it's a weakness to pay too much attention to goodnesses. That attitude smothers our hearts; it's like being color-blind on a brilliant spring day.

Husbands, do we give our wives a full measure of the compliments that exist in our hearts? Mind you, I didn't say, "the compliments she deserves." It's arrogant to judge whether someone deserves a compliment. The question is, rather, "Right now, do I have a compliment in me? How many of these do I give?"

We may be afraid that compliments are feminine. But if we hold back our compliments, our wives won't think we're masculine; they'll think we don't care.

We wives might hold back our compliments for a different reason. "My husband is too cocky as it is. If I ever started praising him, he'd be impossible to live with."

A man can be overflowing with false pride because he doesn't get deep, sincere praise. He's starving for compliments backed by understanding and real affection.

I honestly believe most men get far fewer compliments than do most women, starting in childhood. We'll praise our boys for their accomplishments: for a home run, A's, or putting out the garbage. They have to perform well to be praised, but we compliment girls on who they are. We'll tell them they're pretty or cute, or call them Daddy's girl. True, most of those compliments are physical. Still, they didn't have to be earned.

We also compliment girls on being thoughtful, understanding, and considerate; these are all human qualities. We do give personal, human compliments to our boys, but they're much less frequent. Our men are starved for compliments. That cocky man—or a quiet one—may be like someone who's fasted a long time. If you suddenly give him a thick, rare steak, he won't be able to swallow it as easily as someone who's recently been fed.

Compliments Are Great, But You Have to Accept Them

It's tremendously difficult for many of us to give compliments. It takes effort; we've been trained to criticize, not to look for the good in others. It also takes some courage, because a truly personal compliment makes us vulnerable. If we say, "You are really an understanding person," we really mean, "My heart is touched because you understood me."

It's as tough, or even tougher, to accept a compliment. Most of us will squirm every which way to dodge praise. "Well, thank you, but . . ." we begin. ". . . but I'm not really pretty." "But this is just an old shirt." "But I'm not a forgiving person; I'm really quite a bad person, if you only knew . . ." Our low self-esteem keeps us from accepting the healing we so urgently need.

We must understand what's happening behind the scenes when our lovers cast off our heartfelt praise. They may laugh or say, "You don't mean that," or even "What do you want?"

Have patience. Again, the Lord doesn't say, "Spend your resources when they'll be accepted." He says, "Spend your resources."

There is nothing like praise. Our highest call, in relationship with our Father in heaven, is to praise Him. How can we praise God unless we praise our spouses? Furthermore,

God is really more pleased when we praise the daughter or son He gave us than when we praise Him directly.

Remember, Jesus said, "You must love one another just as I have loved you" (Jn. 13:34). He didn't say, "You must love me just as I have loved you." What a generous God we have.

Now, let's ask ourselves specifically, "Do I give my spouse the praise I have inside? Do I give it all?" We humans tend to hold back; to give praise only when it's appropriate, when we're feeling warm and affectionate, when we've been complimented, or when someone has earned it.

Don't let yourself be satisfied with "Well, yes, I'm a very praising man. I always praise my wife," or "I really do praise my husband. I can honestly say that I give my husband a lot of credit."

Thanks be to God. That's wonderful. Now, is it all you have? Is there any more in you? If there is, spit it out. Don't keep it to yourself; it's just rusting in there. Keeping a compliment inside doesn't help anyone, unless you're praising yourself.

By the way, we should praise ourselves. Not in pride, of course, but in love and acceptance. It's just as important as praising our spouses, perhaps even more so. If we don't recognize our goodness, we'll never recognize our badness.

Beauty Is More than Skin Deep

God gave you physical attractiveness, too. How much of it do you spend every day and how much do you save for special occasions? I think couples should go out on the town in jeans and sweat shirts, and save their party dresses and good suits for time together at home. Am I serious? Not entirely. But am I crazy? Not at all. Why should we dress up to impress acquaintances and strangers, then look like bums when we're alone with the people who matter most?

Why should we wives dress for our husbands in baggy, worn-out sweats? We all know what "at-home" clothes are: they're the clothes we wouldn't be caught dead in at the grocery store. When he hugs you, does he know you're in there, or does it feel like he's hugging the laundry?

Why should we husbands dress that way for our wives? How about the typical male couch potato, lounging around in his shop clothes or his underwear? Does he think he's turning her on? Later that night, is she going to say, "I've been looking at you all evening, handsome, and I can hardy wait"? Or is she going to say, "You know, I really need my sleep."

We men would never dream of going to the office without having shaved, but on Saturday, the family has to stand clear or they'll get scratched to death. That's our "day off," we think. We don't have anyone to dress for. There's just old faithful who's sitting there in the other chair.

Are you spending the beauty God gave you? Don't just ask yourselves if you can stand to look in the mirror.

Our Talents Are for Eternity

We have so many talents, it would take a book to list them all. One of our greatest is our desire to love each other. We do, indeed, wish to put each other first. The difficulties we face in doing so are just that: difficulties. They're not failures. We can overcome our difficulties with prayer, with soul-searching, and by keeping our eyes wide open to the love-killing lessons society has taught us.

The toughest part is facing the fact that, often, we have to give up something in order to have love instead. What makes it tough is that we don't realize how marvelous and fulfilling that love will be. Our present life seems pretty attractive, even if it is somewhat hollow.

Decide what kind of relationship you'd like to have, then go for it. Don't worry about looking back; there are better roads ahead. You'll see.

That brings us back to the subject of time management. In order to love each other, we simply have to spend time with each other, and that may mean cutting something out of our schedules.

I've spoken with many women who want to add passion to their sexual love lives. Some of them will tell me, "I know I should make love to him, but I just get so tired."

The answer's often quite simple, although painful. Change your agenda.

The same answer applies to men.

Who, really, is more important? Your spouse, or your friends, coworkers, fellow volunteers, or children's sports coaches? You didn't marry those people. The Lord is not going to ask how passionate you were about them. Nor will He ask you if you did the laundry, the ironing, the lawn, or the house repairs after you came home from work. He might ask, though, why you didn't put your feet up for an hour after dinner so you'd be enthusiastic about your lover.

We all have beautiful excuses about time, but they aren't cast in stone. We can find enough time with each other. Our problem is that we don't want it: not unless it fits into our current schedules.

That's when we have to cut loose from that love-smothering focus on self; to trust our spouses to make us happy, just as we did when we were first married. We must also trust God, who truly wants us to be happy. He's offering us a way; for heaven's sake, let's take it.

Let's go back to our lists of the talents God gave us. Let's add all the skills, big and little, that we now realize are ours. Take every talent, one by one, and ask, "Am I using every bit of it for my beloved?" not "Am I doing well?" "Is she satisfied?" "Is he content?" and not "Would he understand if I suddenly did all those things?" "Would she be shocked if I became that full-fledged?"

"How much am I keeping to myself? Am I using my talent for the sake of my beloved, or am I just letting it rust, maybe to disappear in bitterness because I haven't been able to live up to my potential?"

Let's ask ourselves if we're ready to stand before the Lord and say, "You gave me this talent of listening. You gave me five shares of it and I have spent five shares. You gave me two shares of sexuality and I spent it all. You gave me five units of understanding and I poured it all out. Now I have ten because You returned it in abundance."

I have faith in you; you are truly good people. Even now, as you spend your talent of hope, remember the Master's promise: "Well done, my son; well done, my daughter. You have shown you are trustworthy in small things; I will trust you with greater; come and join in your master's happiness. To everyone who has will be given more, and he will have more than enough."

Consider these questions privately:

What qualities prompted my spouse to spend his/her life with me? What compliments has my spouse given me that I just pass off?

251

Make a time budget. How much time do I have with my spouse? What can I make more efficient, shuffle around, or omit entirely to give me more time with my lover?

What talents have I been given for my beloved's sake? There are at least three kinds:

Spiritual (like kindness or patience) . . .

Enriching (like creativity, intelligence, or humor) . . .

Uplifting (like lightheartedness, optimism, or sexuality) . . .

Do I use each of these talents for the benefit of my beloved? What can I do to use each one to the utmost?

Share these questions with your spouse:

What compliments do I give you, dear, that you don't seem to believe?

I want to spend more time with you, dear. I'm willing to do these things . . . so we can spend more time together.

My beloved, I yearn to spend more time being intimate with you physically. Why don't we do the following . . . ?

Finally, let us invite God into our marriages:

Loving Father, it is hard for me to truly believe that You have given me so much goodness. Please help me appreciate all the talents You have given me, especially the ones I don't yet see. Let me use these every day, to the utmost, for the sake of my beloved spouse. Let me fill his/her life with warmth and joy and trust. When I believe my talents are lacking, gently remind me that, when I have spent all the talents I have, You will fill me with so many more. Thank You for loving me so much. Amen.

CHAPTER 10

⌒⌒⌒

WE ARE ONE, DEAR

⌒⌒⌒

(1 P. 3:8–12)

Peter's first letter is written to you: you "who have been chosen, in the foresight of God the Father, to be made holy by the Spirit . . . you who are being kept safe by God's power through faith . . ." (1 P. 1:1, 2 and 5).

It really was written for you. You'll find it just as relevant today as it was to the early Christians, who were also bearing "all sorts of trials" (1 P. 1:6).

> Finally: you should all agree among yourselves and be sympathetic; love the brothers, have compassion and be self-effacing. Never repay one wrong with another, or one abusive word with another; instead, repay with a blessing. That is what you are called to do, so that you inherit a blessing. For

Who among you delights in life,
longs for time to enjoy prosperity?
Guard your tongue from evil,
your lips from any breath of deceit.
Turn away from evil and do good, seek peace
and pursue it.
For the eyes of the Lord are on the upright,
his ear turned to their cry.
But the Lord's face is set against those who do
evil.

1 Peter 3:8–12

Here, St. Peter is referring to the whole church. That's a lot to deal with, so let's take it down to the little church: the family. Most specifically, we'll see how Peter's words apply to the husband-wife relationship.

Who Delights in Life, Longs for Time to Enjoy Prosperity?

We certainly don't hesitate to wish for happy lives. As for prosperity, we'd probably translate that somewhat differently from the way Peter would. Still, we do long for an abundance of peace in our households; that is, if we haven't decided it's a hopeless case, so we might as well seek our peace elsewhere.

The key to this prosperity of peace, happiness, and goodwill is found in the next two lines:

Guard your tongue from evil,
your lips from any breath of deceit.

These verses make sense. None of us would defend the virtues of malicious conversation and deceitful talk. We

254

can see the tremendous hurt these bring our loved ones. We're especially aware of hurts inflicted on those in our homes.

Maliciousness and deceit are so repugnant to us, in fact, that we don't apply them to ourselves. It's far more comfortable to see malice "out there" in our coworkers and neighbors. Now, we're not hateful people, but we're not perfect, either.

Maliciousness can crop up when we're hurt, especially if we've evolved a lifelong attitude of defensiveness. It's a way of protecting ourselves, of lashing back—or lashing out first—before someone else runs us down. It can arise when we're called to change but are afraid to let go of the safe and comfortable. It happens frequently when envy gets the best of us.

Personally, I find it difficult to admit I have malice. I don't fall into the trap of claiming I'm perfect, but I do tend to write off the bad things I say: "Well, sometimes I sound malicious, but most of the time it's provoked," or "Maybe I was malicious. But I wasn't nearly as bad as he was. Did you hear *him?*"

But Peter didn't tell me, "Guard your tongue from evil unless you're provoked." Nor did he say, "Make sure your deceit isn't as bad as the other guy's."

I—and most of us, I think—find myself seeing things my way. I don't know why, but I have to explain why I'm justified "I lost my temper," I say. It's even harder to admit that I tend to hold hurts within myself. In a good relationship, I know, you're supposed to be honest and open. Sometimes I am open: too open. "I'm just expressing my feelings," I say. But my openness is opening the other person from stem to stern.

Silence Can Be Golden

In most marriages, there is usually a silent partner and a speaking partner. The roles can switch any time; one spouse might be the silent partner on politics while the other is silent on religion.

That silent partner may be failing to express himself; she may not be open. That can be harmful, but it also has its good points. The silent partner, by keeping silent, is curbing that tendency toward a malicious tongue.

As I mentioned in Chapter 2, I wonder if we underestimate the importance of thinking something out. Silence has a lot of virtues; it applies to St. Peter's lesson, too.

Yet we humans excuse ourselves for thoughtlessly blurting out our problems. After all, we say, we're not "holding it inside." We're certainly not holding back at all.

Perhaps you've had a tough day at work, and you just can't wait to get home and vent your feelings. Wait a minute. Maybe it would be better to wait until tomorrow night, when you have a little more perspective.

Maybe you're the type of person who stores up the frustrations of the day until your spouse comes home. You're not attacking him. You're just telling him what's wrong with your life.

Now, that isn't malice. Is it? Not really; malice has to deliberately try to hurt. But it's close enough.

Imagine it from an outsider's point of view: A husband greets his wife at the door. She's so glad to see him, she's smiling. She's been waiting all day to give him a hug, but he doesn't notice that. His thoughts are full of his stupid boss and that stupid job. He's running scripts in his mind: "I wish I'd quit. I wish I'd *hit* him and then quit . . ." He can't stand it; he has to speak. "What a lousy day," he begins. "You wouldn't believe . . ."

When he's through, what has he accomplished? Among other things, he's made her as miserable as he is. What's worse is that, deep down, he knew he'd be making her miserable before he ever began.

We've all behaved that way at some time, haven't we? It's not that we're mean, it's that we can hardly resist. We know we'll be in pain if we don't vent it on someone, and secretly we decide, "Better them than me."

That takes us back to St. Peter's use of the word "prosperity." Most of us tend to define prosperity in terms of cash, but also in terms of comfort. Now, some of that comfort is material, but some of it is emotional, too.

It's ironic, isn't it? Our very longing for prosperity is what keeps us from having it.

Quantity or Quality?

We truly must examine our consciences when it comes to our conversations with each other. This especially applies to you who are the talkers.

Please believe me: I'm not in any way, shape, or form saying it's wrong to talk a lot. Free speech—and I mean speech free from fear or shyness—is a real grace in a marriage. But we do want to look at the content of that speech. Sometimes, because we so highly praise communication, we underemphasize the virtue of thinking a problem through first.

Our society tends to make a talker feel superior. Those of us who can lay it on the line feel skilled, and may even consider our quiet spouses handicapped.

Not necessarily. First, let's examine the content of what's being said. Take me, for example: I'm a talker, and sometimes it takes someone else one sentence to say what I've said in three pages. I admire the other person for that, but I can't imitate it. I'm much more comfortable with the three pages. On my bad days, I might even say, "He wouldn't have been able to do that if I hadn't spoken first." Of course, that's not necessarily true, nor is it true that my three pages are better than his one-liner.

To find out how much peace and prosperity exist in your homes, study a normal day in your lives. How much does your lover enjoy your company? Not your conversation; communication is beyond conversation. Even when it concerns a tough subject, it's beyond merely venting your anger. To twist the old saying, where there's fire, there's probably so much smoke that nobody can see clearly anyway.

Let's take an imaginary scene again. Supposing, wives, that your husband forgot your birthday. He didn't say anything in the morning and he didn't ask you out to lunch. That evening you waited for your surprise, but surprise! It didn't come. You decided you'd give him until the next morning to shape up, and when morning dawned, he was still out of shape. You went off to work angry, and as the day progressed, you rehearsed the blistering comments you'd make when you both got home that night.

You weren't able to make them, though; you had to work late. Then you realized there was nothing in the house for supper, so you went to the grocery store. By the time you got home, you had to feed the children and put them to bed. You also had time to think—and to cool off; to remember how busy he'd been at work, with the kids, fixing the plumbing. Now you had an honest chance at communication.

If you'd said what you'd originally planned, there would have been no communication whatever. An angry "Did you intend to forget my birthday, or was that just the best you could do?" would provoke nothing but defensiveness and shame.

A comment based on compassion might have had a different effect:

"Yesterday was my birthday, Joe."

"Oh, no. Not the twenty-first?"

"That's right. Shall we do something anyway?"

Joe is a good man, even if he did forget, and this gives him a chance to exercise his goodness: to take you out, bring you belated flowers. It also gives him a chance to apologize, and for you to express your hurt feelings in a nonthreatening way.

Blurting it out isn't always wrong, but it isn't always right, either. Blurting it out has nothing to do with openness, honesty, or communication. It's a knee-jerk response to pain, an action that is supposed to make us feel better. It doesn't, really. It takes away the feeling that we're going to explode, but it causes anguish in the family, and that can't possibly make us feel good.

Sometimes blurting it out does help rid us of negative feelings. It's like writing a hate letter. By the time we've finished the letter, we've changed our minds and maybe feel a little silly.

So write, if you have to. It's much better to wield that poison pen than a malicious tongue. You can always trash the letter, but you can never erase your lover's memory of your harsh words. If you have to, shout at the mirror. Say those angry things into a tape recorder. Then play it back.

Believe me, once you've heard yourself at your worst, you won't be tempted to speak that way again.

Then sit down and think your problem through.

By the way, when I speak of a person who thinks something through, I don't mean someone with a pout a mile long. When you do that, you're talking. You're even shouting. Your face is telling your spouse, "See how miserable I am? I'm not going to *say* anything, but can't you take a hint?"

I also don't want to imply that the thinker is more intelligent than his or her spouse. The thinker is merely a person who, by nature, ponders and examines.

Marriage Means Change

Sometimes malice is disguised as self-awareness. We each have years of experience in knowing which subjects, phrases, or tones of voice will pain our lovers. Still, we yield to the impulse to use them again, saying, "I get it all out on the table. That's the kind of person I am."

How about changing that to "That's the kind of person I am, all right. And I want to do better."

Change is marriage's whole purpose. In matrimony, you become one couple, not two good people being themselves.

The matrimonial union creates a whole new life, just as the sacrament of Baptism does. We may not realize it until years after the ceremony, but baptism is a commitment not to be ourselves anymore. It's a commitment to become bodied with the Lord in His people, to become so much more than we could ever be ourselves. That commitment

doesn't take away our identities or make us less than we
are.

Marriage, in a very real way, is the same. We're called to
become bodied with our beloveds; to become bone of his
bone, flesh of her flesh.

Those are inspiring words. Many of us will read them
with pride and gratitude, perhaps even saying, "Good.
People are finally starting to recognize our dignity as a
married couple." We have to watch, though, that we don't
close this book and return to our old selves: two good
people living side by side, except on special occasions.

It's difficult not to do that, especially when we try to
force virtue on ourselves. We should do it the easy way:
by praying for the grace to become one with our beloveds.

Are We Alike?

We must ask ourselves, "How similar have I become to
my spouse in the last twelve months?" Again, we
shouldn't ask, "Am I satisfied with our marriage?" or "Do
I think I'm a good wife (husband)?" That last question is
a fine one, but it's only a beginning. Let's ask, "How
much of her has become part of me?" "Do I speak as he
does?"

I'm not speaking of tone of voice or even vocabulary,
although I do think we should take on each other's vocabularies. I'm speaking of desiring to converse the way he
converses; talking about her topics in her way. Ideally, it
should happen spontaneously. The more we become like
our spouses, the less malicious we'll be. The more sincerely we enjoy their conversation, the less deceptive we'll
become.

This is not easy. That's why you're a sacrament.

If we're like the pagans—good pagans—we get along well with each other, provided there are some understandings: "He's used to my spouting off." "She has to take my ranting and raving in stride. She knows I get on my soapbox."

Instead, ask, "Am I used to talking to her in the tone of voice and in the way that touches her heart? Am I used to listening to myself with his ears rather than just shouting it out?"

We excuse ourselves for our flaws in conversation. We say, "I'm only human," or "Let's be reasonable. Any man would react the same way," or "I'm not a bad woman, but enough's enough."

First, you're not "only human." The Lord came to make you greater than mere flesh. Second, you're not a man, you're a husband. Any guy can be a man. You're not just a woman, you're a wife.

Your marriage license isn't just a contract to support a family, put out the garbage, and cook the meals.

Your marriage is a call to put him on like a beautiful garment, to make her an integral, intimate part of you. Too many of us really haven't changed much since we were single. Sure, we'd find it difficult to sleep alone. We wouldn't want to sit down to an empty table, and we do like someone to throw our words at, even if that person doesn't listen. Those are good changes; they're a beginning. Now ask yourselves, "How different am I inside, compared with my single days or with any single person?"

"Well, I'm thinking about him all the time." "She's my whole life; she's the reason why I do so many of the things I do." That's great. That's also an exaggeration, isn't it? But it's good; it shows ambition.

It's not enough, though, to be thinking about your lover all the time. You're called to bring her inside yourself, to draw him close. In a very real way she has to be doing some of the thinking for you. He has to be so much a part of you that it's difficult to imagine where you end and he begins. That does lead to prosperity and a happy life.

The Marriage Bomb

It certainly isn't easy to keep the tongue under control. If the tongue were a beast, it would be more of a Komodo dragon than a house pet. St. James puts it bluntly: "Wild animals and birds, reptiles and fish of every kind can all be tamed, and have been tamed, by humans; but nobody can tame the tongue—it is a pest that will not keep still . . ." (Jm. 3:7,8).

That makes us stop and think, doesn't it? It's another statement most of us wouldn't want to debate. We'd probably agree that a thunderstorm is very powerful. But no matter how destructive it may have been, its aftereffects don't compare with the path of destruction wreaked by a truly nasty tongue. That becomes most clear when we look at the damage in our own lives.

Nuclear weaponry is another terrible power. It could wipe out the entire world. Terrorism is a horrible example too. But the vast bulk of unhappiness on earth has come more from malicious tongues than from any other single source.

That's certainly true in marriage. How many of us really work on our tongues? Most of us probably don't, except when it comes to extremes.

Now, remember, I'm not addressing the shrews and spouse beaters who make the headlines in the local paper, and I'm not talking about verbally abusive relationships. I'm talking to you: good people who are nevertheless capable of malice, especially when you're wounded by insult, envy, or what have you.

We all have shameful memories of a quickly slung insult that really made him crumble, a cheap word we know she never forgot. Those memories make us feel awful, and we know to work on that kind of behavior. Let's work, too, on the peace and prosperity of our everyday speech.

Let's examine the power speech has over men and women.

For many women, sex lasts longer than it does with their men. These wives are still basking in the afterglow while their husbands are saying, "Let's do it again."

Likewise, conversation usually lasts longer with a man that it does with a woman. When a wife talks out her problem, the talking itself is her cure. Her husband, though, tends to think out his problem. It may take days.

This trait has both positive and negative implications. If she insults him, he may feel the sting for a long time. If she compliments him, he will savor that goodness for a long time, too.

A really sincere compliment lasts longer with a man than with a woman. That's why our women think their husbands are so sparing with their praise. That accusation baffles their men, who protest, "I *said* I loved you. Didn't you believe me?"

Bite Your Tongue

In Chapter 3, I suggested the silent partner ask his spouse how to converse. Now it's time to turn the tables.

If you're the talker in your marriage, why don't you ask your lover how to stop and think before you talk? After all, marriage is a relationship where we share and learn from each other.

At first, it may sound like asking the leopard to change his spots, but that's not the case. A long history of spouting off isn't virtuous, nor is it cast in stone. It's a powerful reason for change.

Choose a time when the two of you aren't in conflict, then ask: "When you want to blow up at me, how do you stop yourself? I'm sure you have feelings as strong as mine, and I know you'd like to blurt it out sometimes. Yet you don't. How do you succeed?"

Next, ask, "How do you stand it?"

Then listen to the answer. Much of it will probably be along these lines:

First, your spouse trusts you. He (or she) knows you make mistakes, but believes you are a good person who honestly loves him.

Second, calmness and confidence are involved. There will be a solution to your dispute.

Third, follow this two-part rule: One, "Don't sweat the small stuff." Two, "Everything is the small stuff." When you think about it, it really is.

Jesus was the father of stress management, by the way. He spoke against worry on many occasions. In the Gospel according to Luke, he said, ". . . you must not set your hearts on things to eat and things to drink; nor must you worry" (Lk. 12:29). And in St. Matthew's Gospel, he said, ". . . do not worry about tomorrow: tomorrow will take care of itself. Each day has enough trouble of its own" (Mt. 6:34).

Fourth, focus on learning to forgive. Sometimes it can be rough on our pride, but it always pays off. In a real crisis, forgiveness may be a pure act of will. The forgiving person may say silently, "Lord, even though I am furious with this person, I forgive her (him). At least, that's what I want to do, even though I don't feel it now. So help me to really forgive; to really have compassion for her."

Forgiveness also frees us from a myriad of unconscious reactions; it is a way of choosing life-giving thoughts and rejecting the negative thoughts induced by someone else's behavior. If your next-door neighbor drives you absolutely up a tree, forgive him or her; think of pleasant things instead and silently insist that you won't let him bother you.

If you don't do this, you'll remain a puppet on angry strings, dancing to his piping. If you relieve that tension by dumping it on your spouse, both of you will be trapped.

Tonight, Dear, We're Going to Be Happy

Again, I'm not trying to blame the talkers. There's a great deal of virtue in blurting it out. When no one says anything, marriages drift apart, beginning with a "married singles" mentality and ending in divorce, either legal or spiritual.

You who are talkers, though, have an awesome responsibility. In most marriages, you're the one who determines the atmosphere at home. You're the one who decides whether it will be a peaceful night, a joyful night, an angry, frustrated, or worrisome night. You have a profound ability to make your home a place of prosperity—or a place starved for peace.

Let's stop now, and think of the painful moments you and your spouse have had in the last two weeks. If you were the one who blurted something out, imagine what would have happened if you had taken time to think it through first. Could some of that pain have been averted? That isn't pie in the sky, by the way, and I'm not looking for a prefabricated answer. Be honest with yourselves. What could you have done differently?

Maybe you're not a hair-trigger talker. Maybe your temper is more of a slow burn: "Sometimes I think it out and think it out, and then it's a major explosion. It would have been much better if I'd talked it out before it became a megaton bomb."

That's true. I'm not recommending suppression of your feelings; even without the explosion, hidden feelings are the stuff of which bad marriages are made. If you're part of each other, you have to share those feelings. But I am definitely recommending time out to see the other side.

We might excuse ourselves, saying, "Well, with me it's just a quick flare-up and then it's over." But how often do those flare-ups happen? Sometimes frequency is serious, even though the flare-up itself is little. An attack of rage seems far worse than a little impatience. Is it, really? Impatience constantly multiplies. It's worse than rage, if the rage is infrequent.

Discussion or Slander?

Evil or malicious speech isn't always kept within the four walls of our homes. Sometimes we defuse our anger at our spouses by dumping it off with friends. It's all right, we think, because we've purged ourselves of it and now we won't fight with our lovers.

Like nuclear waste, the poison of complaints doesn't just disappear. It can seep and spread and remain constantly virulent. Even the nicest, the noblest, of friends won't refrain from looking at your spouse and thinking, "Why does he leave her at home when he goes out on Saturdays? Just selfish, I guess," or "Boy, I'm glad I don't have old spendthrift pulling the purse strings like he does."

Do your girlfriends wish they had married your husband, or do they think he's a lot like their own men: partly good and partly bad? Is every man at work anxious to see the paragon you go home to, or is she just another woman?

It's ironic; we say things about our spouses that no one else would even dare hint. If a friend said, "Your wife couldn't balance the checkbook if she tried. What an airhead!" we'd bristle instantly. If a neighbor said, "Poor dear. Your husband must not love you very much. He's always going off to play poker," we'd let her have it. But we'll deliver similar insults ourselves. What in the world are we doing?

"I'll talk to my mother about him; she'll understand."

"I can always tell my brother. He knows what women are like."

What kind of reputations are we crafting for our lovers? It doesn't matter if our complaints are true. That just makes us guilty of detraction instead of calumny.

Like nuclear waste, it's difficult to erase the poison once it's spilled. Once we gripe to our mothers, neighbors, bosses, or the people in our car pools, we find it difficult to retract that gripe. We rarely say, "You know, my back was really aching and that's why I was so mad at my wife," or "The kids made bad grades and I was angry.

Then he said one wrong word and I made a whole paragraph of it."

At best, we just don't repeat it again. If our friends bring up the gripe at some later time, we'll probably support it again because we don't want to look spineless or unsophisticated. Especially after ten or twenty years of marriage, we don't want people to think we're too much in love. Too much in love? What a terrible cage we've locked ourselves in.

Of course, when we criticize our spouses to others, we wind up feeling guilty. Whenever we think of our lovers or see those friends we complained to, we remember our hasty words. The result of it all is definitely not prosperity.

Turn Away from Evil and Do Good, Seek Peace and Pursue It

Do we seek peace in our homes or do we seek personal satisfaction?

I keep coming back to this point, but it's a critical one: When someone asks you how your marriage is, how do you answer? Do you say, "Yes, I have a happy marriage," or "Well, it could be better, it could be worse, but in general, I'm happy"?

If you do, it's understandable. It was the way we were taught. But then, the Huns were taught to loot and pillage. Jesus is teaching us a new way to love each other. It's time to cast aside hopeless "common sense."

A man or woman of peace should answer, "I honestly believe my wife is happy"; "I truly think my husband has a happy marriage."

Now, if you believe your husband or wife truly isn't happy, don't feel like a failure. You are here, loving that person, ready to change. Praise the Lord for your goodness.

This focus on self begins in our dating years. When I went on a date, my mother, father, and aunt always waited up for me. "Did you have a good time?" they asked. They were sincerely interested, and that was beautiful.

Never once, though, did they ask if my date had a good time. Maybe it's good that I didn't get married. My whole preparation for marriage was to enjoy myself.

That's an exaggeration, of course. But we are indeed trained to judge our romantic relationships by how well we're satisfied.

That's also true for our priests. If you asked me, "Are you satisfied with your priesthood?" I would not automatically look at you, my people, and ask in return if you're pleased with me. Instead, I'd say, "Well, gee, I couldn't imagine myself doing anything else. I feel very fulfilled. I have tremendous opportunities I wouldn't have anyplace else. I seem to be fairly successful."

My answer is a denial of our relationship. It becomes "my" priesthood, not "ours." Then it's reduced to a ministry instead of a network of love relationships.

Likewise, a marriage becomes "my" marriage instead of "our" marriage. It becomes a list of duties, balanced by the benefits of your living up to your responsibilities, too. That's good business. True peace in the home comes, instead, when we find satisfaction and joy by experiencing our spouses' happiness.

We have to bow reverently to our husbands when it comes to lovemaking. Most good husbands simply don't enjoy sex unless their wives do. Without her delight, he has only the minimal physical satisfaction. To him, that isn't truly satisfying. That's beautiful, isn't it?

Conversation should be the same way. Is it? Too often, we evaluate a conversation by asking, "Did she listen to me?" "Did he understand what I was saying?" Instead, we should be thinking, "I truly believe I understood her tonight"; "I really think I listened to him." That's when conversation brings joy.

Peace Be with You

Our homes aren't truly at peace when we're merely getting along or when we've succeeded in hashing out an issue. Peace doesn't come when we're doing all the right things by each other. Peace comes when we're more interested in our lovers' well-being than in our own.

It sounds great on paper, but when we try to live it, we find ourselves saying, "Yes, that's nice, but it's unreal. I'd like to be that way, but I'm human and I fail."

We keep concentrating on our humanity. Remember, Peter said, "You are a chosen race, a kingdom of priests, a holy nation, a people to be a personal possession to sing the praises of God who called you out of the darkness into his wonderful light. Once you were a non-people and now you are the People of God . . ." (1 P. 2:9,10).

He didn't say we're people. He didn't even say we're good people. He said we're a holy people, a people to be a personal possession of God.

Frankly, we don't accept that. We don't deny the theology of it, but it sounds too good to be true; like we're saints or something. Why not take Peter's word for it? We're so used to limiting ourselves. In material possessions or career goals, our society is insatiable, but when it comes to something like love, we throw up our hands and say, "Infatuation doesn't last forever, you know. Real love is—uh, comfortable."

Are we living in God's light by the way we love our spouses?

You Should All Agree Among Yourselves

Peter's first letter was directed to the whole church. But certainly if it applies to the whole church, it applies to our fellow Christians with whom we sleep.

In Chapter 4, we spoke briefly on this. Now we'll go into greater detail.

How much do we agree among ourselves? How much do we disagree? Maybe we even take pride in our disagreements. We say, "Ah, but opposites attract." That explains why we get married. It doesn't explain why we're still married and reading this book today.

After one, ten, or thirty years together, are we still opposites? In marriage, we're not called to be rugged individualists. We're called to be one in the Lord, models of how Jesus loves His church. He is one in mind, in heart and affection with us.

Again, do we live in harmony, or do we ascribe to the "separate but equal" philosophy: "She takes care of this part of our life together and I take care of the other part." Do we agree among ourselves or do we just avoid fights? "I'll go along unless she pushes too far," or "He's a good man; I'll give in."

Giving in isn't enough. That's a good start, but we have to become part of the other person.

An obvious area is the one we've just been working on: the struggle between a silent partner and a talker. If a talker is overwhelming a thinker, we must both examine that situation and decide how to fix it. The thinker can't just say, "Well, he (she) always takes the stage. I'll just have to live that way." That's not agreement. That's toleration.

Another area of disagreement may be lovemaking. One partner may have more physical desire than the other. That's fine; that's where we start. After ten years, the gap should have narrowed a great deal. Has it?

Sex with teeth gritted and a false smile would be a form of prostitution. You don't have to pretend, though; it can happen naturally. You can pray for passion. You can ask your spouse how to yearn more for him or her. If exhaustion or worry is sapping your energy, you can address those issues as well. You can also work at it. In this case, practice has a great deal to do with desire. It really does. But too often, the person who doesn't have the desire says, "Well, when I get the desire, I'll practice."

There are a myriad of other possible disagreements. For example, how do you both feel about a wife working outside the home or working inside the home? How about overtime, hobbies, furniture buying, faith, friends? In Chapter 4, you found a list of possible disagreements. Go back and read them over with a new eye.

Now then, ask yourselves where you need to agree more. Don't ask what conflicts you need to resolve. Many of your disagreements will be hidden within your lifestyles. They don't always surface as conflicts. After all, you are good couples, and whether or not you realize it, you've already begun your search for peace.

Over the years, there's been a great deal of polarization of views in the Catholic Church. Many Catholics, weary of it all, have taken refuge in indifference. Have you settled

into indifference about in-laws, money, the number of
your children, the raising of those children? That's not
agreement.

Sure, I'll Agree, Dear—Whenever You're Right

Remember, I don't recommend artificial smiles pasted
over angry faces. Start with "I want to agree with you."
That may sound trivial, but it isn't. Once we say, "I don't
agree with you," we've closed a door. We don't even want
to agree.

So, first, build up the desire to agree, not because our
lovers are right but because they're our lovers. Loving
each other will help us agree.

Don't think, "I'll lose my integrity if I knuckle under all
the time." As a married couple, your integrity is formed
not by maintaining opinions but by becoming one with
each other. Think instead, "I just can't understand why
she feels this way, but I want us to work it out." "I love
him so much, I don't want there to be anything between
us."

Of course, we're not talking about violations of conscience. If your spouse wants to rob a bank, agreement is
not an issue. Instead, we're talking about minor opinions,
and they're a dime a dozen. What isn't a dime a dozen is
your spouse. He or she is infinitely precious.

That's why St. Peter calls us to agree among ourselves.

You Should All Be Sympathetic

In this section, St. Peter is telling us not to take each
other's sacrifices for granted, no matter how everyday they
seem.

How often do we simply expect our lovers to fulfill their responsibilities? We know we're taking them for granted when our thoughts begin with "Of course . . ."

"Of course she has dinner ready when I come home. That's why she stays home all day."

"Of course she cleans house after she comes home from work. That's what she's supposed to do."

"Of course he goes to work even when his back is hurting him. How would we eat if he didn't?"

"Of course he comes home every night at five forty-eight. Where else would he go?"

How sympathetic are we, and not just toward the stupendous virtues?

Perhaps your husband's most magnificent trait is his consistency. In fact, that was what attracted you to him. You knew he would never let you down. Do you still delight in that, or do you sometimes feel there's no excitement in your life?

Perhaps you married your wife because she was so practical and level-headed. You knew she'd take good care of a family. Do you still bless her for that, or do you feel weary because she keeps suggesting financial and home improvement projects?

Too often, we can ignore the goodness that we deliberately brought into our lives. Instead, we focus on the miserable. That isn't realistic, either. It's just miserable.

How sympathetic are we toward our lovers' trials and responsibilities? Sometimes we're too envious to be sympathetic. So often, we believe our lovers' ways of life are much easier than our own. We can all relate to the struggle for sympathy between a working husband and a wife who works in the home:

"He has it easy," she says. "He's surrounded by all

those gorgeous secretaries and eats lunch at a nice restaurant every day. All I have is the leftover peanut butter and jelly. I haven't had a new dress in three years. People respect him because he 'works.' But when I go to a party, people ask if there's anything I *do*."

Meanwhile, her husband says, "She has it easy. If she doesn't want to do the laundry today, she doesn't have to. I have to do this tough job every day, whether I like it or not. I have to get up in the morning. I have to go out when it's zero. She can stay in the house."

It's silly, isn't it? We even laugh about it, but we do it, nevertheless.

Instead of being so aware of our own sacrifices, we should be aware of the sacrifices our spouses make. If our spouses didn't love us, they wouldn't go to that job every day, clean the house, or take the children to school. They'd sit back, relax, and say, "Why should I be unhappy? Let him shoulder the load"; "Let her bring in all the money."

Our lovers' responsibilities are more than drudgery. They're gifts. Unfortunately, though, we rarely see them that way. Instead, we're always focusing on what we don't have. Deep down, we think we're supposed to be that way. If we're too grateful, someone might say, "Pollyanna, get your head out of the clouds."

We deliberately torture ourselves with hurtful fantasies; ones that aren't even true. How about the old classic "I wish I'd married . . ."

Maybe you envy your girlfriend who married a doctor. If someone told you, "Look, dear. He's never at home, he ignores his family, and in five years he'll be bald as a billiard ball," you'd call that person a spoilsport.

Or take the case of the man who wishes he'd married the sexy dish at work. Imagine that's you. Now imagine a friend telling you, "Know why she looks so good? Because she puts her face in a mudpack every night. That hair costs five hundred dollars a year. And when her husband wants to make love, what's she doing? Her nails." You probably wouldn't believe it.

So on we go, having our "fun," making ourselves feel terrible. That isn't what Christ called us to do. Even if He'd remained silent on the issue, it would be pretty silly behavior.

Are you sympathetic toward your lover? I'm speaking of more now than pitching in with the housework or watching the family budget. You must let your lover know you appreciate his or her work. You must find meaningful ways to express thoughts like this one: "I'm so grateful that you do all these things for me, and for the children, too. You do them so well, and I know they're not easy." Now, this must be more than an occasional pat on the back or a nice word that almost sounds dutiful.

Quite a while ago, I was at a convention where hugs were the customary form of greeting. I hugged people whether I knew them or not and said, "Hi, I'm Chuck Gallagher." Often, a man I was hugging would immediately push me away and say, "You're Chuck Gallagher? I want to shake your hand." The hug was all right until it really meant something.

You see how gestures and even words become so customary with us? They lose their meaning.

Sympathy needs a little imagination. To convey it, speak your thoughts a little differently from the way you otherwise might; use, maybe, a change of intonation or facial expression. Your lover is used to hearing you say, "Yeah, thanks." You want to convey an added message: "How wonderful you are to do that."

Love the Brothers, Have Compassion

Compassion is deeper than sympathy. Husbands, do you really know your wives' pain? Wives, do you experience your husbands' suffering?

All of us are mature adults. We can't have lived as long as we have without accumulating a fair number of scars.

How compassionate are we because her father never hugged her; because she just doesn't feel comfortable with her body? How much tenderness is in our hearts because his mother nagged him to pieces? Any time he hears a feminine voice, he cringes.

It doesn't have to be that extreme. Maybe a husband just doesn't see himself as all that lovable, or a wife doesn't see herself as all that capable.

Maybe our lovers' wounds are long buried, but still alive and painful. Our lovers probably don't complain of them; they don't realize how much they hurt. Maybe he lost his father at twelve, or she always wanted a sister; she was raised with six brothers. Maybe he was an only child.

We can't rectify these lifelong hurts, but we can help the healing process by giving our lovers our compassionate hearts today.

Maybe our lovers' hurts are physical. We're usually more compassionate about physical pain, but how often do we stretch ourselves to be as compassionate as we can be?

It's especially hard when physical pain becomes a way of life. Maybe a wife has constant migraine headaches. After a while her husband gets used to them. He encourages her to lie down; he takes over around the house, then entertains himself with the paper until she's up and around again. He isn't fully suffering with her.

What happens when a husband has a touch of bursitis? Perhaps his wife thinks, "What can I do about it?" She notices the flash of pain across his face and says, "Pretty bad tonight, isn't it?" She's sympathetic, but she isn't fully suffering with him, either.

In both cases, their actions are good. They're probably better than someone else's actions, but they're not filled to the brim with compassion. Again, we have much more compassion than we use. As in the parable of the talents, we're asked to use that compassion to the full.

Be Self-Effacing

This command of St. Peter's is probably the hardest one in this Scripture passage. Can we honestly say we're self-effacing?

Now, I'm not speaking of a milk toast or a nothing. I'm speaking of a person like John the Baptist. If you'll recall, his thundering denunciations and unswerving proclamation of the Lord's message were anything but spineless. He was a fireball. He was also self-effacing. In John 3:30, he said of Jesus, "He must grow greater, I must grow less."

I'm not speaking of becoming a slave to others or encouraging the children to pay attention to the other parent instead. I'm speaking of selflessness, of seeing that our lovers get the attention, affection, and healing they need, while we cease being preoccupied with our own.

For instance, who gets the attention at home? Maybe we make sure it's us.

On the other hand, maybe we're a bit shy, so our spouses really do get the lion's share. That may not mean we're self-effacing. We may merely lack assertiveness. Perhaps we don't need much attention, but when we do, everything screeches to a stop while the family gives us our due.

On the other hand, people who are not self-effacing—let's call them proud—may not demonstrate that pride by ranting and raving and demanding. The proud person can be a quiet type who controls the atmosphere in the home by his or her very quietness. The proud person can be dedicated to fairness or even generosity. "I will always give you equal measure," he or she seems to say. "In fact, it will be pressed down and overflowing. I'll give you even more than you give me, but I have to have mine."

Incidentally, we need to look at that middle-class Madison Avenue notion we've all been bombarded with lately: "You deserve it." We "deserve" all kinds of things that cost money; everything from hair color to exercise equipment. In order to get the things we "deserve," we work harder and harder at jobs we like less and less. We set our sights on objects like restaurant meals and cars and clothes; there's no time or energy left for the God-given people in our lives. Like a car on an icy road, we feel more and more out of control, so we wander the shopping malls in search of inner peace. "After all," we say, bewildered, "everyone else gets to eat out (a new car/a hot tub) . . . I deserve that much." Oh, do we? When we're exhausted, frazzled, and broke, have we gotten what we deserved?

"Deserve" crops up sometimes as an excuse. "I deserve some attention. After all, I'm home all day," or "Well, after all, I earn the living. I do deserve a little respect when I come home," or "I pull a double shift. I deserve a break now and then."

When it comes to God's generosity, none of us is more

deserving than the rest. If we struggle for what we "deserve" in a relationship and that struggle deprives us of God's peace, what do we deserve? The whole argument begins to sound like a parody of *Alice in Wonderland*.

Let's not ask ourselves what we deserve. Let's ask, instead, "Is my life about him, is my life about her? Or is it about myself?"

We have a natural tendency to think that happiness starts with ourselves. "If I'm happy," we think, "I'll make her happy. If I'm pleased, I can be so much more responsive to him." Unfortunately, it doesn't work that way.

Now, I'm in no way, shape, or form suggesting that you allow yourself to live in anger, unforgiveness, or self-loathing while trying to please others. Not only is that hurtful, it isn't necessary. If your focus is on the loves in your life, you will naturally be happy. You'll be like a physically healthy person who feels great without thinking about it. If you're constantly focused on your need to be happier, you'll be like a hypochondriac who's miserably absorbed in minor aches and pains.

Let's say, instead, "If I please her (if I make him happy), it will be so much easier for my love to respond to me."

Never Repay One Wrong with Another

Now St. Peter's really hitting below the belt, isn't he? We don't like to think we do this. The truth is, we will graciously put up with a certain amount of trouble. Then our dignity's at stake. After all, you can't allow a woman to pull you around by the nose. You can't let a man walk all over you. "If I lose my self-respect," we think, "I won't be worth anything."

This is especially easy to do when we're under attack. Suddenly our husband or wife is angry. He's furious; she's shouting, and not kind words, either. What do we do? Shout back. Tell them off. After all, they have no right to do this to us.

We're responding to a challenge to fight. What we're not doing is thinking. On a calmer day, we'd realize he or she is naturally a good, loving person who doesn't really hate us. So what's wrong? It must be something.

In full, this passage of Peter says, "Never repay one wrong with another, or one abusive word with another; instead, repay with a blessing."

What does he mean? That we should be mealymouthed? Not at all. St. Peter is not recommending this type of exchange:

"You silly ninny. Can't you do anything right?"

"God bless you, dear."

That's not good-hearted; it's unnatural. Instead, St. Peter wants us to respond with a kind word, a gentle word, a soft word. That will, indeed, turn away wrath. We're called to see behind the anger, to learn what our lovers are really trying to say.

If you do this, Peter says, you inherit a blessing, because the eyes of the Lord are on the upright, His ear turned to their cry. That means He won't abandon you to an eternally angry spouse.

Now You Are the People of God

Are we really taking our values from the Lord, or are we taking our values from the world around us and saying, "Well, I'm not doing badly"?

282

You are a holy people. You are not called to be a "not bad" people. You are saints. I'm not just writing nice words to close out Chapter 10, and I'm not just repeating them because they were good enough for Peter. They really come from the depths of my heart because I couldn't have written these words to any but a holy people.

Consider these questions privately:

When have my words at home caused unhappiness or hurt? What would have happened if, instead of blurting it out, I had taken time to think? Exactly how would I have done that?

When have I complained of my spouse to others? How could I have stopped myself?

What are my spouse's hurts and responsibilities? How can I show sympathy and compassion for my spouse?

What steps can I take to be more in unity and agreement with my spouse?

Share these questions with your spouse:

Each of us takes turns being the speaking partner and the silent one. With that in mind, ask: Dear, how do you keep from blurting out harsh words?

St. Peter said we are a holy people, meant to sing the praises of God who called us into His wonderful light. How would I think, speak, and act if I really believed that?

Finally, let us invite God into our marriages:

Glorious Father, we ask You to be present in our marriage this day and always. Thank You for Your gift of grace, which allows us to see our flaws and gives us the courage to become more loving and selfless. Help keep us from hurting others with our anger. Let us see each other's goodness so we can speak gently and with love. Give us Your peace and prosperity, and help us to truly become one. Amen.

INTRODUCTION TO CHAPTERS 11 AND 12: SCRIPTURAL MARRIAGE

(Ep. 5:21–33)

In these last two chapters, we're tackling that most mis-understood passage in the New Testament, the one where St. Paul is supposed to tell husbands they have dominion over their wives, and that wives should be their submis-sive servants.

Do I have your attention?

Honestly, St. Paul doesn't say that at all. The Scriptures were inspired by God, that same loving God of Genesis. That first book of the Old Testament says:

God created man in the image of himself,
in the image of God he created him,
male and female he created them.

. . . God saw all he had made, and indeed it was
very good.

Genesis 1:27 and 31

Under His influence, St. Paul was inspired to make not
a document of slavery but a case for equality of the sexes.
He's recommending peace and love and great respect;
something far better than an uneasy détente of war and
chores.

Trust Him as you read this passage of St. Paul's letter to
the Ephesians:

> Be subject to one another out of reverence for
> Christ. Wives should be subject to their husbands as
> to the Lord, since, as Christ is head of the Church
> and saves the whole body, so is a husband the head
> of his wife; and as the Church is subject to Christ,
> so should wives be to their husbands, in every-
> thing. Husbands should love their wives, just as
> Christ loved the Church and sacrificed himself for
> her to make her holy by washing her in cleansing
> water with a form of words, so that when he took
> the Church to himself she would be glorious, with
> no speck or wrinkle or anything like that, but holy
> and faultless. In the same way, husbands must love
> their wives as they love their own bodies; for a man
> to love his wife is for him to love himself. A man
> never hates his own body, but he feeds it and looks
> after it; and that is the way Christ treats the Church,
> because we are parts of his Body. This is why a man
> leaves his father and mother and becomes attached
> to his wife, and the two become one flesh. This
> mystery has great significance, but I am applying it
> to Christ and the Church. To sum up: you also,

each one of you, must love his wife as he loves himself; and let every wife respect her husband.

Ephesians 5:21–33

What Does It Mean?

In a nutshell, St. Paul's message is this: Husbands, be
one with your wives; love them as fully and completely as
Christ loves His church. To you, wives, he says, let them
love you as Christ loves His church.

Neither of these commands is easy. They both require
dying to self. But as you well know, dying to self means
opening your heart to others and especially to our good
God. It's like Jesus' parable of the mustard seed. That
smallest of seeds—our sin-bound, hurting self—when
healed and allowed to bloom, becomes the biggest of trees.

In a moment, we'll examine in detail the husband's role:
how he can more fully love his wife the way the Lord
intends. Afterward, we'll examine the wife's role, including a detailed explanation of what the Lord did *not* intend.

But first, let's reexamine our call to the sacrament of
Matrimony.

Marriage Is a Prayer

Do we believe our marriages are spiritual?

Are we sure? It's easy to say a quick yes.

Marriage is spiritual twenty-four hours a day, not just
when the children are neat and clean in their best clothes.
It's not spiritual just at Christmas, at mass or church services, or after a wonderful sexual experience. Marriage is
spiritual on Tuesday—any Tuesday—even if it's spaghetti

night and the food is all over the floor. It's spiritual on Friday when we come home shell-shocked from the week.

Too often, we see God's plan as a list of sentences beginning with "not" or "shouldn't." We shouldn't fight, we shouldn't be angry with one another or hurt one another because God wants us to love one another.

God's definition of love, though, isn't like calf roping at the rodeo. We're not supposed to subdue our anger and annoyance like a wild, panicked beast. We're supposed to transcend our humanity by, again, dying to self and believing in the wonderful goodness of our lovers.

That translates into spirituality. If a stranger asked, "What spiritual things do you do?" would we answer, "Well, I'm marrying her"; "I'm marrying him"? Or would we list Scripture reading, prayer, or the sacraments?

We Catholics are invited to attend mass and receive the Eucharist every day. We consider the Eucharist a sacrament. Matrimony is a sacrament, too. Whether we're Catholic or Protestant, do we see marriage as a grace we receive daily?

Sometimes we think loving others is more in tune with the Gospel message than loving our own spouses is. If someone works in the inner city, Appalachia, or the local Sunday School program, we think they're being especially spiritual. If we, on the other hand, spend time with our families, we're only doing what comes naturally.

Do we realize our marriages are spiritualizing us, or do we merely see our spirituality helping our marriages? There's a difference.

Do we realize that our marriages are our fundamental prayer, or do we merely believe prayer helps our marriages?

Of course, we should certainly use prayer to help our

marriages, but our first prayer is our relationship with one another.

Prayer is a way of acknowledging God and reverencing Him. The best way husbands and wives can acknowledge God is by loving one another in His name.

Take an ordinary day, perhaps a normal Wednesday. We haven't had a bad day and nothing is happening tonight. We're just going to sit around and talk. During the evening, are we different from a good, loving pagan couple?

By the way, we have to understand what pagan means. Pagan has nothing to do with goodness. Pagans can be magnificent people who accomplish wonders, but they simply don't know they are children of God.

Our relationship is more than a series of actions that please God; it's more than doing the right thing, as He commanded us. It's an act of liturgy. All the normal little everyday acts of love in the living room, bedroom, dining room, and kitchen are religious acts because we are faithful couples.

Gone with the (Spiritual) Wind

We fail to live up to our potential because we don't believe Scripture is practical. After all, there are bills to pay; there are children to feed. There is so much to do. We have families to relate to, neighbors to respond to.

Because of this, we see Scripture as a beautiful dream, like a holy *Gone with the Wind*. We read, "Husbands should love their wives just as Christ loved the Church. Husbands must love their wives as they love their own bodies," and we respond as if we're watching a romantic movie.

"It's almost like paradise," we say. "Weren't Adam and Eve lucky; why did they mess it up? But the world isn't like that anymore." We decide this spiritual fantasy is meant to be read, not lived.

We use Scripture as an idea book, sifting through to see which ones apply—and which ones we can handle. If a Scripture passage seems to fit our lives, we pay attention. If it doesn't, we finally decide, puzzled, that either the writer was exaggerating or the culture has changed so much, it doesn't matter anyway.

The idea of husbands loving their wives as they love their own bodies—or of trusting husbands to do that— seems so extreme that we tune it out. It's like one of those old-time prayers we Catholics used to say after Holy Communion. They sounded beautiful and they were appropriately spiritual for the occasion, but we had no serious intention of living the type of life they spoke of.

Are We a Gospel People?

The Gospel isn't a book we read; it's a book we live. The very credibility of the Christian religion depends on how well we live it. Jesus is fleshed in us; He's placed Himself in our hands. He calls all people to experience Him by experiencing us. That's a serious responsibility—and a great honor, indeed. Furthermore, He believes we're up to it.

That means we have to live His way. To use an analogy, the Gospel is like a diet book. If we say, "Hey, I bought this diet book and it's really great reading," no one will be impressed. But if we say, "I followed the recipes, and see? I've lost fifty pounds in two months," we'll have plenty of converts.

As I mentioned in Chapter 7, we're extremely quick to say, "Oh, that passage of Scripture? I've heard it before." In our hearts, maybe without even knowing it, we add, "So I don't need to pay much attention." When we do this, we miss the whole point. It's not what's new in the Book, but rather what's new in our understanding of its message.

In other words, when we hear Scripture proclaimed, we should check ourselves out. Where do we stand in relation to both the believing people of God and these particular prophetic words? Does this Gospel speak to us? Are we experiencing it in our daily lives? How real is it for us, and how real does our example make it for the rest of our Christian community?

The Gospel is meant to be proclaimed, and that means communication. We aren't communicating if we shout the Gospel on a mountaintop while no one is around. We have to elicit a response.

In a very real way, all the Gospel statements end with a question mark. "Where do you stand with this?" they say. "Are you living this yet? Do you believe it?" The Lord is looking for our "Amen," our "I believe." That belief is more than an intellectual assent. "That sounds logical to me" simply doesn't work. "I believe" means something like "Wow! This message of the Lord is so right, so true, I have to go live it out."

Are We Saved Yet?

If the Gospel doesn't usually inspire us that way, it's probably because we have trouble believing in our own salvation. Do we believe we *are* saved, not just that we will be? Remember, Jesus already died on the cross to save us. He isn't waiting until we die. We're already free.

Now, we can't just say, "Yes, I'm saved," then sit on our laurels. We must be living that salvation.

Ask yourselves, "Does my belief in salvation affect my entire being? Can people see it because of the way I conduct myself?"

People who are hearing St. Paul's message for the first time shouldn't think it sounds bizarre. When they hear, "Husbands should love their wives, just as Christ loved the Church; wives should be subject to their husbands as to the Lord," they should be able to say, "Oh. You mean Christ loves the church as much as Joe loves Mary? And we can respond to God as Mary responds to Joe? You know, that's really something."

If people ask, "What do Christians believe about marriage?" we can't just answer, "Listen to this. This is what St. Paul says." We must say, "Come and see. Look at us."

He's Serious About This

Sacred Scripture really does give couples a vocation to love each other with the same passionate faithfulness that exists between Christ and His church. Imagine St. Paul looking you right in the eye and saying, "Will you love her as you love yourself? Will you treat him as you'd treat Jesus?" Not just "Are you doing a good job?"

We, the people of the church, are calling you to a totally different relationship. It's not a lofty ideal that an occasional saint or two might embrace. It's just as attainable as reconciliation with God, Holy Communion, or the sacrament of Baptism.

When you're baptized, you seek admission into the community of God, the very body of Jesus. We, the church, respond to you with trust and confidence. We baptize you into the death and Resurrection of Jesus: we immerse you in the saving waters of baptism.

That's not fantasy; that's a fact. When we call you a matrimonial sacrament, that's a fact, too. When we say that we, God's chosen people, believe you are to love each other as Jesus loves His church, that's not an exaggeration. We're serious.

We Christians can't be married like pagans, even good, loving pagans, nor can we simply do better at our marriages, using the world's standards as a yardstick.

We are called to be prophets. A prophet, despite the popular misconception, is not someone who predicts the future. A prophet is someone who announces God's presence in our midst by living an exemplary life. As married couples, we are specifically called to live out those words of St. Paul's. We are called to a scriptural marriage, not just a human marriage.

That means a total life-style change; it's more than being a little kinder to each other today. We can read love poetry and be moved toward kindness. Instead, we're called to be moved toward God.

Well, God, How Did I Do?

It's important not to rank and rate ourselves on this. Don't ask yourselves, "Do I have ten degrees of Ephesians 5 in me?" or think, "If that lady at church has twenty-five and the man across the street has four, I'm not as good as she is, but I sure am better than him."

We all fail. We're all sinners. The only question we should ask is: "Am I the kind of spouse I honestly want to be?"

We never have to count the number of times we fall. Did we stand up one more time? If so, we're successful.

Still we keep focusing on our achievements rather than on our yearnings. We're off base there. If we want to tell who a person really is, we can learn much more by studying that person's dreams than his or her accomplishments. Some presidents of companies have crude, impoverished souls, and there are ditchdiggers who reach the stars.

Some men and women do all the right things by their spouses and yet have no ambitions for their relationship. Others fail a lot and yet dream magnificent dreams of love.

Ask yourselves, "Do I share the world's view of marriage, or do I reach for God's?"

Who Am I?

Imagine yourself being interviewed by a newspaper reporter.

He's saying, "My editor thought your life would be worth a story. Why don't you tell me about it?"

What would you tell him? Would your story center around your job, your avocation, or outside interests? Better, you might mention a cause you've lived for or some people you've served with responsibility and love.

Even better, you might describe your personal qualities: "I'm Joe Smith and I'm a very gentle person," or "I'm a very prayerful woman," or "I'm really good with children." Now, that's an improvement, but still, is that all?

Would you tell this reporter, "The most important thing I've ever done is become Mary's husband (Joe's wife)"?

Maybe a better question for this section would be, "Who are we?"

Too often, we think marriage is something each of us accomplishes separately: The wife does wifely things and her husband does husbandly things. The two halves somehow equal one whole.

It doesn't work that way. Marriage is purely a relationship, and that relationship is determined by how much we become each other.

Do you really want to become that intimate? Sometimes we say, "That's an impossible dream," but deep down, we really feel it's a frightening one. Do you want to be that much his? Do you want to be enfleshed in her? Or do you want to be your own boss?

Our single mentality inevitably holds us back. No matter how long we've been married or how married we believe we are, we're still living with a singles orientation. All our objections to unity are based on maintaining our own thoughts or independence of life-style. We haven't really made the leap into marriage.

The heart of matrimony is the community of life we establish in each other. The key to that community of life is not merely to live in the same house, sleep in the same bed, eat at the same table, or go together to the same party—and even stay together during the party. The key is to have the same goals and values. It's not merely avoiding conflicts or disagreements; it's two hearts beating as one. It has to be a constant effort, not just something that's nice when it happens. We have to make a deliberate choice to dream her dreams, to make his hopes ours.

We may have very good and lofty dreams; probably the dreams we had even before we were married. We should take on our lovers' dreams, not because the dreams are so good, but because our lovers are.

We husbands must believe that we are enfleshed in our wives just as Christ became fleshed in His Church. We wives must trust our husbands to make us glorious in a relationship that reflects His great love.

This kind of unity is possible, but we must be open to God's grace. St. Paul admits that this is not something we would think of ourselves. He says this is a mystery of great significance. He also explains why we are called to it. When we accomplish this or even strive to accomplish it, we are revealing Jesus' love relationship with His church.

The next chapter will be written for husbands, and the one following, for wives. It would be a good idea for everyone to read both chapters. Although they're written to an individual marriage partner, the human traits described will apply to both spouses. And that means you!

Chapter 11

Enfleshed in Love

(Ep. 5:21–33)

It had been an exhausting day; Jesus had been swamped with paralytics and cripples, sinners and Saducees. All he wanted now was to soak his feet, smoke a pipe, and curl up with the daily paper.

"Bad day, eh?" said one of his apostles.

"Not a bad day," Jesus replied, "but I sure am shot."

"Can I talk to you for a minute?" the apostle said. "I'm exhausted, too. I had some problems expelling demons and I want to confess my sins."

"Yeah, great," Jesus mumbled, his nose in the paper. "Just a minute. Hey, you wouldn't mind getting me some supper, would you? We can talk then."

"I guess so," the apostle said. "You know, I also wanted to talk about us. You've been pretty busy—"

"That's for sure."

"—But I really feel—"

"By the way," Jesus interrupted, "you'd better start getting things ready for the Passover, okay? Don't want anything to go wrong on the big night."

By now, you've realized that's not really Jesus. He wouldn't behave that way. He doesn't recommend that husbands behave that way to their wives, either. For one thing, their wives would quickly consign them to a place God doesn't deserve to go, even in a parody.

For another thing, such high-handed behavior obviously isn't His way. Remember Him washing His apostles' feet?

In all seriousness, what is His plan of life for husbands? Let's repeat this portion of Ephesians 5:

> Be subject to one another out of reverence for Christ
> . . . Husbands should love their wives, just as Christ
> loved the Church and sacrificed himself for her to
> make her holy by washing her in cleansing water
> with a form of words, so that when he took the
> Church to himself she would be glorious, with no
> speck or wrinkle or anything like that, but holy and
> faultless. In the same way, husbands must love their
> wives as they love their own bodies; for a man to love
> his wife is for him to love himself. A man never hates
> his own body, but he feeds it and looks after it; and
> that is the way Christ treats the Church, because we
> are parts of his Body. This is why a man leaves his
> father and mother and becomes attached to his wife,
> and the two become one flesh. This mystery has great
> significance, but I am applying it to Christ and the
> Church. To sum up: you also, each one of you, must
> love his wife as he loves himself . . .
>
> Ephesians 5:21–33

Did He Say Anything About Men?

We've all heard this Gospel before, but we probably didn't listen to its message because we were distracted by those words that came just before: "Wives should be subject to their husbands as to the Lord."

As soon as we men hear that, we're thinking, "Oh, oh." She's sitting there rigid and we're trying to disappear. We don't want it stirred up.

Even back in blatantly sexist days, we didn't pay attention to the second part of this passage because it just didn't grab us; the other statement was so strong and attention-getting.

We also tune out the second part because it concerns marriage. Marriage is a woman's occupation, or so we think. Almost anything about marriage is written for women. Even if it isn't, women are usually the only ones who read it.

Really, men, if we were as current on our jobs as we are on our marriages, we'd be on the unemployment line. Isn't that true? What do we read about? Sports; politics, perhaps. What serious reading do we do? Maybe not any. Even when we do, it tends to be something to help us get ahead—and getting ahead doesn't involve marriage.

The Gospel is calling us to take the lead in creating a total environment of love in our marriages.

A total environment of love?

It sounds like a fairy tale. We'd rather be reasonable— remember reasonable?—and do what's expected, then relax until she complains. In other words, we'd rather be irresponsible.

That kind of behavior makes a wife question her ambitions for the marriage. She carries a tremendous burden of doubt. "Why am I always the one who isn't happy?" she thinks. "Why am I the one who's looking for more?" She begins to wonder if something is wrong with her.

The answer, usually, is that something's wrong with us men. We're not putting enough emphasis on our marriages. We're finding our fulfillment in other things. Then we blame her either explicitly or implicitly because she's not satisfied. This wouldn't happen if we listened to St. Paul.

Me First, Dear

We must take St. Paul's teaching to heart. He says, "Husbands should love their wives, just as Christ loved the Church . . ."

How did Christ love the church? He "sacrificed himself for her." In other words, he submitted Himself to her. Scripture shows this quite clearly.

From the very beginning, Jesus submitted Himself to His people. He came down to earth and became one of us. As a child, and even as an adult, he was subject to Mary and Joseph. He was also obedient to His Father's will. In John 8:28,29, He said, ". . . I do nothing of my own accord. What I say is what the Father has taught me; he who sent me is with me, and has not left me to myself, for I always do what pleases him."

He died in submission to us, too. He didn't have to be mocked, beaten, and crucified, but He let us do that to Him. You'll recall that when Jesus was betrayed by Judas in the garden of Gethsemane, one of His followers cut off the high priest's servant's ear. In Matthew 26:53,54, Jesus asked that disciple, ". . . do you think that I cannot appeal to my Father, who would promptly send more than twelve legions of angels to my defence? But then, how would the scriptures be fulfilled that say this is the way it must be?"

Do you see? In everything, He submitted to His people and His Father's will.

If a husband is to answer the Lord's call to sacramental marriage, he must take the leadership in submitting himself to his wife, exactly as Jesus submitted himself to the church. He must surrender himself profoundly, relentlessly, and totally to this woman who is flesh of his flesh.

A sacramental wife is called to subject herself to her husband *in response to his subjection to her*. If she seems to have difficulty doing this, it's because she has no model. The Lord says that model is you. He's calling you to take the lead.

In this chapter, we'll discuss what form that leadership takes.

Husbands Should Love Their Wives, Just as Christ Loved the Church

How exactly did Jesus sacrifice Himself for us, submitting Himself to His church? Was He merely good to us? Did He just drop in to spend some time with us, then go about His business? Did He lay down a list of rules to be followed—or else? No; He immersed Himself in a total, all-consuming passion.

Jesus took us on; He became one with us. He said about us, the Church, "This is my Body." He showed this not just in His actions, but in His whole way of life. He became the God-Man.

Jesus wasn't just a good provider who lived, preached, died, and was buried, then rose again because it was in the script. He was a lover who pitched His tent among us. Not only did He become a real, flesh-and-blood human being, but He delighted in His humanity. He lived our way of life, and He finds His very identity in us.

What did He call Himself? The Son of man.

A name is a very precious thing. Most of us dearly love our names, and many of us have traded the formal names we were given for nicknames. All my life, until adolescence, I was called Charles, and I was really a Charles kind of kid. But one loving teacher saw the man who was trying to emerge. He called me Chuck, and that name is now very precious to me. I don't want to be a Charles. I don't even want to be a Charlie.

Some people call me Charlie. I don't want to make an issue of it, but I stiffen up every time. If you call me Charlie, I think, you don't know me.

We have trouble knowing Jesus because we don't call Him by name. We just call him God. He is God, of course, but He prefers our name: the Son of man. He summons all men and women throughout the world to find Him through us, the church. We are His Body.

I can't discover you unless I respond to your body. How can I know your soul if I don't listen to the words you speak, watch your face, see the way your hands move, sense the way you feel, and learn how you touch? I may say instead, "We have a spiritual relationship." That means I don't know you.

Why Don't You Tell Me About Your Life, Mr. Christ?

Remember the reporter who asked us, in the last chapter, what was significant in our lives? Suppose he turned his attention now to Jesus.

What would our Lord say? "Well, I started a worldwide religion; I was a great healer. I even brought people back from the dead. I saved a lot of souls . . ." No; He wouldn't say that.

Jesus finds His success not in the things He has done, but in how we respond to Him. That is also a husband's vocation. A man has to examine himself according to his standing with his wife. She is bone of his bone, flesh of his flesh.

Does he find his identity in her response or in some other standard of success? Is he as single-minded in his relationship with his wife as Jesus was with us? Is he as complete in making no distinction between his wife and himself?

Ask yourselves, "Am I trying to become one with my wife or am I simply living harmoniously with her?" The point isn't whether she voices any complaints; it's whether we, the church, do. We call you to be a sacrament, to treat her as Jesus treats the church.

A sacramental marriage calls a man to become incarnate with his wife just as Jesus enfleshes Himself with us. I can't state it too strongly: a sacramental husband makes no distinction between his wife and himself. St. Paul says, ". . . husbands must love their wives as they love their own bodies; for a man to love his wife is for him to love himself."

Ask yourselves, "Do I see her as my body, or as an important but very separate person?"

We husbands may acknowledge our responsibilities toward her and admit we have opportunities to make her life more pleasant. We may want to do that; we really do care for her. Beyond that, though, we live our own lives because we don't want to take on too much responsibility.

We don't want the kind of overwhelming intimacy Jesus is calling us to.

If we could listen to our wives' hearts, we would hear a constant, painful cry of desire to be closer to us. The words of Scripture are not foolish. They're rooted in human experience.

We husbands are tempted to say this total intimacy isn't real; it's something no one really does. Before we actually voice those words, let's take a good look at our wives. Do we see their pain, their desperate search for oneness?

A man has to ask himself, "How married am I?"

Sure, we do a lot of married things and we've stopped a lot of single ones, but are we living a married way of life? Or are we merely two nice people who have affection for each other, some concern, a history together, and are living side by side in peace and harmony? At least, is that how it seems to us?

Those last few words are important. We've described the marriage as we see it, not necessarily as our wives do. A man has to be very cautious when he evaluates his marriage. Masculine goals in marriage do not necessarily match feminine ones. In general, wives' ambitions for their marriages are much higher than their husbands' ambitions. We husbands must listen to our wives and respond on their terms.

Are There Still Male Chauvinists?

Yes, indeed. In fact, male chauvinism is still the biggest barrier to God's plan for husbands.

The expression has gone out of style, and in a sense, that's good. Male chauvinists are a vanishing breed; that is, if they're the men who make wise-guy remarks like "Darn right. Keep 'em barefoot and pregnant."

But the superiority is still with us; it's merely become sophisticated.

To some degree, all of us have been trained to be chauvinistic. We may view women as good people with nice ideas who are unfortunately ill equipped to face the grit and challenge of the real world. Then we're protective— and superior. We may not believe we do this, but who counts the collection baskets after church? Who's in charge of the parish council?

Most men have poor personal self-images but feel great pride in men. They're like the Irish. Most Irishmen feel lousy about themselves but think the Irish are great.

We men may not feel all that good about ourselves, but we certainly think men are the world's movers and shakers.

Sometimes we use equality to become more discriminatory than ever. "I support her career," we might say. "I'll let her do anything she wants, whatever she finds fulfilling." That's not as liberal as it sounds. Men have done that for centuries. They simply stayed away from anything women were interested in.

Today, their grandsons are proud progressives. "Sure, dear," they say. "Go ahead, pursue your goals; good for you." Then they walk away. They're no more part of their wives than their grandfathers were, nor are they allowing their wives to be part of them.

Sometimes there's an unspoken finish to these comments: "If she finds her own interests, she'll leave me alone," or "If she has to wrestle a boss like mine, maybe she'll understand me better." With this attitude, we're not accepting our wives any more than before, nor are we respecting them. We're just avoiding a fight. If they're upset about something, whether it's equal pay or respect for those who work in the home, we decide we'd better let them have their own way. That must infuriate our women.

I'm a Man's Man, and Proud of It

Too many husbands form their identities by watching other men rather than by becoming one body with their wives. These men tend to judge success by their nonmarital accomplishments.

You might say, "Well, that's understandable. You don't go to a woman and ask, 'What's a man?' " But you do, because if there weren't any women, a man would be just a human. The very notion of maleness is based on relationship with women.

If a man chooses to be single, he can determine his own male life-style, but as a husband, it's she who tells him who he is. He's not *a* man, he's *her* man, and that's personal and very precious. It takes him out of a category and makes him an individual.

Most men won't discover themselves through their wives. Sure, they'll adapt to their wives—often, a form of superior toleration—but that's not the same.

If a man lets other men determine his identity, his wife is merely an outside interest. She has her rights, and he respects these. She has her needs and desires, and he knows he has a responsibility to respond. He does his best, but his wife is definitely a distinct entity. Why? Because women aren't males; they're different. Sometimes they're almost alien.

This attitude undercuts St. Paul's whole message. If she's different and distinct, she's not part of a man's own body. She's a separate body, albeit an attractive one. She's a responsibility, probably his prime responsibility.

In a discriminatory setting, the man customarily fits his wife into his life-style rather than his life-style into his relationship with his wife. Now, he'd never put it in those terms. He'd say, "Gee, honey, we have to have bread on the table. I've got to do the job . . . We have to move to this other city because this promotion offers so much for us . . . I have to get my rest. I can't sit up all night and talk . . . You can't expect me to be that involved with the kids. I've been working all day."

Think about it.

She Pays Great, but How Much Does She Love You?

A husband can use his job as a smoke screen to avoid an intimate relationship. "I'm doing this for you, dear," he says. "Everything I do is because I love you." Usually he's quite sincere. There's no doubt: material support is part of his responsibility and he is very faithful to that. In fact, he's usually faithful even if it's destroying him.

His work may be terrible, but it's not absolution. Too often, he excuses himself from relationship with her because he handles the job well.

Many men are married to their jobs. That's a timeworn old expression, isn't it? It won't go away until we do something about it.

We can't just say, "Well, that's the way men are." St.

Paul is saying very clearly that sacramental husbands are *not* supposed to be that way.

We can allow the job to keep us from relationship in other ways. For instance, we can bring the job home with us.

Sometimes we do it literally: "I just have a few plans to make, honey," or "I have to go over these reports," or "I have a workshop to prepare," or "I have to go over those figures because the audit is coming up."

Even worse, we bring home the job's atmosphere. This happens more frequently, drowning the whole family in work-related anger or depression. Maybe the foreman's been on our back, or maybe we're the foreman and we've been on everyone else's back. When we come home, everybody has to deal with our job traumas.

Our male superiority leads us to ascribe emotionalism to women, and only to women. "Women have their moods, you know," we say wisely on the train going to work. "Men have to look at a problem objectively, then make a logical decision. We can't afford to be moody." We men are unreal. Sometimes we actually believe that nonsense. We don't realize how all-pervasive our own moods can be.

We use the pressures of work to excuse our lack of involvement at home. We blackmail our wives by letting them know how good we are to support them. "You think I like that job?" we say indignantly. "Remember, I'm doing it for you." Now, that can be true, but not when we say it that way.

We haven't fooled our wives, either. In the last twenty years, they've been reading between the lines. "Oh, you hate it, do you?" they've responded. "I could do with that kind of misery." And they've demanded equal careers. They refuse to be little girls waiting for handouts.

We men have to change.

Consider the Source

Frequently we men find more fulfillment in the good opinions of our bosses and coworkers than we do in our wives' compliments.

A wife can praise her husband to the skies and he'll take it very much in stride, but when a boss passes him in a corridor and says, "Nice work, Jack," he'll live for months on that. He'll say, "I was talking to the big boss in the company the other day"—actually, it was two years ago—"and do you know what he said to me?"

How many times does a man brag to his friends about some compliment his wife gave him?

Not very often. His friends would probably laugh at him. Even if they didn't, he still wouldn't take her praise seriously. Compliments at work are much more important. Many men live for those moments of recognition, and that's sad.

Periodically we evaluate whether we're close to the next promotion or even closer to the pink slip. How frequently do we inventory our relationships with our wives?

Do we ever ask others how to be better married? I don't mean casually, with the people standing in line at the cafeteria, but with good friends. Sure, we discuss what wives are like and where they're putting the pressure on us. Then we encourage one another to resist that pressure. Do we ever talk, not about how she doesn't understand us, but about how we can help her understand us better?

She doesn't understand us because we don't tell her much. She has to guess what's going on inside us. How many times are our conversations with our wives limited to injustices in the office, descriptions of some guy we don't like, lectures about money or the kids? Those conversations aren't personal. Since we aren't being open and intimate, there's no fear of rejection.

Do we talk about promoting our marriages with the same seriousness as promoting our products? That job is our biggest cover, no question about it. What have we done about it?

You Can't Afford to Be Out of Body

These deep-seated attitudes of superiority encompass more than our jobs. They also crop up at home. An ideal husband is supposed to be generous—on a man's terms. That is, materially. We measure this ideal by asking what kind of presents he gives her and how much they cost, where he took her for dinner and how extravagant the vacation was.

A husband sees himself as a provider, a present giver, a janitor and a caretaker, a gofer, an escort, an entertainer, an assistant baby-sitter—by the way, isn't this dehumanizing?—but on many nights, he simply is not present to her. He's living his own way of life, and she's his companion. He's not even beginning to answer St. Paul's call to make no distinction between his wife and himself.

Many of us have trained ourselves to memorize the last five words she says. When she complains, "You're not listening to me," we can say, "I certainly am. This is what you just said." But we're not really there for her, and she knows it.

We seal our fates by thinking that's the way men are supposed to be. We men are objective, not subjective. We have thoughts rather than feelings, and we wouldn't want to trade. We may generously say, "Well, Sandy is the feeling one in our family," but there's a lot of superiority in that kind of remark. We're really saying, "I'm the one who has the head on my shoulders," or "Feelings are little fluffy things and they're for women."

Too often, we don't think of our wives as unique individuals. They're members of a category. We do this when we say, "Aren't women so . . ." "Women usually . . ." or "Isn't that the truth about women . . ."

We defeat her with that kind of mentality. After all, she is a woman, but she's not all women and she's not just any woman. She is "my woman." She's not someone outside, but someone who is flesh of our flesh.

Don't be afraid you can't change. Have some faith in your own initiative. If your training as a doctor, a salesman, or a construction man were becoming obsolete, you'd darn well take refresher courses. You'd make sure the opportunity for retraining didn't pass you by, because you can't afford to be out of work. You can't afford to be out of body either, and that means you have to bring your wife inside. You can do it, too; St. Paul wasn't just killing time by writing a love story.

After You, Dear

Paul, by the way, would also disapprove of the attitude that the man takes care of the woman. Isn't that arrogant? She's no little girl in patent-leather shoes, needing only suitable ribbons to tie in her hair and a husband to pacify her.

If a man does this, he keeps his male role at the expense of unity. Marriage becomes recreation rather than a way of life. It's something he does after his day is over; after he's accomplished his events of importance. It's for weekends and off-hours. It's where he gives what he has left over.

We may say that marriage is our most important accomplishment and the most vital part of our lives, but we certainly don't live that way, and actions speak louder than words. Our wives come second. Usually we don't even think twice about it. Only when she raises a big storm do we even realize there may be a problem.

We wouldn't treat our bodies that way. We're very sensitive to every little ache or pain that interferes with our physical well-being. We have to be just as sensitive toward our wives.

When we embrace a discriminatory attitude, we come to believe in a division of labor—and love. The bills and his job are a man's responsibilities, but the home front and the marriage are hers to command. If she's not complaining, the marriage must be fine.

Some of us will say, "Women are never satisfied; they always have a gripe." Perhaps we have to hear gripes before we'll move. Maybe if we took the initiative, our homes would be at peace.

St. Paul is calling us to take the initiative in examining our marriages. When we do, we need to understand the tremendous love that dwells in our wives' hearts.

She's not asking more *from* us; she's asking more *of* us. After a while, of course, a woman may give up. She realizes she isn't going to get us, so she has to make do with the things we're willing to give her. We heave a sigh of relief and say, "Well, finally things are settled down." They are; about six feet deep. We can't see it, but we're sinking. She's our last hope. If she gives up, we'll wander adrift in a duty-filled, impersonal marriage.

312

The Lord's call to be a husband is a glorious one. It asks us to make no distinction between our wives and ourselves. When we hear the statement "What God has united, human beings must not divide" (Mk. 10:8), we assume it applies only to divorce. Actually, in most homes, we husbands are dividing what God has united because we want to live a male way of life with a woman on the side.

To Be One in Tenderness

Physical, mental, and spiritual tenderness is such a beautiful gift from a man to his woman. Sometimes we husbands are tender physically but not mentally. Tenderness means so much to a woman. Ask any woman, married or unmarried, young or old, what qualities she wants in her lover, and tenderness is always there.

Some women will say they want a certain standard of living. Others will insist he has to be blond, six feet tall, or both. Some women say he has to have brains, he has to be in a certain type of profession, care for people, love children, or be religious. But all look for tenderness in their men.

How desperately she seeks our tenderness.

We're inclined to be tender only when we feel like it. If we're in a tender mood tonight, we show our tenderness. But that's a response to ourselves, not to our lovers.

Tenderness, whether mentally, physically, or psychologically, can be a decision. Its reward isn't the mere pleasure of feeling tender but the fulfillment that tenderness gives her and the unity it helps achieve.

Tenderness is important. We shouldn't merely nod, saying, "Yes, that's sweet. Women do like that, and I try to be that way." Most likely we only try when it seems important: when she's distraught or we're in a particularly tender mood.

We have to start thinking about how we can improve our tenderness quotient. We have to force ourselves to do this just as we force ourselves to jog, study for an exam, or drag into the office when we're sick. We can ask for the grace to create an environment of tenderness within our homes. It won't happen overnight, but each day we'll improve a little. In time, we will truly see the results.

First, we must remember when we've been tender, what helped create that feeling and helped express it meaningfully to our wives. We should recall what destroys a tender mood or an attitude that would lead to tenderness. Then we must take steps to eliminate those destructive influences, thoughts, or behaviors.

We men are called to take the lead in creating that tender environment in the home. To do so, we have to be as willing to work on tenderness in our marriages as we are to work on success in our jobs. We can't leave our marriages at the mercy of accidental happenings, and we shouldn't leave the initiative to our wives.

Tenderness of heart and soul, mind and conversation, is an inestimable gift to our beloved wives. To give it, we should place three thoughts where we'll never forget them: a memory of how anxiously she desires our tenderness, how significantly that tenderness changes her whole day, and how much more it would mean if she could look forward to tenderness as a normal, everyday occurrence.

This tenderness shouldn't be intermittent or merely a

special bonus in her life. It should be as free and all-encompassing as the air she breathes.

The Unity of Joy

Most husbands do a wonderful job when it comes to selflessness. I've mentioned some of these before, but I want you to know, again, how genuinely good you are.

You truly seek your wife's happiness in sexual intercourse. It's a rare husband who isn't disappointed if his wife isn't pleased with their lovemaking.

Another of your beautiful qualities is your lack of jealousy. In social events, you honestly don't want the attention for yourself. You'd much rather have people pay attention to your wife; you're delighted when someone thinks she's funny or a good cook, is dressed nicely or knows how to run a party.

You also feel it's much more important for your wife to be pleased with your home than it is for you to like it. Now, sometimes this comes from indifference, but it's usually caused by your real tenderness toward her and a willingness to sacrifice your comfort or taste to suit her desires.

You really want your children to be tender and loving toward their mothers. You're much more upset when they don't reverence your wife than when they show lack of respect for you personally.

St. Paul really cares for you and your wife. He offers his words to give you hope and direction and a goal that will lead to greater happiness.

We should keep this in mind all the time. His letter to the Ephesians isn't a burden; it's a game plan for joy. We have to work to get rid of our own game plan and the world's game plan. We have to integrate the Lord's plan into our way of living.

If Your Wife Is Your Body, Better Give 'er a Pinch

When you get up in the morning, you mentally check yourself out. Maybe it takes a little while to get the sand out of your eyes. It could be halfway through shaving or after you get out of the driveway, but at some point you decide how you are that day.

You'll say, "I feel pretty good," or "Uhh, I feel shot," or "What a boring day it's going to be." Your body's mostly responsible for that conclusion. Either it's sluggish or coursing with blood; either you feel chipper or you have stiff knees and a bit of a headache.

When you check how you're feeling, you should be checking with your wife. How is she, and not just physically? How fully does she feel loved by you? Does she know what it's like for her lover to treat her as he treats himself?

Your day should be determined by your evaluation of her happiness. That way, you make no distinction between your wife and yourself. That's a powerful statement, but it can be true if you want it to be.

Heavenly Treatment

Since we've been called to treat our wives as Jesus treats the Church, let's examine Jesus' life. What did He do, exactly? Let's take some cases in point.

*   *   *

In John 15:15, He said, ". . . I have made known to you everything I have learnt from my Father."

Do we men let our wives know what is inside us? Many husbands keep private places within themselves. Can we truthfully say to our beloved wives, "I have told you everything that's inside me. There isn't any of me today that you don't know"?

"But that isn't so easy to do," you might want to say. "I'm naturally not too reflective a guy. I don't look inside myself that much, much less talk about it."

That's all right. That's where you are right now. But you should start being different for your wife's sake. She needs to be part of you, and she can't be part of you unless you tell her what's in there.

In John 10:10, Jesus said, "I have come so that they may have life and have it to the full."

Why have you come into marriage?

Many husbands don't understand that their life's purpose is to give their beloved wives abundant happiness. They believe they can add to her well-being and they really want that. But her fulfillment is her own responsibility, they think.

Jesus didn't think that way, though. Our whole way of life is different because He has been to us. He didn't come to teach us a little more than we knew before; He didn't come to improve things around here. He came to give us a totally new way of being, and He did this because we are His flesh.

Likewise, men, your wife's whole life should be totally different, fresh and new in hope and joy because she is one with you. You have let her into your life so she wouldn't be alone any longer. Now she is full of you and your love for her; she doesn't have to make it on her own anymore.

Jesus said, "Come to me, all you who labour and are overburdened, and I will give you rest" (Mt. 11:28).

Many husbands offer their wives every refreshment but themselves. They suggest a night out with the girls, a trip to the mall, freedom from the children for a Saturday.

But Jesus didn't say, "Boy, do I have a way to take your mind off your troubles." He said, "Come to me and I will give you rest."

When our wives are frazzled, lonely, disturbed, or not feeling up to par, do we say, "Come to me," or do we offer them all sorts of suggestions to take them outside themselves? We do this largely because we don't believe in our power to heal. St. Paul doesn't agree. Neither does the Lord. They not only believe we can do it, they are calling us to.

Without question, our wives' heaviest burdens are the children. That's partly because of the children's natural demands, but mostly because they don't have full-time fathers. I mentioned this in detail in Chapter 4, but it bears repeating: Many husbands are good men. They're well-intentioned, but they're not really there.

A wife is not fundamentally refreshed if her husband pitches in only when she's desperate, or if he gives her little rewards like praise and an occasional dinner out. The only true refreshment a loving husband can give is to become an actively involved father.

A woman can't believe her husband truly loves her unless he loves those children. No matter what else he may do, she's going to feel deserted and alone.

Women receive a lot of put-downs about having children, especially if there are more than two. These insults come from family, friends, neighbors, even strangers. It hurts our loves when others think they are foolish or lacking independence and creativity because they have families.

If a woman's husband is as involved with the children as she is, those attacks don't bother her. When they do sting, it's because they are echoed at home.

In John 10:14, Jesus said, "I am the good shepherd; I know my own and my own know me."

Often, husbands don't really know their wives. Do you *really* know your wife, not just know about her?

"Sure, I know her; we've been married for twenty years. She likes to sleep with the window open and she likes anchovy pizzas. She gets mad when I'm five minutes late and even madder when she hears about cruelty to animals . . ."

That's fine; it has to start there. But really knowing the other person is a much deeper matter. Often, a husband doesn't take enough time for that.

Jesus was referring to the Lord's knowledge: the knowledge of belonging. He said, "I know my own," not merely "I know this person because we've lived side by side for two decades." Do we know with intimacy, and do ours—our wives—know we belong to them, or are we very much our own men? We may do all the right things by them; we may live up to our responsibilities in marriage. That's good for a start, but Jesus went much further when forming a love relationship with His church.

In John 15:11, Jesus said, "I have told you this so that my own joy may be in you and your joy be complete."

How often do we talk to our wives to bring them joy? In comparison, how often do we talk to provide information, instruction, or a suitable response?

Do we even want our speech to make our beloved wives joyous? Of course we do. Then that's where we must concentrate. It isn't as difficult as it seems, nor does it call us to do all sorts of exotic tasks. We must simply tell her who we are. We must believe our wives have a beautiful need to know us. Nothing brings a wife more joy than for her husband to let her inside.

You're at the Starting Gate, And the Race Is . . . On!

In 2 Timothy 4:7, St. Paul wrote, "I have fought the good fight . . . I have run the race to the finish; I have kept the faith . . ."

When I hear these words, husbands, I really think of you. You're at the starting gate and there's no reason in heaven why you can't win.

When we do fail, it's because we don't see the tremendous power that is in us and how eager our wives are to respond. Nor do we truly understand that the Lord has placed our beloved wives' fullness in life directly in our hands.

Partly, this is because, deep down, we think our professions as lawyer, doctor, foreman, or line worker are more significant than our calling as husbands.

Actually, the greatest careers in the universe can't compare with the responsibilities and opportunities of matrimony. In St. Paul's letter to the Philippians 2:7, he said of Jesus, ". . . he emptied himself . . ."

Our call as husbands is to empty ourselves of superiority, to belong to our beloved wives rather than to the society of males. A lover wants to live in the mind of his beloved and to possess her heart.

Hey, Honey, It's Not Me!

St. Paul, in describing his relationship with Jesus, said, ". . . it is no longer I, but Christ living in me. The life that I am now living . . . I am living in faith . . ." (Ga. 2:20).

Can we speak these same words of oneness about our love relationships with our beloved wives?

Jesus spoke our language; He came as one of us. Many men simply do not speak their wives' language: the language of feelings. They believe feelings aren't masculine. That's tragic. They're depriving not only their wives, but themselves as well.

Millions of people can have the same thoughts, but each person's feelings are absolutely unique. No one else feels pain or elation, satisfaction or contentment, peace or blueness, the way you do. That particular richness is the most delightful gift you can give your wife.

Wouldn't it be tragic if a wife spoke only English and her husband spoke only Italian? Think of how that would cripple their relationship. Well, few men are fluent in the language of feelings. At best, they speak it with a heavy accent. That's so debilitating in a relationship; we simply have to become bilingual.

Let's say to ourselves, "It is no longer I, but my beloved living in me." Now, how does that phrase fit? What can we do to make it fit better?

St. Paul was no fool. He knew how much he was asking of us. The great love he describes doesn't happen easily.

We have to work at it, keep it in our minds and hearts, and pray over it.

And the Two Become One Flesh

Near the end of St. Paul's passage on married love, he wrote, "This is why a man leaves his father and mother and becomes attached to his wife, and the two become one flesh."

If I were to ask whether you were living in accordance with this passage, you'd sincerely say yes. You'd be puzzled, wondering why I even asked. After all, you left your father and mother's house years ago.

Why not put a new slant on the question? Ask yourself this: "Have I left myself and my habits, attitudes, and demands? Have I left my single way of life and become one with her?"

"This mystery has great significance," Paul added. A mystery is never understood completely; it's only gradually revealed. That's why the Lord gives you fifty years to love your wife.

Consider these questions privately:

Below is a list of Scripture passages. Each describes Christ's intimate love for His church.

Read and interpret each of these. How do they apply to your relationship with your wife? What are you doing well? What can you do better?

Matthew 11:28: "Come to me, all you who labour and are overburdened, and I will give you rest."

Matthew 19:13, Mark 10:13–16, Luke 18:15–17: Jesus
and the children.
Matthew 26:6–11, Mark 14:3–6, John 12:1–7: The
woman and the oil.
Luke 10:38–42: Martha and Mary.
John 8:2–11: The adulterous woman.
John 13:3–16: The washing of the feet.
John 13:34, 35: "Love one another as I have loved
you."

Share with your spouse:

After you and your wife read Chapter 12, write to each
other on these themes:
Beloved, you are such a delightful spouse; I have such
wonderful memories of your goodness. I can see you following God's plan for our relationship when you . . ."
(Write on more than one if you wish.)
My dear, I realize I haven't always followed God's plan
for our relationship. I am going to make the following
change(s). This makes me feel . . .

Finally, let us invite the Lord into our marriages:

Almighty Father, I truly want to follow Your plan for
our marriage. I know that, without your help, I don't have
the grace to do what you ask of me. Please send me your
Spirit so I can fully live out Your plan with my beloved
wife.
I thank you for her beauty and goodness, and for the
graces you have already given me: the grace of openness
to Your word, the grace of trust, the grace of generosity,
the grace of hope. Thank You; praise You for Your gifts to
my beloved and myself. Amen.

CHAPTER 12

I AM HERE, BELOVED, TO GIVE YOU LIFE

(EP. 5:21–33)

Wives, the Lord is using St. Paul to give us a message. It's best described by taking liberties with another Bible story. This one begins with John 13:1:

Before the festival of the Passover, Jesus, knowing that his hour had come to pass from this world to the Father, having loved those who were his in the world, loved them to the end.

They were at supper, and the devil had already put it into the mind of Judas Iscariot, son of Simon, to betray him. Jesus knew that the Father had put everything into his hands, and that he had come from God and was returning to God, and he got up from the table, removed his outer garments, and, taking a towel, wrapped it around his waist; he then poured water into a basin and began to wash the disciples' feet and to wipe them with the towel he was wearing.

He came to Simon Peter, who said to him, "Lord, are you going to wash my feet?"

Jesus answered, "At the moment you do not know what I am doing, but later you will understand."

"Never!" said Peter, "You shall never wash my feet."

Jesus fixed his gaze on him. "Why not?"

Peter was flustered. "Well, because—I just can't stand it, that's all. I should be doing things for you, not the other way around."

"Peter, I know why you feel that way. Do you want to know too?"

Peter nodded grudgingly.

"Because as long as you keep washing my feet instead of the other way around, you aren't risking anything in our relationship."

Peter was instantly angry. "You're saying I don't love you. You think that little of me—"

Jesus silenced him with an upraised hand. "If you let me do something for you, you become vulnerable. You have to trust me then. And you don't trust me, Peter."

"Trust you? Lord, I would lay down my life for you."

"Yes, but you still wouldn't trust me. It's probably because you were hurt—maybe in your romantic relationships, maybe as a child. Somewhere, you got the idea that people aren't to be trusted, especially people who say they love you. You couldn't stand their rejection, so you don't give them a chance to fail."

Peter scratched his head.

"Or you could think you don't deserve their love," Jesus added. "Your self-opinion is so low, you can't stand to let people love you. You're judgmental and con- demnatory—of yourself. Actually, Peter, I doubt that's your problem."

Peter grinned.

"There are lots of reasons why you don't let me love you," Jesus said. "But no matter what they are, unless you let me love you the way the Father says, you can have no share with me."

Peter was caught off guard. "What?"

"As long as you won't let me love you, you're keeping me outside. You've locked yourself into a shell of mistrust and self-shame and fear. It's safe there, but it's not very glorious. Peter, I have many things for you to do in my community of faith. But if you just sit there, huddled in- side yourself and thinking you're in good spiritual shape, you'll never be able to do them."

"Oh." Peter felt ashamed—and rebellious. He, have scars? He had no scars at all—and he knew it would take years to heal them. But it occurred to him that, with Jesus' love, he ought to succeed. Why not? he thought. "Well, then, Lord, wash not only my feet, but my hands and my head as well."

It May Look Like Freedom, but See That Barbed Wire?

If only we could shed our humanity that easily. Accept- ing love doesn't come naturally to most of us. We'll accept as much as we think we deserve—or we'll accept a pleasant amount, but not so much that we let down our defenses.

People who don't need others aren't the freewheeling, self-sufficient independents society thinks it's celebrating. They're hurting, wounded little children, hiding behind well-designed masks. If the masks are thick enough, they won't even know they're there.

St. Paul's Scripture passage calls us not to servitude, but to healing. Our Lord wants us to be free to live in the warmth of His love, and He shows us that love through our beloved husbands. He wants us to be free; free to share ourselves with others, free to believe we are wonderful and good, free to accept and give love, free to use our talents as whole human beings.

Let's review that Scripture passage again. Some of it describes what the Lord is asking us to do. The rest describes His promise.

> Be subject to one another out of reverence for Christ. Wives should be subject to their husbands as to the Lord, since, as Christ is head of the Church and saves the whole body, so is a husband the head of his wife; and as the Church is subject to Christ, so should wives be to their husbands, in everything. Husbands should love their wives, just as Christ loved the Church and sacrificed himself for her to make her holy by washing her in cleansing water with a form of words, so that when he took the Church to himself she would be glorious, with no speck or wrinkle or anything like that, but holy and faultless. In the same way, husbands must love their wives as they love their own bodies; for a man to love his wife is for him to love himself. A man never hates his own body, but he feeds it and looks after it; and that is the way

Christ treats the Church, because we are parts of his Body. This is why a man leaves his father and mother and becomes attached to his wife, and the two become one flesh. This mystery has great significance, but I am applying it to Christ and the Church. To sum up: you also, each one of you, must love his wife as he loves himself; and let every wife respect her husband.

Ephesians 5:21–33

The Lord Takes Away Wrinkles?

In other words: "My blessed daughter, I want to make you whole. Your husband is to wash you in the cleansing water of his love and approval, so you will be glorious, with no speck or wrinkle or anything like that, but holy and faultless. Let him; help him."

How much heartburn do we suffer because we truly aren't faultless? How many romance novels do we read, envying the heroine who's long-legged, blue-eyed, and glorious? And how much of our gross national product goes into making us "with no speck or wrinkle"?

All this time, our husbands were supposed to be doing all that for us—and making us holy as well.

For years, many of us have listened to Ephesians 5 in anger and despair. We thought it was just another put-down; another demand that we continue to be passive.

It's not that at all. Allowing yourself to be healed and loved is anything but passive. It's tremendously hard work. It will take everything you've got, spiritually, intellectually, and emotionally. It's rather like a crisis, except that exhilarating things are happening instead of traumatic ones.

I Am Here, Beloved, to Give You Life

The sad truth is, many people will never be healed. Terrified of trust, they develop alternate ways of dealing with—and sometimes manipulating—others. Each victory through masquerade or manipulation is another nail in their spiritual coffins. Ultimately they can turn away from God and humanity, living half-lives of empty loneliness or black despair.

If you've read this book thus far, or even if you're only reading these pages, that isn't happening to you. You have the courage to change.

Allowing yourself to be healed and loved, though, takes more than courage. It takes self-confidence, love, and trust. All these are graces from God, and we should pray for them. God loves it when we ask for His graces. He'll give them to us every time. Pray for them every day; it may take hours, weeks, or even a few months, but you'll begin to notice changes. Grace, by the way, snowballs. It may start small and slow, but if you're willing, it picks up depth and speed until it's a magnificent avalanche.

Some of you must be wondering why the Lord places such emphasis on self-stroking. If our purpose on earth is to love others, why are we wasting time in these selfish pursuits?

Now, that's a put-down par excellence. Who are we to say we don't deserve healing and wholeness? The Lord made us, he wants to heal us, and that should be enough.

There's another reason why we should allow ourselves to be whole: we must be healed and loved before we can give love. Maybe it doesn't seem logical, but it's like this: Trying to love others while neglecting your inner self is like trying to draw water from an empty well. You can put mud in the bucket instead, but people who drink it will be able to tell the difference. Now, won't they?

329

Let's explore the idea of being subject to the healing power of God through our beloved husbands.

It's Not Just Your Healing

Now that we've talked about your individual healing, let's apply that to you as a couple. In fact, reread the previous section, applying it to the union of yourself and your husband.

Go ahead; do that.

Now, then. The Lord is calling you as a couple to be healed; to be one whole body, just as Jesus is one with His church. He wants you to give each other His life to the full. When that happens, you can show His love to all other people.

Before we tackle the world at large, though, we should be healing our husbands. Many of our husbands have wounded children hidden inside, too, and are suffering from lack of love. Our power to heal will be a constant thread through this chapter. As you both begin to grow, him loving you, you accepting that love and loving in return, your bond of oneness will grow stronger.

By the way, your husband needs love the way he defines it. That's not because his idea is right and yours is wrong. It's because love happens not with the giver but with the receiver. For instance, imagine you and your spouse have been conversing, and he was doing most of the talking. Now, have you listened to him? Only he can say for sure. You can tell him, "I have tried to listen to you," but only he can say, "I feel listened to." Likewise, you can say, "But I did love you. Didn't you feel it?" He's the one who decides, "Yes, I feel loved by you," or "No, it's not getting through to me."

Of course, it goes both ways. Only you can decide whether you're feeling his love.

If It's Too Easy, It Probably Isn't from God

Jesus seems to have a penchant for difficult, even shocking, lessons. Remember the Last Supper? People today are familiar with the belief that Christ really is embodied in the bread and wine. But can you imagine the apostles' reactions when, in the middle of an elegant, formal dinner, Jesus began talking about eating His body and drinking His blood? They probably shuffled their feet, looked at the ground, and tried to change the subject. There He was, going off the deep end again.

Jesus baffled them—and us—another time when he met that rich young man who wanted to possess eternal life. "If you wish to be perfect," Jesus told him, "go and sell your possessions and give the money to the poor, and you will have treasure in heaven; then come, follow me" (Mt. 19:21).

After the young man went away, sad and bewildered, Jesus astonished his disciples by remarking, "It is easier for a camel to pass through the eye of a needle than for someone rich to enter the kingdom of Heaven" (Mt. 19:24).

His words clash with our modern, materialistic culture, just as they clashed with His own. The apostles expected their messiah to be a rich and powerful king. They couldn't fit this simple man of poverty into their mold, so they tried to modify Him.

So do we. Fear of the unknown is probably the greatest challenge of a thinking creature, and spiritual growth definitely involves a leap into the unknown. Sometimes we wish the Lord would behave as we expected and stop asking for difficult changes.

We will change, though, whether we want to or not. The status quo is a delicate high wire of security and safety, fear and frustration. It is anything but a steady perch. We can't remain there. We'll either fall into hopelessness—disguised as sophistication, common sense, or cynicism—or we'll reach for positive change. So let's go. We begin with trust of our Lord, who is stretching us so we'll be happier; more in harmony with Him and His world. He doesn't plan to bludgeon us for the good of our souls.

Remember, He said, "Come to me, all you who labour and are overburdened, and I will give you rest. Shoulder my yoke and learn from me, for I am gentle and humble in heart, and you will find rest for your souls. Yes, my yoke is easy and my burden light" (Mt. 11:28–30).

Ponder these words of St. Paul's. Pray over them; talk about them with each other, with friends, and with other couples in your church communities.

Pass the Dynamite, Dear

Before we do some honest soul-searching, let's blast, once and for all, some centuries-old misconceptions about this passage of Ephesians.

First, it doesn't mean that the husband is Lord. It doesn't say the husband's decisions, ideas, or attitudes represent the will of God.

Second, this passage is concerned only with relationships, not sexes. It certainly does not say, "Women, be subject to men." That would be completely out of character with the freedom and dignity Jesus offers all men and women. The idea of prostrating oneself before another in order to be dominated is alien to the message of the Gospel. Thomas Merton, one of the best-known thinkers in the contemporary church, writes, ". . . there is only one will in whose service I can find perfection and freedom. To give my freedom blindly to a being equal to or inferior to myself is to degrade myself and throw away my freedom."

None of Scripture relegates women to the role of passive rag dolls. Women played an active role in Jesus' life and He always responded with reverence and respect. Subjection, as expressed in Scripture, cannot mean a lessening of women as persons.

Paul's words, then, speak to a woman who has chosen a man to love. He and she have already established a relationship of understanding, communication, and responsiveness. They're totally committed to each other. Only then could he consider treating her as he treats his own body; only then could she be called to be subject to his love as she is to that of Jesus.

Because of the uniqueness of sacramental marriage, a wife's role is shaped by her interaction with her husband. She can't be subject to him unless he draws forth that response. The two of them must be bonded together in making this happen.

This bonding happens in love. The husband loves his wife as his own body; he gives himself up for her. The wife becomes subject to that love because its invitation at this depth is irresistible. Her joyous response inspires an even deeper love from him.

A wife who actually experiences this kind of love would have no problem in responding totally to her husband. This total response is the subjection St. Paul calls for.

Unless we see our marriages in these terms, we can't really respond to the invitation "Beloved wife, be subject to your husband's gift of total love." We won't even hear it that way. We'll hear, "Woman, be subject to this man," and we'll see it as an invitation to slavery.

You should fill your names in when you read this Scripture passage. For instance, "Terry, be subject to Joe as to the Lord. Joe, love Terry, just as Christ loved the Church and sacrificed Himself for her."

Terry might be tempted to tell Joe, "But you're not loving enough." Meanwhile, Joe might say, "Well, you're not responsive enough, either." That's human nature. We all want to examine the other person's conscience.

Be Still . . . and Know that You Are Loved

St. Paul's message calls us to accept our husbands' love, to let them consider us part of their own bodies and to make absolutely no distinction between us and themselves.

After all, we're celebrating the sacrament of Matrimony. It's much more than marriage, which is a secular contract. In marriage, two people who love each other merely come together to their mutual advantage. Instead, we've taken on a whole new way of being; we're living in, with, and through the other person.

Matrimony is not two people doing nice things for each other. It is two people *being* each other. This is St. Paul's meaning when he says the two become one flesh.

The Gospel calls your husband to live for you. It asks you to let him make you his world and his happiness. You are the woman for whom he pours out his life, just as Christ poured out His life for His Church. As his center, you are the place where he discovers his true identity. Your scriptural call is to accept his gift and support him in giving it.

St. Paul calls each of you to complete, absolute, and relentless responsiveness to your chosen husband. You must draw from him a willingness to share totally in your life. Ask yourselves, "How can I belong more deeply to my husband?"

As you read this, you may be thinking, "I just can't respond that way forever. It's too much."

But you can respond today. We live only in the present; right now, today's love is all that matters. C. S. Lewis, in his book *The Screwtape Letters,* says, ". . . the Present is the point at which time touches eternity . . . in it alone, freedom and actuality are offered . . ." Tomorrow doesn't exist yet, and the past is over. Besides, God gives us graces on a daily basis. He even told us that the burden of our whole future is too much for us to bear.

Follow the Leader? What If There's No Leader?

By the way, what if your husband isn't impressed with God's plan and isn't interested in following it?

Then you are called to pray for him, and for yourself. Not a prayer like "Dear God, make him do what he's supposed to do," but a prayer to bless him, to surround Him with God's infinite love, and to help him feel that love. He needs compassion, as much as you can give. He isn't making the first move for a number of reasons.

First, he may not know what he's supposed to do. If he does, he may believe it's too challenging or too wonderful to be real. He may be alienated from God by suffering or negative experiences with organized religion.

Perhaps you have been sending out signals that say, "Love me, but don't get too close." Maybe you unknowingly have sent him the message that his best—that is, what he considers his best—isn't enough for you. Perhaps he feels inadequate.

Perhaps he needs healing. This will come with time, prayer, and effort.

Perhaps he needs empowerment.

Perhaps he's afraid of the depth of involvement that would happen if he followed St. Paul's message. Not only would it drain his resources, he wouldn't know how to handle it.

Each husband may have a different combination of reasons for reluctance. In all cases, your prayer is a good first step. Especially, pray for compassion. As Jesus said in Matthew 6:8, ". . . your Father knows what you need before you ask him." And as he said in Luke 11:9,10, "Ask, and it will be given to you; search, and you will find; knock, and the door will be opened to you. For everyone who asks receives; everyone who searches finds; everyone who knocks will have the door opened."

If your husband is unwilling, you might reread Chapter 6's section on "How to Grow a Lover."

The Many Faces of Anger

Now let's examine the ways in which we fail to follow God's plan for our marriages.

First, especially in a hypersensitive subject like this one, we tend to finger-point: "Yes, women do *this*, but it's because men do *that*."

Be careful not to think that way, in either this chapter or Chapter 11, because it will throw a whole lot of heat and not very much light. If you tried to keep score, you would have to list which of his actions caused the flaws he's accusing you of: "Sure, I yell sometimes. It's because he doesn't care; but he doesn't care because . . ." You'd need a full notebook to keep track of all the blame and misery, and when you finished, you'd have two wounded hearts and no resolutions, except for the mistaken assumption that you didn't love each other as much as you thought you did.

The second way we lose track of God's plan is in our expression of anger.

When we speak of anger, we're usually speaking of fights. Let's examine how each partner reacts to a fight, and how these natural, harmful reactions damage love relationships and clear no air anyway. In most fights, good men and women will behave in ways that only worsen the conflict.

Men and women feel anger differently. A man's anger usually says, "Get off my back." When his wife, boss, or coworker does that, his anger fades away.

A woman's anger, on the other hand, is much more long-lasting. The reasons for this are subject to debate. Perhaps it comes from a deep-rooted feeling of powerlessness and a desperation to have some effect on the "tougher" partner. But women don't realize how much power we do, indeed, have, and how much ability we have to inflict hurt. Men dread their wives' anger; it makes them feel hopeless and leaves heavy lumps of anguish in the pits of their stomachs. Worse, it makes them feel unloved.

Anger is a feeling, and feelings are neither right nor wrong. But these by-products of anger are definitely worth giving up:

First is the desire for retaliation. Perhaps a man hurts his wife by being indifferent to her needs; by ignoring her, working overtime, whatever. She feels betrayed; she believes he doesn't care. There's no way she can *make* him care or repent his actions. He just has carte blanche to walk all over her any time he feels like it. So, partly in despair, partly in indignation, she delivers verbal punishment for his crime.

Second is the urge to provoke guilt. If a wife yields to this impulse, her husband will feel like an absolute blockhead by the time the fight is finished. This is certainly easy for a woman to achieve, and a natural human impulse, but it doesn't come from God. She would never do it in cold blood; if a friend tried to make him feel equally worthless, she'd go in swinging to defend him. After the fight is over, the man may insist he still feels good about what he's done, but he nevertheless feels like garbage. This lowers his self-respect and his ability to love. It starts a downward spiral.

Third, this anger can be ongoing. We don't think, "Yes, he failed me, but that's okay. It's over. I'll forget it." Instead, we have a panic reaction: "Dear God, he really worked me over. Is this a trend? I have to deal with it or my life will fall apart." The hurtful emotions that accompany this don't rise to the conscious surface, but they do come out in the fight.

In a fight, a woman's emotions are in full swing. She's upset; she's hurt; she's afraid and downright furious. She gives vent to most of her impulses. That is, she shouts. After all, how can she really hurt this big male creature who doesn't show much emotion and deals so capably with the world?

The man, who, no matter what he says, isn't that confident, feels attacked. The person he loves most in the world suddenly hates him from the inside out. He knows that isn't really true, but if she doesn't hate, loathe, or blame him, she's certainly giving a good imitation of it. He decides to stay calm; his getting angry won't solve anything. He tries to apologize, calm her down, tell her the situation isn't that bad. In other words, he placates her.

This makes her angrier. Who does he think he is to be so indifferent, so all-knowing or logical? This is proof positive that he really doesn't care how she feels.

The fight escalates from there until the man really is angry. As his adrenaline flows, he wants to fight or flee. He can't do either. If he leaves, the trouble will be waiting when he comes back. And he certainly can't hit her. All he can do is survive the situation and swallow that heavy pit in the center of his stomach.

Eventually, harsh words fly back and forth. Everyone is hurt; both parties wish it had never happened.

So often, though, it happens again.

What can be done about it?

There's no quick answer. Understanding and compassion for each other work; so does prayer. So does a calm, nonfrantic life-style. The biggest healer, though, is trust.

What Are My Odds, Doc?

Trust is like quadruple bypass heart surgery. If you don't get it, you'll live a restricted life and you may even die. But the thought of climbing onto that operating table is equally terrifying.

Many of our women don't trust. They're terrified of emotional surgery.

In many of us is a deeply ingrained fear that we don't have equilibrium in the relationship. The details are different for each woman. Perhaps there's a fear of being mastered, of losing our identity, of being taken for granted or becoming a servant. Certainly there's the fear of not being loved and cherished. Often, at the bottom of it is a feeling of worthlessness—that we're not as important as our husbands and deserve no more than second-rate love. We're constantly on the watch for skirmishes on the disputed territory of self-worth and lovableness. If we can defend ourselves vigorously enough, maybe that empty feeling inside us will go away.

It all boils down to lack of faith in our men. Because we cannot trust, we deny ourselves the life-giving, self-affirming knowledge that our husbands will always love us and will be there for us, no matter what.

"But he does let me down. I'm not imagining that."

That's true. But you let him down, too. You're both good, imperfect people who love each other. Flaws don't stop healthy, whole people from trusting. None of us can earn trust; it's a free gift. In fact, it's an essential gift if we want to follow God's plan.

This trust is, in a nutshell, the subjection St. Paul speaks of. Paul asks us to say to our beloved husbands, "I am yours; I belong to you. I find my true self in your love. I place myself in your hands and I give myself over to you. You will determine the quality of my life."

The reward for trusting him isn't betrayal; it's peace of

mind. It's happiness. It's trading that heavy burden we all drag around for the lighthearted freedom of God's plan.

I'm More Inferior than You Are

What an awful debate that would be. Yet men and women have been having it since before the birth of modern psychology. Without trying to reenact it here, let's once more examine superiority and inferiority in a husband-wife relationship. Keep in mind that this topic isn't an academic sparring match between the sexes. It's pivotal in our fear of trust.

In the public domain, men are kings. They can be expert manipulators, steel-shelled and bristling with verbal and financial weapons. Even if they're not grand movers and shakers, men are good at mastering feelings, applying logic, coming to quick decisions, and getting things done that have dollar signs attached.

As I mentioned in previous chapters, women are seen as superior in the private domain, especially when it comes to goodness. Women are better at child care; they're more tender, kind, loving, sympathetic, and sensitive. Those are God-approved behaviors, so they must be closer to Him. Women are more civilized, too; they wash more thoroughly and spend more attention on themselves and their surroundings.

John the Baptist may have dressed in camel skins and eaten locusts—which was pretty uncivilized behavior—but we know he was close to God. Ordinarily, though, cleanliness is next to godliness. If John had had a wife, she would have knitted him a tunic, fed him a good breakfast, and made him trim his beard. "You think that dirt's impressing someone?" she would have said. When a man calls his wife his "better half," he probably isn't joking. He feels inferior.

Further, relationships—like marriage and child-raising —are women's turf, and he feels inadequate. The baby won't stop crying, the older ones complain that he just doesn't understand them, his wife doesn't have faith in him, and no matter how hard he tries, he just isn't "good" enough to rise above it all. He feels like a failure. Perhaps he even believes he doesn't have what it takes to be a good husband and father. Paralyzed from this self-limiting attitude, he can hardly even try.

The Absentminded Husband

In many ways, men have little control over their own lives. They work until they're wrung out, and when that's over, they're only too willing—or resigned—to let us shepherd their remaining hours.

Who keeps the social calendar? We do. Most husbands will call during the day and ask, "What's on for tonight?" Either they don't know or they don't remember.

This herding phenomenon can even be seen in a couple's spiritual life: "Prayer meeting at seven, dear." "Let's say the rosary." "I've signed us up for a retreat." "Remember, we agreed to work on that project at church."

Ours may be benign rulership, but it's rulership nonetheless. No one deserves blame here; it doesn't matter whether it was prompted by our husbands' faults or our own. Now it's a problem that needs to be solved.

Maybe our husbands like having social and spiritual secretaries. Maybe, though, that rejection of responsibility is prompted by feelings of surrender—and generosity to-

ward us. Maybe if they had their choice and enough lei-
sure time to choose, they'd structure their spiritual lives
differently.

We can't force them to be enthusiastic if they really
aren't, but we can be supportive of their spiritual growth.
We can make sure they have every chance to move in faith
the way the Lord is calling. This may take a while; feelings
of powerlessness take time to heal.

Male Bonding: Is It Anything like Glue?

How often do our husbands go out with their own
friends? For all the talk about nights out with the boys, it's
probably pretty seldom. Often, when a man gets married,
his whole social life becomes restricted to his wife and her
choices of what to do.

Take one example: wilderness trips. They're a typical
male recreation, but many men don't get to experience
them because of their responsibilities at home. If he goes
off with the boys to fish or hunt, he feels guilty because his
wife is left at home with the children. But often, he can't
take her with him because she doesn't enjoy the rugged
outdoors. Now, she rarely says, "Don't you dare do that
to me." She may not even mind if he goes, but after years
of her unenthusiasm, he is so dispirited, he decides he
doesn't want to do it anyway. It remains a wistful dream
or a memory of his youth.

A lack of enthusiasm, by the way, is devastating. It's
every bit as effective as disapproval; it just takes a little
longer. If you hear yourself laughing about "men's stuff,"
take note of it. Stop, because once he's convinced that the
things that turn him on are worthless, he'll be partly dead

inside. You'll then have less of a husband. He'll love himself less, and he'll be less capable of loving you the way God wants.

A lack of enthusiasm is particularly devastating in sex. When a wife tells her man "No," or even "Oh, I suppose so," he feels alone, even abandoned. Especially if he's a macho sort, he's afraid to speak of his love and desire for unity, so he expresses it physically. When you imply "I'm not really interested in you right now," you've done more than deprive him of his evening's entertainment; you've told him you don't love him. He takes it personally, and he's right to do so.

The Hebrew word for *memory* means "make me present to you." In sex, you make yourselves totally present to each other through your bodies, which are no longer your own but are given up for the other. When you make love to your husband, you are saying, "I have given up my body for you. It is yours. Make me present to you, and become present to me, as we speak to each other physically."

It sounds like a paradox, but we humans are happiest when we forgo control and become truly one with our lovers. If the oneness is a coming together in sex, it suffuses our being for a long time afterward. We are not lonely because we are no longer alone.

For God's Sake, Woman, I Just Want Some Peace

"So do I," she responds. "That's why I want to get this problem solved."

That, in a nutshell, is the difference between men's and women's views of peace. What's defined as "quiet" to a man is, to a woman, the final solution. To her, remaining quiet when there's an unresolved problem is as silly as sweeping dirt under the rug. Her husband, though, just wants time to think. How can he solve anything when he doesn't even have the silence he needs to ponder the problem?

Wives, let's have compassion on them. Let's understand they're not stonewalling us; they do sincerely love us. They just work differently. They crave that silence; they need it in order to love us as Christ loved His church. Even if it feels sometimes as if we're living with the emotionless Mr. Spock from "Star Trek," let's give them thinking space.

Both husbands and wives need an atmosphere of peace and harmony in order to let Christ's love flourish in our homes. Only when there's peace—peace as he defines it, because right now we're showing compassion for him and aiding his journey to the Lord—can he work on loving you as he loves himself.

Peace? I Don't Have Time for It

Peace is particularly difficult to find in our tense, driven society. We don't allow ourselves any time to think, and we make sure our lives are crammed full; so full, our tempers fray. "I shouldn't feel this upset," we tell ourselves. "Mary (Melissa/Joanne/whoever) works much harder than I do. *Plus* she has an exercise program and that wonderful hobby. She seems so happy and cheerful. Why can't I do it, too?"

Of course, that other woman isn't as happy and cheerful as we imagine. She's working like a field ox; how can she possibly be happy? She—and we—are like Richard Cory. Do you remember the Simon and Garfunkel song based on the poem by E. A. Robinson? Richard Cory was the rich man who had everything: women, money, honor in the church, the respect of his fellow men. But, as the song says, Richard Cory went home one night and put a bullet through his head. He ought to have been happy, with all his achievements and luxuries, but in fact, he was in despair.

We simply can't be superheroes, yet we don't allow ourselves the dignity of our own limitations. We deny our feelings of frustration, and instead, dance to the piping of "You'd better do it or you'll be inadequate."

Let's ask ourselves a question: "What do I need to do in order to feel really good about myself?" Most likely, the answers will be in the form of exacting demands: lose twenty pounds, dress better, have thicker hair, wash out that gray, make more money, be able to do more work in a day, take up an exotic hobby like jewelry making, increase my IQ . . . The grind goes on and on. When we do get a color, lose twenty pounds, and buy some clothes, we'll find another reason to feel inadequate.

Of course, the problem goes much deeper. At the root of it are two facts: we don't value ourselves as ourselves, and we are lonely in our personal relationships. If we asked ourselves, "Would I rather lose twenty pounds and keep my relationship with my husband just as it is? Or would I rather my husband was wildly romantic and after me all the time just as I am?" what would we answer? We'd have to think about it, wouldn't we?

What are we doing to ourselves? We're saying, "No, I won't subject myself to freely given love. It can't be worth anything unless I earn it."

We don't seem to place a very high value on plain and simple happiness. Furthermore, we don't even know what it is. We think happiness comes when we have what we ought to have. The idea that we ought to take time to watch the sun go down sounds romantic and rather frivolous. We don't do it very often because it wouldn't get us anywhere.

Declaration of Independence

Part of our pain exists because we think we're not worthwhile people unless we do worthwhile things. We have to have our own hobbies, do our own housekeeping and child-raising, make our own money. It's like a computerized formula for self-worth.

Imagine feeding this into the computer: "My greatest accomplishment is loving my husband with everything I've got." Where does that fit in?

In our society, it doesn't compute. If we said it out loud, people would answer, "What are you talking about?" or "Oh, you can do that anytime."

It's time to reprogram ourselves.

We're happiest when we're in love. Remember your courtship and your honeymoon? People are desperate to recapture that feeling. They'll rip their lives apart trying to do so. That's why there are so many divorces, so many affairs, so many lonely women lost in beautiful novels. We all wish like crazy to be in love, but we work like crazy at things that drive us apart. We love love, but it isn't "worthwhile" according to society's standards. We don't agree out loud, but our actions speak louder than words. Love is a waste of time, a waste of ambition.

Now, I'm not saying we should abandon our talents. God gave them to us to be used. I am saying that your transcendent calling in life is to love that man; your calling as a couple is to echo Christ's passionate love affair with His church.

Are you ready? The world—and your lovers—are waiting.

You Are the Light of the World

Dear wives, dear husbands, it has been such a pleasure writing these words to you. So much of God's presence in this world is shown through loving couples like you who are willing and courageous enough to embrace His way. The world needs you so much; your spouses need you; your children need you. Our society desperately needs you as an example and a guiding light. We hope these words will take root and grow in you, so that Christ's joy may be in you and your own joy may be complete.

Love, Chuck and Mary Angelee.

Consider these questions privately:

Below is a list of Scripture passages. Each describes a response to Christ's love for His church.

Read and interpret each of these. How do they apply to your relationship with your husband? What are you doing well? What can you do better?

Trusting the goodness of our spouse:
> Matthew 11:28: "Come to me, all you who labour and are overburdened, and I will give you rest."

Accepting unconditional love:
> John 13:3–16: The washing of the feet.

Relentless love:
> John 13:34, 35: "Love one another as I have loved you."

Oneness:
> Acts 4:32–35. The early Church.

God's will for our love:
> Romans 8:28–39.

God's great love for us and our response:
> 1 John 4:7–19.

Share these thoughts:

After you and your husband read Chapter 11, write to each other on these topics:

Beloved, you are such a delightful spouse; I have such wonderful memories of your goodness. I can see you following God's plan for our relationship when you . . ." (Write on more than one if you wish.)

My dear, I realize I haven't always followed God's plan for our relationship. I am going to make the following change(s). This makes me feel . . .

Finally, let us invite the Lord into our marriages:

Dear Father, I truly want to follow Your plan for our marriage. Please help me to trust my husband's goodness; give me Your peace, Your patience, and enthusiasm for

Your will. Please send me your Spirit so I can fully live out Your plan with my beloved husband.

Thank you for his wonderful goodness and for the graces You have already given me: the grace of openness to Your word, the grace of compassion, the grace of generosity, the grace of hope. Thank you; praise You for Your gifts to my beloved and myself. Amen.